Roman Law and Maritime Commerce

Roman Law and Maritime Commerce

Edited by Peter Candy and
Emilia Mataix Ferrándiz

EDINBURGH
University Press

Edinburgh University Press is one of the leading university presses in the UK. We publish academic books and journals in our selected subject areas across the humanities and social sciences, combining cutting-edge scholarship with high editorial and production values to produce academic works of lasting importance. For more information visit our website: edinburghuniversitypress.com

Edinburgh University Press Ltd
The Tun – Holyrood Road
12(2f) Jackson's Entry
Edinburgh EH8 8PJ

Typeset in 10/12 Goudy Old Style by
IDSUK (DataConnection) Ltd, and
printed and bound by CPI Group (UK) Ltd,
Croydon, CR0 4YY

A CIP record for this book is available from the British Library

ISBN 978 1 4744 7814 4 (hardback)
ISBN 978 1 4744 7816 8 (webready PDF)
ISBN 978 1 4744 7817 5 (epub)

Contents

Acknowledgements

This book found its inception in the shared interest of the editors in the relationship between law and society in the Roman world, ancient maritime trade and the exciting possibilities presented by interdisciplinary research and the integration of a wide range of evidence into the writing of legal history. The production of this volume would not have been possible without the help and support offered by many people and institutions. We are very grateful to the ERC project *Law, Governance and Space: Questioning the Foundations of the Republican Tradition* (headed by Kaius Tuori) and to the Helsinki Collegium for Advanced Studies, for their generous support toward the organisation of the seminar 'Law, Trade and the Sea: Discovering Maritime Trade in the Roman World', which took place in Helsinki on 12–13 September 2019, at which many of the papers included in this volume were first presented. We would also like to thank the School of Law at the University of Edinburgh, St Catharine's College, Cambridge, and the Eurostorie Centre of Excellence in Law, Identity and European Narratives (founded by the Academy of Finland) for supporting our research in a myriad of different ways. We are especially grateful to Professor Paul du Plessis, who provided much useful advice in organising the conference and for sharing his editorial experience. The labour of editing would have been much harder for us without the kind help of Heta Björklund, Sara Heinonen, and Ida Karjalainen, from the Eurostorie Centre of Excellence. We would also like to offer our warmest thanks to the editors of Edinburgh's University Press, Laura Williamson and Sarah Foyle, for guiding us along the route to publishing this volume, as well as to the series editors and anonymous readers for their useful comments and advice.

PC and EMF

Illustrations

FIGURES

TABLES

List of Contributors

P. Campbell is a Lecturer in Cultural Heritage Under Threat at the Cranfield Forensic Institute, England.

P. Candy is a Fellow in Roman Law and European Legal History at the University of Edinburgh, Scotland.

G. Cifani is a Researcher in Classical Archaeology at the University of Rome 'Tor Vergata', Italy.

R. Fiori is a Professor of Roman Law at the University of Rome 'Tor Vergata', Italy.

É. Jakab is a Professor of Roman Law at the University of Szeged, Hungary.

A. Marzano is a Professor of Ancient History at the University of Reading, England.

E. Mataix Ferrándiz is a Postdoctoral Researcher at the University of Helsinki, Finland, and Research Fellow at the Käte Hamburger kolleg in Münster, Germany.

G. Purpura is a Professor Emeritus of Roman and Ancient Law at the University of Palermo, Italy.

A. Tarwacka is a Professor of Roman Law at the Cardinal Stefan Wyszyński University in Warsaw, Poland.

Abbreviations

All abbreviated references to authors from classical antiquity and their works follow the standard conventions in the Oxford Classical Dictionary (4th edn). All abbreviated references to ostraka and papyri follow the standard conventions in these disciplines.

AE	*L'Année épigraphique: revue des publications épigraphiques relatives à l'antiquité romaine* (Paris 1888 →)
Aespa	Archivo Español de Arqueología (Madrid 1940 →)
AJAH	American Journal of Archaeology (Boston 1885 →)
AJLH	American Journal of Legal History (Philadelphia, PA, then Oxford 2016 →)
ANRW	Aufstieg und Niedergang der römischen Welt (Berlin 1989 →)
Arch. Class.	Archeologia classica (Rome 1949 →)
AUPA	Annali del seminario giuridico dell'università degli studi di Palermo (Palermo 1916 →)
Bas	Basilica
BIDR	Bullettino dell'Istituto di diritto romano (Rome 1888 →)
CIE	Corpus Inscriptionum Etruscarum
CIL	Mommsen, Th. et al., *Corpus Inscriptionum Latinarum*, 17 vols. (Berlin 1863 →)
C	Codex
CGG	Cahiers du Centre Gustave Glotz (Paris 1991 →)
Coll	Mosaicarum et Romanarum Legum Collatio
CP	Classical Philology (Chicago, IL 1906 →)
CTh	Codex Theodosianus
CQ	Classical Quarterly (Cambridge 1907 →)
D	Digest
DAGR	Daremberg, C., and Saglio, E. (eds) (1900) *Dictionnaire des antiquités grecques et romaines* (Paris: Hachette)
DHA	Dialogues d'Histoire Ancienne (Besançon 1974 →)
FIRA	*Fontes Iuris Romani Antejustiniani*
G	Institutes of Gaius
IDélos	Dürrbach, F. et al., *Inscriptions de Délos*, 7 vols. (Paris 1926–1972)
IG	Dittenberger, W. et al., *Inscriptiones Graecae* (Berlin 1903 →)
IJNA	International Journal of Nautical Archaeology (New York 1972 →)
IK	Inschriften griechischer Städte aus Kleinasien (Bonn)

ILS	Dessau, H., *Inscriptiones latinae selectae*, 3 vols. (Berlin 1892–1916)
Index	Index: quaderni camerti di studi romanistici (Naples 1970 →)
Inst	Institutes of Justinian
IRAT	Inscriptions Romanes Ager Tarraconensis
IVRA	Iura: rivista internazionale di diritto romano e antico (Naples 1950 →)
JJP	Journal of Juristic Papyrology (Warsaw 1946 →)
JLH	Journal of Legal History (London 1980 →)
JRA	Journal of Roman Archaeology (Ann Arbor, MI 1988 →)
JRS	Journal of Roman Studies (London 1911 →)
Labeo	Labeo: rassegna di diritto romano (Naples 1955 →)
Lenel, EP	Lenel, O. (1927) *Das Edictum Perpetuum* (Leipzig: Tauchnitz)
Lenel, *Pal*	Lenel, O. (1889) *Palingenesia Iuris Civilis*, 2 vols. (Leipzig: Tauchnitz)
MBAH	Münstersche Beiträge zur antiken Handelsgeschichte (Marburg 1982 →)
MEFRA	Mélanges de l'école française de Rome – Antiquité (Rome 1881 →)
Mon. Eph.	Monumentum Ephesenum
Nóm. naut.	Nómos Rhodíōn nautikós (= Rhodian Sea Law)
OGIS	Dittenberger, W., *Orientis graeci inscriptiones selectae*, 2 vols, (Leipzig 1903–1905)
PS	*Pauli Sententiae*
RA	Revue Archéologique (Paris 1844 →)
RAN	Revue Archéologique de Narbonnaise (Narbonne 1968 →)
RDN	Rivista del Diritto della Navigazione (Rome 1935 →)
RHD	Revue d'Histoire du Droit (Leiden 1918 →)
RIDA	Revue Internationale des Droits de l´Antiquité (Brussels 1948 →)
SDHI	Studia Documenta Historiae et Iuris (Rome 1935 →)
SEG	*Supplementum epigraphicum graecum* (Leiden (Vols 1–25); Alphen aan den Rijn (Vols 26–27); Amsterdam (Vols 28–51); Leiden-Boston (Vols 52 →) 1923 →)
TAPhA	Transactions of the American Philological Association (Baltimore 1869 →)
TH	Tabula(e) Herculanensis(es)
TLL	Thesaurus Linguae Latinae
TPSulp	Tabula(e) Pompeiana(e) Sulpiciorum
ZPE	Zeitschrift für Papyrologie und Epigraphik (Bonn 1967 →)
ZRG RA	Zeitschrift für Rechtsgeschichte. Romanistische Abteilung (Weimar 1880 →)

Chapter 1

Introduction: Roman Law and Maritime Commerce

Peter Candy and Emilia Mataix Ferrándiz

It is a curious fact that the two seminal studies of the last century to work at the interface between Roman law and maritime commerce were both written by scholars based at the Université de Lyon: the first, Paul Huvelin's study of the history of Roman commercial law (*Études d'histoire du droit commercial romain*), which was published in 1929, five years after the author's premature death at the age of fifty-one; and the second, Jean Rougé's *Recherches sur l'organisation du commerce maritime en Mediterranée sous l'empire romain*, which was published in 1966. The two works, written by a jurist and historian respectively, provide a useful starting point for considering the potential and pitfalls of an interdisciplinary approach to the study of long-distance trade. Though they were written some fifty years apart, the structure of each work shows a similarity of approach that has continued to have a lasting impact on the study of the subject to this day. A brief examination will therefore serve to provide context to the studies in this volume, which represent a move toward a holistic, interdisciplinary approach to the study of Roman law and maritime commerce.

To begin with Huvelin's study, this was divided by the author into two parts: the 'external history' (*histoire externe*) and the 'internal history' (*histoire interne*) of Roman commercial law. In the first part, Huvelin sought to locate the law's development within its broader historical context. To this end, he divided Rome's history into four periods, beginning with the origins of Rome to the end of the First Punic War and ending with the late empire, with the death of Justinian. For each period, he wove together aspects of Rome's political, social and economic history in an attempt to throw light on institutional questions integral to the development of the city's commercial law. The topics addressed included, among other things, the institution of *commercium*, procedural developments and the internalisation of the *ius gentium*. In the second part, Huvelin turned to the internal history of Roman commercial law. This he understood as consisting in a large part of maritime law (*droit maritime*), which he proposed was generally concerned with three issues: (i) the exploitation of the ship; (ii) the juridical acts required to carry out the intended enterprise; and (iii) contractual and delictual liabilities incurred during the course of navigation. Under these heads, Huvelin variously discussed the *actiones furti et damni adversus nautas*, the *receptum nautarum*, the *actiones exercitoria* and *institoria*, the *lex Rhodia de iactu* and *nauticum foenus*.

In terms of structure, the manuscript, which Henri Lévy-Bruhl stated in the preface had been published with only minor alterations, provides no explanation as to the rationale behind the division of the study into two parts, nor of the author's conception as to the relationship between them.[1] The conceptual origins of the *Études d'histoire*, however, can be detected (at least in part) in Huvelin's earlier work. In the introduction to his doctoral thesis, a historical essay on the law of Mediaeval French markets and fairs, the author distinguished between the law's external history ('the circumstances which have influenced the running of fairs . . . and, particularly in France, the influence that has had on their development in connection with the Crown, the Church, and the constitution of society') and its internal development ('the internal organisation of these fairs and . . . all the privileges which give the life of fairs an original character'), and divided the study along these lines.[2] Some seven years later, Huvelin went on to adopt the same distinction in a broader study of the history of commercial law, which dedicated:

> 'One part to the history of our law, that is to say to the examination of the influence that the various manifestations of economic and social life have had on commercial institutions. The external history of commercial law is therefore based on the very history of commerce and trade policy. It must review the various civilisations, and draw attention to the significance and the forms that commercial law has taken in each of them. . . Another part to the internal history of commercial law, that is to say, to the historical study of each commercial institution taken independently, showing the general progress of the institution, and the immediate precedents of its modern form.'[3]

The significance of Huvelin's choice of structure emerges from the context of the distinction between external and internal methods in the writing of legal history. In a chapter published in the *Oxford Handbook of Legal Studies* in 2005, D Ibbetson explains that:

> 'A convenient and conventional division can be made between 'internal' and 'external' legal history. The former, we might say, is the history of lawyers' law, of legal rules and principles. Its sources are predominantly those that are thrown up by the legal process: principally statutes and decided cases, supplemented where possible with lawyers' literature expounding the rules and occasionally reflecting on them. The latter is the history of the law in practice, of legal institutions at work in society rather than legal rules existing in a social, economic, and political vacuum. The former, defined by its own terms, is bounded within its own field of reference; the latter, in its very nature, is necessarily unbounded.'[4]

Ibbetson wrote this passage principally in the context of the common law tradition. However, as M Hoeflich has shown, the distinction had its origins in civilian juridical thought long before Langdell, Maitland and Ames were laying the foundations of modern legal history in the common law world.[5] According to L Raggi, the distinction can be traced back to Gottfried Wilhelm Leibniz, who before he turned his considerable powers to mathematics had studied (Roman) law and philosophy at

Leipzig (1661–1663), before publishing a series of jurisprudential treatises shortly thereafter.[6] According to Leibniz, a natural lawyer, the internal history of law concerned the history of the development of the law's substance (that is, its principles and legal rules, through a process of reasoning), as opposed to its external history (that is, connected political and historical events), which though necessary for understanding that development, provided only the supporting structure (*adminiculum*) within which that development took place.[7] As Raggi noted, it was a corollary of this view that the motivating principle for the development of the law was considered internal to the law itself; the law's 'external history' providing only the framework within which legal change occurred on a rationalistic basis.[8]

By the time Huvelin was writing over two centuries later, Leibniz's thought, though influential on other natural lawyers and the Pandectists, had since been transformed by Friedrich Carl von Savigny. Savigny, the founder of the German 'historical school' of jurisprudence, believed that law was not merely an emanation of reason (*ratio scripta*), but rather could only be understood, in the words of A Rahmatian, as 'the product of history and an organic development which embodies the culture, tradition and character of a people'.[9] One consequence of this new understanding was to bring the law's external history into closer contact with the history of its internal development: no longer was history simply a prop but indispensable to reaching an understanding of a nation's 'sources' of law, which were the *fons et origo* of its legal rules and principles.[10] In maintaining the distinction between the generation of legal principles (a product of history) and their analytical and systematic refinement (a matter of legal science, or *Rechtswissenschaft*), Savigny therefore simultaneously maintained, albeit on a different footing, the distinction between the external and internal history of law. In France, this approach was taken up by (among others) the jurist Henry Klimrath (1807–1837), who argued for a programme of research into the history of French law in which lawyers studied both the external history of law ('the history of the sources of law and the political and social events necessary for their explanation') and its internal history ('the substantive history of the law, its provisions and its principles').[11]

From this perspective, Huvelin's decision to adopt the internal/external distinction can be understood as the application of a conventional methodological approach to a subject of contemporary historical interest. As F Audrun has observed, the choice to study first markets and fairs, and later the history of commercial law more generally, was inspired by the German, Belgian and French historiography of the period, which was breaking free from the orthodoxy of composing national political histories to forge new paths in the study of social and economic history. Huvelin, in taking up a topic that had yet to be subjected to holistic analysis, nonetheless treated it within a traditional legal historical framework.[12] It was probably this feature that led Henri Pirenne, one of the leading contributors to this new historiography, to comment that although he thought Huvelin's early work 'remarkable', it also came across as 'abstract' and 'systematic'.

The same bipartite division is also exhibited by Rougé's study into the organisation of maritime commerce during the high Roman Empire. A historian trained at the Sorbonne in Paris, Rougé was taught by renowned scholars such as Gustave Glotz, Jerome Carcopino, and André Piganiol, the latter of whom, as the supervisor of his dissertation on the Ostian corporations, inspired his passion for Roman economic and social life.[13] In the introduction to the *Recherches*, Rougé drew attention to the near total absence in contemporary studies of ancient commerce of, in his words, a focus upon 'the internal structure and infrastructure of maritime commerce, that is to say, its organisation'.[14] Instead, these studies tended either to have been composed in a sweeping style, particularly those written before the advent of modern economics, or, if they did take account of modern economic science, to focus upon the agricultural economy so that maritime commerce was treated only briefly and with a degree of superficiality.

Two works, however, were excluded by Rougé from criticism: the introduction to Levin Goldschmidt's *Handelsrechtsgeschichte* (1891) and Huvelin's 'magisterial work', the *Études*.[15] These, the author suggested, were a reminder that even if the history of maritime commerce during the Roman period remained in a large part to be written, still there was one aspect of its operation that had long been the focus of attention: the study of its law. Besides these exceptional works, however, Rougé was quick to point out that the legal historical studies into the subject tended mostly to be fragmentary and failed to provide an insight into the general conditions of maritime commercial activity.

Rougé's project was therefore to integrate the different aspects of the organisation of Roman maritime trade into a coherent whole. To this end, he divided the work into three parts: first, the infrastructure of maritime commerce (the sea, the ship, sailing routes, and ports); second, the 'structure' of maritime commerce (as he put it) or 'les gens du commerce'; and third, 'les problems économico-juridiques', which the author stated would be addressed 'as far as possible from the point of view of the historian and not the jurist'.[16] In the introduction to the third part, however, Rougé explained that though the book was divided into three parts, these fell into two overarching sections: first, 'the study of maritime trade in an external way: the study of its infrastructure, the study of its personnel'; and second, 'the problems posed by the practice of maritime trade both from a strictly legal and from an economic point of view'.[17] Though Rougé therefore adopted the same broad framework as Huvelin, his focus upon the process by which maritime trade was conducted rather than upon the internal history of the law's development (in the author's own words, a study of the law 'properly so-called'), led him to keep his treatment of the legal materials on a 'purely historical level': that is, the 'study of the texts and institutions not in and for themselves, but only to try to extract from them living data, apt to show us the problems that a merchant in the Roman period had to solve'.[18]

THE PRESENT VOLUME

Taken together, both Huvelin and Rougé were conscious of the need for a holistic approach to the study of the relationship between Roman law and maritime commerce. Each, however, was constrained by the internal/external distinction in their treatment: the former focusing upon the law's internal history, the latter upon the insights the legal texts could yield into the social and economic reality of long-distance trade during the Roman period. The present volume makes no pretension at seeking to overcome this distinction, which has its roots in both the development of legal history as a discipline and philosophy. One limitation of earlier studies, however, which modern scholarship is beginning to address, concerns the range and treatment of a variety of different kinds of evidence. Though Rougé, for example, acknowledged the importance of archaeological, epigraphic and papyrological evidence, these were only treated briefly in the introduction under the heading of the 'auxiliary sciences' and subordinated throughout the work to the textual evidence.[19]

Since the publication of these authors' works, however, the availability of new evidence, together with the development of new methods by which to study and interpret the sources, has opened up exciting possibilities in the study of Roman law and maritime trade from a holistic perspective. The advances in our knowledge of the conduct of ancient long-distance trade, particularly in the past sixty or seventy years, have been propelled to a large extent by archaeological research. The growth of maritime archaeology, which Rougé regretted was only in its infancy at the time he was writing his own work, has provided access to the wealth of material remains preserved at shipwreck sites in both the Mediterranean basin and the Black Sea. These sites, the great majority of which consist of the remains of clay amphorae deposited on the seabed (sometimes preserving parts of the hull underneath), provide unparalleled insights into the technological aspects of ancient shipping, including construction and stowage techniques.[20] Moreover, the composition of the cargoes and the patterns of their distribution help toward an understanding of sailing routes, trade flows and the economics of maritime trade more generally.[21] In terms of the infrastructure that supported the distribution of these commodities, research into ports around the Mediterranean seaboard and beyond has yielded new insights into their capacity and operation. Owing to the Portus-Limen project, for example, we now possess a much better understanding of the roles and connectivity of early ancient ports in their Roman and Mediterranean context.[22] Similar developments can also be traced in connection with the study of storage and warehousing, which has moved beyond the study of individual sites toward understanding their role within extended supply chains, in addition to a new appreciation of their social and economic importance.[23]

The discovery and publication of epigraphic sources has also contributed greatly to our understanding of the human context of maritime commerce during the Roman period.[24] The great variety of funerary inscriptions, together with those associated with the *collegia*, provide a unique insight into the world of *les gens du commerce* and the life of ancient port communities. Another epigraphic source consists in the remains of *tabulae* on which the written record of contracts and other arrangements were preserved. Alongside *tituli picti* (that is, markings made on the side of containers during the distribution process), these take us into the heart of the transactions that were the lifeblood of maritime trade. Occasionally, too, the discovery of official inscriptions furnishes evidence of the institutional architecture governing trade: such as the regulations concerning the collection of customs duties at Ephesus, fragments of Diocletian's Price Edict, and now a new inscription discovered at Rhodes, which (if authentic) would provide unique evidence of the text of the so-called *lex Rhodia de iactu*.[25]

Finally, engagement with the papyri has opened up a rich and important source of evidence to renewed scrutiny.[26] Papyrological sources provide a unique insight into contractual arrangements between merchants, carriers and financiers operating in Egypt during the Ptolemaic, Roman and Byzantine periods. Though these documents, which range from dossiers connected with financing agreements (*nautikai syngraphai*) to freight contracts (*naulotikai*), were once considered special to the Egyptian context, new research has shown that the mutual interpretation of these different sources alongside Roman juristic texts can yield productive results.

Building upon the works of Huvelin, Rougé and the scholarship of the half century just past, the papers in this collection proceed on the basis of a commitment to interdisciplinary engagement, particularly between specialists in a variety of different sources of evidence and legal historians. The arrangement of the chapters broadly follows the different kinds of evidence with which each of our contributors have engaged (literary, archaeological, epigraphic, papyrological), which both allows for some fluidity but also draws attention to some of the common historical questions that arise out of the mutual interpretation of different bodies of material.

In Chapter Two, Gabriele Cifani combines the evidence of archaeological and literary sources to argue that archaic Rome had already developed a maritime culture, owing to its participation in wider patterns of trading activity across the Mediterranean basin from as early as the sixth century BC. Peter Campbell (Chapter Three), meanwhile, takes the literary and archaeological evidence in a different direction, arguing for a new theory of 'contingent movement', which seeks to explain the process of navigational decision-making as a series of responses to the changing maritime environment in a commercial context. Turning more squarely to the literary sources, Anna Tarwacka (Chapter Four) draws attention to the legal questions that arose concerning the status of individuals captured by pirates and the juridical implications of their release. In Chapter Five, Annalisa Marzano demonstrates the importance of personal and social ties to the viability and conduct of maritime enterprise during the Roman period, supported in a large part by the evidence of inscriptions. Next, Emilia Mataix Ferrándiz (Chapter Six) draws our attention to the interface of public and private in the context of the *annona*, with particular reference to monumental inscriptions and the *tituli picti* inscribed on Dressel 20 amphorae. In Chapter Seven, Gianfranco Purpura demonstrates the indispensable role of written documentation in the context of transport in bulk, achieving at the same time the integration of the papyrological texts with a full suite of archaeological, epigraphic and juristic material. Next, Éva Jakab (Chapter Eight) examines the relationship between the financing of maritime trade and warehousing arrangements through the lens of the epigraphic evidence supplied by the tablets in the archive of the Sulpicii; and in Chapter Nine, Peter Candy stays with the theme of maritime credit to offer a new interpretation of *TPSulp*. 78, one of the *tabulae* preserved in the archive. Finally, in Chapter Ten, Roberto Fiori shows how the traditional trichotomy used to distinguish different configurations of the contract of letting and hiring is not sustainable in light of the approach taken by the Roman jurists to the interpretation of maritime freight agreements, such those preserved in the papyri.

As the range of papers in this volume shows, the collection is intended as a demonstration of the potential for interdisciplinary engagement between Romanists and scholars in other disciplines with a common interest in Roman legal, social and economic history. U Babusiaux recently remarked that:

> 'The task of future research on Roman law can only be to combine the traditional dogmatic study of private law with the impulses offered by the ancient history of law and modern trends in ancient studies. These two perspectives are not opposites, but can be mutually productive and lead to new questions when joined, which in turn also lead to new insights.'[27]

In these terms, research into the relationship between Roman law and maritime commerce represents an excellent opportunity to integrate the study of different sources of evidence in the writing of legal history and to bring these two perspectives – the internal and the external – together in new and productive ways.

BIBLIOGRAPHY

Armgardt, M. (2014), 'Leibniz as Legal Scholar', *Fundamina* 20, pp. 27–38.

Arnaud, P. (2011), 'Ancient Sailing-Routes and Trade Patterns: The Impact of Human Factors', in D. Robinson and A.I. Wilson (eds), *Maritime Archaeology and Ancient Trade in the Mediterranean* (Oxford: Oxford Centre for Maritime Archaeology), pp. 61–80.

Arnaud, P. and Keay, S. (eds) (2020), *Roman Port Societies: The Evidence of Inscriptions* (Cambridge: Cambridge University Press).

Aubert, J.J. (2020), 'Law and Life in Roman Harbours', in P. Arnaud and S. Keay (eds), *Roman Port Societies: The Evidence of Inscriptions* (Cambridge: Cambridge University Press), pp. 198–215.

Audren, F. (2001), 'Paul Huvelin (1873–1924): juriste et durkheimien', *Revue d'Histoire des Sciences Humaines*, Vol. 4, pp. 117–130.

Babusiaux, U. (2016), 'The Future of Legal History: Roman Law', *AJLH* 56(1), pp. 6–11.

Chankowski, V., Lafon, X. and Virlouvet, C. (eds) (2018), *Entrepôts et circuits de distribution en Méditerranée antique* (Athens: École française d'Athènes).

du Plessis, P.J. (2020), 'Modes of Roman Legal Reasoning in Context: A Brief Survey', in B. Spagnolo and J. Sampson (eds). *Principle and Pragmatism in Roman Law* (Oxford: Hart Publishing), pp. 27–36.

Goldschmidt, L. (1891), *Handbuch des Handelsrechts* (Stuttgart: F. Enke).

Harris, W.V. and Iara, K. (eds) (2011), *Maritime Technology in the Ancient Economy: Ship-design and Navigation* (Portsmouth, R.I.: JRA).

Hoeflich, M.H. (1986), 'Law & Geometry: Legal Science from Leibniz to Langdell', *AJLH* 30(2), pp. 95–121.

Huvelin, P. (1897), *Essai historique sur le droit des marchés et des foires* (Paris: A. Rousseau).

Huvelin, P. (1904), *L'histoire du droit commercial* (Paris: Cerf).

Huvelin, P. (1929), *Études d'histoire du droit commercial romain (histoire externe-droit maritime)* (Paris: Recueil Sirey).

Ibbetson, D. (2005), 'Historical Research in Law', in M. Tushnet and P. Cane (eds), *The Oxford Handbook of Legal Studies* (Oxford: Oxford University Press), pp. 863–879.

Keay, S. (2020), 'The Context of Roman Mediterranean Port Societies: An Introduction to the Portuslimen Project', in P. Arnaud and S. Keay (eds), *Roman Port Societies: The Evidence of Inscriptions* (Cambridge: Cambridge University Press), pp. 1–35.

Klimrath, H. (1843), 'Programme d'une histoire du droit français (1835)', in *Travaux sur l'histoire du droit français*, Vol. 1 (Paris-Strasbourg: Joubert), pp. 88–112.

Langlois, C.V. and Seignobos, C. (2014), *Introduction aux études historiques* (Lyon: ENS Éditions).

Leibniz, G.W. (1771), *Nova methodus docendae discendaeque iurisprudentiae* (Pisa: Aug. Pizzorno).

Leibniz, G.W. (2017), *The New Method of Learning and Teaching Jurisprudence According to the Principles of the Didactic Art Premised in the General Part and in the Light of Experience*, trans. C.M. de Iuliis (New Jersey: Talbot Publishing).

Meyer-Termeer, A.J.M. (1978), *Die Haftung der Schiffer im griechischen und römischen Recht* (Zutphen: Terra).

Raggi, L. (1959), 'Storia esterna e storia interna del diritto nella letteratura romanistica', *BIDR* 62, pp. 199–222.

Rahmatian, A. (2007), 'Friedrich Carl von Savigny's Beruf and Volksgeistlehre', *JLH* 28(1), pp. 1–30.

Rice, C. (2016), 'Shipwreck Cargoes in the Western Mediterranean and the Organization of Roman Maritime Trade', *JRA* 29, pp. 165–192.

Richard, F. (1991), 'Jean Rougé (1913–1991)', *Revue des Études Augustiniennes* 37(2), pp. 196–198.

Rougé, J. (1966), *Recherches sur l'organisation du commerce maritime en Méditerranée sous l'Empire romain* (Paris: S.E.V.P.E.N.).

Van Oyen, A. (2020), *The Socio-Economics of Roman Storage: Agriculture, Trade, and Family* (Cambridge: Cambridge University Press).

Virlouvet, C. and Brigitte, M. (eds), *Entrepôts et trafics annonaires en Méditerranée: antiquité-temps modernes* (Rome: École française de Rome).

Wilson, A.I. (2011), 'Developments in Mediterranean Shipping and Maritime Trade from the Hellenistic Period to AD 1000', in D. Robinson and A.I. Wilson (eds), *Maritime Archaeology and Ancient Trade in the Mediterranean* (Oxford: Oxford Centre for Maritime Archaeology), pp. 33–59.

NOTES

1. In the preface, Lévy-Bruhl explained that the manuscript consisted of notes written in the period between the outbreak of the Great War and 1920. Apparently Huvelin had not intended the work for publication: Huvelin (1929), pp. v–vi.
2. Huvelin (1897), pp. 30–31:

   'l'histoire externe des foires, des circonstances qui ont influencé sur la marche en avant depuis l'antiquité, et, particulièrement en France, de l'action qu'ont eu sur leur développement la royauté, l'Église et la constitution de la société ... l'histoire interne des foires, c'est-à-dire de leur organisation propre, et de l'ensemble des privilèges, qui, en donnant à la vie des foires un caractère original, assuraient avant tout la régularité du commerce'.

3. Huvelin (1904), p. 26:

   'Une partie consacrée à l'histoire de notre droit, c'est à dire à l'examen de l'influence que les différentes manifestations de la vie économique, sociale, ont exercée sur les institutions commerciales. L'histoire externe du droit commercial est donc basée sur l'histoire même du commerce et de la politique commerciale. Elle doit passer revue les diverses civilisations, et mettre en relief l'importance et les formes que le droit du commerce a prises dans chacune d'elles ... Une partie consacrée à l'histoire du droit commercial interne, c'est à dire à l'étude historique de chaque institution commerciale prise séparément, en dégageant la marche générale de cette institution, et les précédents immédiats de sa forme moderne'.

4. Ibbetson (2005), p. 864.
5. See, generally, Hoeflich (1986).
6. Raggi (1959). For a brief but comprehensive biography, Armgardt (2014), pp. 28–33.
7. Leibniz (1771), II.28–29; and for the following translation, Leibniz (2017):
   'Now we must turn to the Historical aspects. Historical Jurisprudence is both internal and external: the former penetrates the very substance of the Jurisprudence; the latter is only a support, and necessary ... The External History, necessary for jurisprudence, is the Roman History which helps to understand Civil Law, the Ecclesiastical History to penetrate Canon law; the History of the middle ages to decipher Feudal Law, and of our time to comprehend the Public Law'.
8. Raggi (1959), p. 207.
9. Rahmatian (2007), p. 5. For a general overview, du Plessis (2020), pp. 30–33.
10. Raggi (1959), pp. 215–216.
11. Klimrath (1843), pp. 96–97.
12. Audren (2001), pp. 117–118.
13. Richard (1991), p. 196.
14. Rougé (1966), p. 8.
15. Rougé (1966), p. 9; Goldschmidt (1891).

16. Rougé (1966), p. 9.
17. Rougé (1966), p. 325.
18. Rougé (1966), p. 326.
19. Rougé (1966), p. 26. This attitude found its origins in the French approach to the study of ancient history at the time, which began with the interpretation of the textual sources and only later expanded to the material evidence furnished by the so-called 'auxiliary disciplines' (i.e. the 'école méthodique française'). See, e.g. Langlois and Seignobos (2014), Ch. 2.
20. See, e.g. Wilson (2011), pp. 33–59; Harris and Iara (2011).
21. See Arnaud (2011); also, Rice (2016).
22. Keay (2020).
23. On warehousing, see Virlouvet and Brigitte (2016); Chankowski, Lafon and Virlouvet (2018); also, Van Oyen (2020).
24. See, generally, the papers collected in Arnaud and Keay (2020).
25. On the Rhodian inscription, see Aubert (2020).
26. The seminal papyrological study from the perspective of Roman law and maritime commerce is Meyer-Termeer (1978).
27. Babusiaux (2016), p. 10.

Chapter 2

Aspects of the Origins of Roman Maritime Trade

Gabriele Cifani

The economy of early Rome is often represented in primitivistic terms of subsistence and basic pastoralism, with very little attention paid to transmarine trade.[1]

As a matter of fact, early Roman engagement in maritime trade is often denied in the literary tradition, probably in order to avoid any connection between the idealised image of austere Roman ancestors (imagined as shepherds, farmers, soldiers and honest citizens) and maritime trade or piracy.[2]

This tradition had a strong influence on the historiography of early Rome, and even the first modern works on Roman history tended to deny any involvement of the city with the sea until the Punic wars, as shown by many works from the eighteenth and nineteenth centuries.[3] Such a reconstruction now seems implausible, however.

The importance of Rome as the emporium of the whole of Latium and the relevance of the maritime activity of the early city had already been stressed by Theodor Mommsen,[4] and by the Italian archaeologist Giovanni Pinza, who first described the Greek and Phoenician importation to early Rome as evidence of long-distance trade.[5]

After the Second World War this picture became clearer following new discoveries at the site of Rome, investigations of coastal settlements and sanctuaries like Gravisca, Caere and Castrum Inui,[6] and, last but not least, with increasing knowledge of Etruscan and Phoenician trading activity. Furthermore, the archaeological findings of the last two decades offer direct evidence of Rome as an active Mediterranean emporium and site of cultural and trade interaction from the late Bronze Age onwards.[7]

It is useful to recall that the site of Rome, lying along the most important river in central Italy and just thirty kilometres from the sea, reveals that maritime trade was already important for the earliest communities. It should also be emphasised that the high cost of land transportation in antiquity made any position along rivers and close to the sea very important economically. This aspect was emphasised by Aristotle and later by Cicero.[8] The maritime activity of Rome is quite clear from the fourth century BC onwards.

According to Theophrastus, Latium itself was considered a land with timber resources useful for shipbuilding. The same author reports an attempt by the Romans to establish a colony in Corsica, while the Periplus of the Pseudo Scylax indicates Rome as the main harbour between Etruria and Campania.[9]

For the Archaic Period, archaeological evidence allows us to propose a reconstruction of Roman trade activity as part of a broader mid-Tyrrhenian network, which included the traders of the southern Etruscan coastal cities and Latium.

The lower course of the Tiber was certainly navigable in small flat-bottomed fluvial boats (*caudicariae*) or in shallow-draft oared ships like the archaic penteconters.[10]

Ships soon became a symbol of wealth and part of the elites' self-representation, as shown by the numerous images of such vessels found in funerary contexts of the southern Etruscan area. It is possible that these images were also a metaphor for the journey to the afterlife.

A noteworthy example is a *kantharos* from the middle of the seventh century BC found in a tomb in the territory of Veii, just eleven kilometres northwest of Rome.[11] The vase is decorated with a detailed image of a transport ship. This is represented as having a square-rigged central mast and at least two decks, with horses on the lower deck and armed men on the upper; the bow of the ship is reinforced with a ram.

Furthermore, the mouth of the Tiber was characterised by two large coastal lakes that were linked to the sea by two artificial channels presumably constructed between the ninth and the sixth centuries BC, as indicated by a recent analysis of the delta evolution of the river.[12]

Both ancient lagoons were possibly used as coastal harbours, but they were also privileged areas for trade, fishing and salt production.

The fact that this area had been important since the origin of Rome is confirmed in the literary tradition with the reference to the age of Romulus and the account of the rivalry with Veii for access to the resources of the Tiber delta, from the period of Ancus Marcius until the fourth century BC.[13]

The mouth of the Tiber also played an important role as a landmark for coastal navigation.

Figure 2.1 Representation of a ship on a *kantharos* from the territory of Veii (after Arizza et al. (2013)).

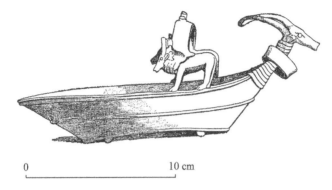

Figure 2.2 Bronze model of ship from the area of Portus (after Depalmas (2005)).

It lies at the mid-point of the Tyrrhenian coast and opposite the Strait of Bonifacio, the ancient *fretum gallicum*, which represents the most direct sea route between central Tyrrhenian Italy and the south of France.[14]

The close relationship between the lower Tiber valley and Sardinia is attested by the presence of imported Sardinian bronze objects in the early Iron Age contexts of Latium and Southern Etruria, including a bronze model of a ship from the area of Portus.[15]

In addition, recent surveys on the island of Tavolara, near the Strait of Bonifacio, discovered an Iron Age settlement with many fragments of Villanovan pottery. This reveals the importance of the Strait in sea trade activity from the early Iron Age onwards.[16]

Early Rome controlled the mouth of the Tiber through the fortified settlement of Ficana. Furthermore, the area between the Capitolium and the Aventine was the ancient cattle market (*Forum Boarium*) as well as the earliest fluvial harbour of the city, from where the sea could have been easily reached. There is little knowledge of this area for the Archaic Period, but the main evidence is offered by the remains of one temple of the sanctuary of Fortuna and Mater Matuta, which was built and restored in the course of the sixth century BC.[17]

During the same century we can identify possible exportation from Rome to the central and western Mediterranean and to Sardinia. The distribution of the Etrusco-Corinthian Human Mask Group vases produced mainly in Rome – or at least in the lower Tiber Valley – in the first half of the sixth century BC, reveals two maritime trade routes partially controlled by the city.[18]

The first, across the Tyrrhenian Sea, linked the mouth of the Tiber with Campania (Stabia) and Sicily (Palermo). The second was a route from the mouth of the Tiber to Sardinia and thence to Massalia, and possibly other sites in the Languedoc.

Figure 2.3 Distribution map of the finds of Etrusco-Corinthian vases of the Human Mask Group and possible sea routes in the sixth century BC (image by the author).

Within this framework, we can contextualise the problematic account of an alliance between the Phocaeans and Rome in the age of Tarquinii, later reported by Pompeius Trogus:

> 'Temporibus Tarquinii regis ex Asia Phocaeensium iuuentus ostio Tiberis inuecta amicitiam cum Romanis iunxit; inde in ultimos Galliae sinus nauibus profecta Massiliam inter Ligures et feras gentes Gallorum condidit . . .

> In the time of King Tarquinius, a company of Phocaeans from Asia, sailing up the Tiber, formed an alliance with the Romans, and proceeding from thence to the inmost part of the gulf of Gaul . . . '[19]

Despite the critical interpretation of this paragraph, which was presumably influenced by the political aim of Pompeius Trogus to stress the ancient links between Rome and Massalia,[20] the source could reflect the existence of a treaty between the two cities that controlled a vital sea route between the mouths of the most important rivers in the western Mediterranean basin: the Rhône and the Tiber.

The archaeological evidence currently available also permits us to reconsider the main document concerning archaic Roman trade: the first treaty between Rome and Carthage, as reported by Polybius in the second century BC.

His description is as follows (Polyb. 3.22):21[21]:

'The first treaty between Rome and Carthage was made in the year of Lucius Junius Brutus and Marcus Horatius, the first Consuls appointed after the expulsion of the kings, by which men also the temple of Jupiter Capitolinus was consecrated. This was twenty-eight years before the invasion of Greece by Xerxes.

Of this treaty I append a translation, as accurate as I could make it, for the fact is that the ancient language differs so much from that at present in use, that the best scholars among the Romans themselves have great difficulty in interpreting some points in it, even after much study. The treaty is as follows:

There shall be friendship between the Romans and their allies, and the Carthaginians and their allies, on these conditions:

Neither the Romans nor their allies are to sail beyond the Fair Promontory, unless driven by stress of weather or the fear of enemies. If any one of them be driven ashore he shall not buy or take aught for himself save what is needful for the repair of his ship and the service of the gods, and he shall depart within five days.

Men landing for traffic shall strike no bargain save in the presence of a herald or town-clerk. Whatever is sold in the presence of these, let the price be secured to the seller on the credit of the state—that is to say, if such sale be in Libya or Sardinia.

If any Roman comes to the Carthaginian province in Sicily, he shall enjoy all rights enjoyed by others. The Carthaginians shall do no injury to the people of Ardea, Antium, Laurentium, Circeii, Tarracina, nor any other people of the Latins that are subject to Rome.

From those townships even which are not subject to Rome they shall hold their hands; and if they take one shall deliver it unharmed to the Romans. They shall build no fort in Latium; and if they enter the district in arms, they shall not stay a night therein.'

The treaty defined areas with different rules and privileges. The first area is Latium: an area under the hegemony of Rome, where piracy or any hostile acts by the Carthaginians was forbidden and where presumably Punic traders could benefit from the same rights as the Latins. The second is Western Sicily and, presumably, Carthage, where Romans and Latins had the same trading rights. The third is Sardinia and the coastal area of North Africa, west of the Fair Promontory (Cape Bon), where trade by Latins was permitted only under strict control and was presumably taxed by the Punic authorities. The fourth is the region of the Emporia, east of the Fair Promontory (corresponding to the historical region of Tripolitania, in modern Libya) where the Romans and their Latin allies were not admitted at all, except in the case of *force majeure*.

In order to evaluate the political meaning of the treaty we should consider it in the context of trade in the late Archaic Period.

It should be recalled that from the beginning of the sixth century BC onwards, trade throughout the Mediterranean was conducted in a new way, as revealed mainly by the Greek sources, which distinguish between two models: *prexis* and *emporia*.[22]

Table 2.1 Prexis and emporia

Mediterranean models of trading		
	prexis	*emporia*
approximative chronology	8th–7th century BC	6th–5th century BC
traders	aristocrats	aristocrats and professional traders: *emporoi, naukleroi*
ships	10–30 tons; one mast	up to 40 tons; one or two masts
merchandise	First: precious items, e.g.: metals, fine ware, perfumes, spices, fine textiles. Secondly: oil and wine.	First: staples, e.g.: cereals; wine; oil. Secondly: precious items.
places of trade	harbours; aristocratic dwellings.	harbours; monumental sanctuaries
rules	personal agreements between aristocrats	official treaties between states
authorities	aristocrats	public magistrates

Prexis refers to the traditional manner of conducting maritime trade, which is well-described in the Homeric poems. Based on small fleets headed by aristocrats, who owned the ships and maintained personal contacts in the harbours of arrival, it typically included the giving of gifts, exchange and mutual hospitality, and piracy among the aristocrats themselves (*xenia*).

The identification of individuals of similar status and their descendants or representatives for the purposes of mutual hospitality was emphasised by the exchange of special tokens called *tesserae hospitales*, which bore the names of the host and guest. It is worthy of note that one specimen, datable to the sixth century BC, was found in the sanctuary of Fortuna and Mater Matuta in Rome and bears the Etruscan inscription of a man (*araz silqetanas spurianas*), presumably a foreign trader.[23]

The model of *prexis* implies that transported goods were perhaps limited to metals or precious items. The gross tonnage of the ships used between the eighth and seventh centuries BC, as reconstructed from the remains of shipwrecks, still lay within a limited range of between ten and about thirty tons, even though the cargo was characterised by an increasing standardisation of transport amphorae.[24]

3 cm.

Figure 2.4 Ivory lion plaque from the area of S. Omobono (after Cristofani (1990)).

We could consider *prexis* as a typical way of trading in the Iron Age and until the seventh century BC, while during the sixth century maritime trade gradually evolved into *emporia*.

The goods to be exchanged were now not only precious items, but also large amounts of wine, oil and grain, which were part of the food supply of communities living in major urban settlements. The activity was now carried out by professional traders (*emporoi*) using rented ships owned by other businessmen (*naukleroi*), with a greater degree of organisation.

Bigger ships could reach coastal trading settlements (*emporia*) where trade was controlled and guaranteed by local authorities.

Significant changes in shipbuilding had also taken place by the end of the sixth century BC.

Evidence from Archaic shipwrecks in the Mediterranean reveal vessels up to twenty-five metres in length (for example, Grand Ribaud F; Gela 1), weighing up to forty tons and carrying about 1,000 amphorae, while iconographic sources provide evidence of two-masted ships.[25]

In the Mediterranean basin the increase in sea trade activity is also shown by the dramatic rise in the number of shipwrecks dating from the second half of the sixth century onwards.[26]

Trade agreements were no longer made between aristocrats but were ruled by the central authorities by means of official treaties with neighbouring communities.

The widespread diffusion of fixed units of value as means of exchange was a further step in the movement of trade accounting towards the public sphere.

The general model, as seen in the late Archaic Greek world, was that each community exercised stronger control over maritime trade and piracy become less frequent. Territorial borders, reinforced by fortresses and new sanctuaries,

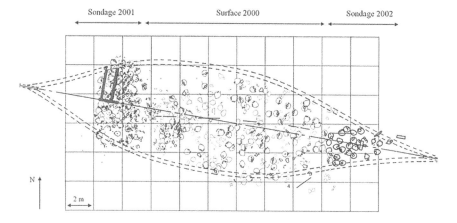

Figure 2.5 Grand Ribaud F shipwreck (after Long et al. (2006)).

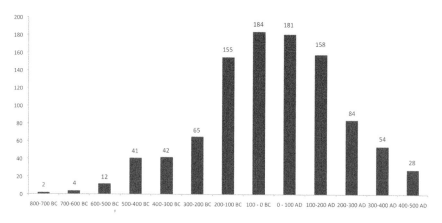

Figure 2.6 Histogram of shipwrecks (after Parker (1992)).

were more visible and more defended, which emphasised the political identity of the territory. Finally, the business of trade protection began to be managed as a monopoly by the public authorities, who levied specific taxes and decided who could be admitted to their own *emporia*.

Connectivity between cities was increased and transaction costs reduced, bolstering trade across the Mediterranean Sea.[27]

In the sixth century BC the new way of doing trade (*emporia*) certainly increased the economic activity of the whole of central Tyrrhenian Italy, including, obviously, that of Rome, which held the political hegemony in the area.

Within this framework of maritime supremacy, the Carthaginians would have negotiated new alliances with the mid-Tyrrhenian communities, including Rome, in order to counterbalance the rising naval power of the Greek traders in the Tyr-rhenian Sea. As agreed by treaty, the Latins (and possibly the Etruscans) would have been prevented from trading autonomously in the less stable territories con-trolled by Carthage, that is, Sardinia and, above all, the region of the *emporia* in Libya. This was a strategic area, where in 525 BC an attempt by the Spartan Prince Dorieus to found a Greek colony at the mouth of the Kynips River was promptly rebuffed by the Carthaginians.[28]

However, the text of the first treaty allows us to assume that Rome possessed a maritime trade activity based first on the natural harbour provided by the mouth of the Tiber, but also on the fleets of the allied Latin communities along the coast, such as Ardea, Antium, Laurentium, Circeii and Tarracina.

Regarding Archaic Rome, our consideration of maritime trade activity must include not only navigation for the transport of goods to be sold or exchanged, but also the mooring of foreign ships in the harbour, their supply of food and water, their escort along the mid-Tyrrhenian coast and possible piracy.

In fact, piracy was common in the ancient Mediterranean, and even in Greek culture from Homer to Thucydides it was considered to be legitimate when its purpose was to protect the territory or maritime trade of a polis.[29]

It was only from the sixth century BC onwards that the centralisation of power in political communities resulted in new rules regarding maritime trade. The main focus of these was the reorganisation of a network of *emporia* controlled by the cit-ies, in parallel with treaties and alliances between the major sea powers.[30]

This new institutional framework for maritime trade may have led to a reduc-tion in piracy, the economic importance of which was partially substituted by tolls and port duties paid to public authorities.

Furthermore, we should consider the complex and mixed nature of archaic Mediterranean trade, involving the co-operation of people from different ethnic areas and the movement of goods from various regions.

An example is offered by a western Greek wine amphora found in the Grand Ribaud F shipwreck, from the beginning of the fifth century BC. The vase bears the inscription '*maniies*', which is the Etruscanised name of a Latin sea trader, while the inscription 'CCCCCCCCCII' on the same amphora is clearly the number 902 in the Latin writing system.[31]

To sum up, our knowledge of the origins of Roman sea trade institutions can only be acquired from a comparison of archaeological data and literary sources.

However, from the sixth century BC onwards, widespread Mediterranean inter-actions and the existence of treaties with the main maritime powers, which had a considerable degree of sophistication in terms of political and trade agreements, confirm that archaic Rome was already, in cultural terms, a maritime society.

BIBLIOGRAPHY

Ampolo, C. (1994), 'Tra empòria ed emporìa: note sul commercio greco in età arcaica e classica', *Annali dell'Istituto Orientale di Napoli*, n.s. I, pp. 29–35.

Arizza, M., De Cristofaro, A., Piergrossi, A. and Rossi, D. (2013), 'La tomba di un aristocratico naukleros dall'agro veietano. Il 'kantharos' con scena di navigazione di via D'Avack', *Arch. Class.* 64, pp. 51–131.

Arnaud, P. (2012), 'L'homme, le temps et la mer: continuité et changement des routes maritimes de et vers Portus', in S. Keay (ed), *Rome, Portus and the Mediterranean* (London: British School at Rome), pp. 127–146.

Bravo, B. (1984) 'Commerce et noblesse en Grèce archaïque. À propos d'un livre d'Alfonso Mêle', *DHA* 10, pp. 99–160.

Brocato, P., Ceci, M. and Terrenato, N. (eds) (2016), *Ricerche nell'area dei templi di Fortuna e Mater Matuta (Roma)* (Arcavacata di Rende: Università della Calabria).

Camous, T. (2004), *Le Roi et le fleuve: Ancus Marcius Rex aux origines de la puissance romaine* (Paris: Les Belles Lettres).

Cassola, F. (1962), *I gruppi politici romani nel III secolo a.C.* (Trieste: Università degli studi).

Cifani, G. (2012), 'Approaching Ethnicity and Landscapes in Pre-Roman Italy: the Middle Tiber Valley', in G. Cifani and S. Stoddart (eds), *Landscape, Ethnicity and Identity in the Archaic Mediterranean Area* (Oxford: Oxbow Books), pp. 144–162.

Cifani, G. (2020), *The Origins of the Roman Economy: From the Iron Age to the Early Republic in a Mediterranean Perspective* (Cambridge: Cambridge University Press).

Cifani, G., and Munzi, M. (2003), 'Alle sorgenti del Cynips', *Libyan Studies* 34, pp. 85–100.

Colonna, G. (2006), 'A proposito della presenza etrusca nella Gallia meridionale', in *Gli Etruschi da Genova ad Ampurias. Atti del XXIV Convegno di Studi Etruschi ed Italici* (Marseille Lattes, 2002) (Pisa: Istituti editoriali e poligrafici internazionali), pp. 657–678.

Dell'Amico, P. (2011), 'Appunti sulle naves caudicariae', *Archeologia Marittima Mediterranea* 8, pp. 185–192.

Depalmas, A. (2005), *Le navicelle di bronzo della Sardegna nuragica* (Cagliari: E. Gasperini).

di Gennaro, F. (2019), 'Uno stanziamento 'etrusco' del X sec. a.C. a Tavolara', in S. Rafanelli (ed), *Alalìa. Etruschi, Greci e Cartaginesi nel Mediterraneo del VI secolo a.C.* (Monteriggioni: Siena ARA edizioni), pp. 54–57.

Drakidès, D., Nantet, E., Gras, M., and Esposito, A. (2010), 'Échanges et circulation', in R. Etienne (ed), *La Méditerranée au VIIe siècle av. J.-C. Essais d'analyses archéologiques* (Paris: De Boccard), pp. 91–135.

Ferrer Albelda, E. (2013), 'La piratería en los tratados entre Cartago y Roma', in A. Álvarez-Ossorio Rivas, E. Ferrer Albelda, E. García Vargas (eds), *Piratería y seguridad marítima en el Mediterráneo antiguo* (Sevilla: Universidad de Sevilla), pp. 95–126.

Fiorini, L. (2005), *Topografia generale e storia del santuario. Analisi dei contesti e delle stratigrafie* (Bari: Edipuglia).

Gabrielsen, V. (2013), 'Warfare, statehood and Piracy in the Greek world', in N. Jaspert and S. Kolditz (eds), *Seeraub in Mittelmeerraum. Piraterie, Korsarentum und maritime Gewalt von der Antike bis zur Neuzeit* (Paderborn: Verlag Ferdinand Schöningh), pp. 133–153.

Gras, M. (1985), *Trafics tyrrhéniens archaïques* (Rome: École Française de Rome).

Höckman, O. (1995), 'Some Thoughts on the Greek Pentekonter', in H. Tzalas (ed), *TROPIS III. 3rd International Symposium on Ship Construction in Antiquity (Athens 1989, Proceedings)* (Athens: Hellenic Institute for the Preservation of Nautical Tradition), pp. 207–220.

Horden, P. and Purcell, N. (2000), *The Corrupting Sea: A Study of Mediterranean History* (Oxford and Malden, MA: Blackwell).

Hultsch, F.O. and Shuckburgh, S.E. (eds) (1889), *The Histories of Polybius* (Cambridge: Cambridge University Press).

Krämer, R.P. (2016), 'Trading Goods – Trading Gods. Greek Sanctuaries in the Mediterranean and their role as emporia and "Ports of Trade" (7th–6th century BCE)', in *Distant World Journal* 1, pp. 75–98.

Mele, A. (1979), *Il commercio greco arcaico. Prexis ed emporie* (Naples: Institut Français Napoli).

Mele, A. (1986), 'Pirateria, commercio e aristocrazia: replica a Benedetto Bravo', *DHA* 12, pp. 67–109.

Mengotti, F. (1803), *Del commercio dei Romani ed il Colbertismo* (Venice: Antonio Graziosi).

Michetti, L.M. and Belelli Marchesini, B. (2018), 'Pyrgi, porto e santuario di Caere. Tra conoscenze acquisite e ricerche in corso', *Annali della Fondazione per il "Museo Claudio Faina"* 25, pp. 245–280.

Mommsen, T. (1888), *Römische Geschichte. Erster Band, bis zur Schlacht von Pydna* (Berlin: Weidmann).

Montesquieu, C. (de Secondat Baron de) (1734), *Considérations sur les causes de la grandeur des Romains et de leur décadence* (Amsterdam: Jacques Desbordes).

Nantet, E. (2016), *Phortia. Le tonnage des navires de commerce en Méditerranée du VIIIe siècle av. l'ère chrétienne au VIIe siècle de l'ère chrétienne* (Rennes: Presses universitaires de Rennes).

Niebhur, B.G. (1828–1832), *Römische Geschichte* (Berlin: Realschulbuchhandlung).

Parker, A.J. (1992), *Ancient Shipwrecks of the Mediterranean and the Roman Provinces* (Oxford: British Archaeological Reports).

Pinza, G. (1905), 'Monumenti primitivi di Roma e del Lazio antico', *Monumenti Antichi dei Lincei* XV, cc.1–844.

Scardigli, B. (1991), *I trattati romano-cartaginesi* (Pisa: Scuola Normale Superiore).

Sourisseau, J. C. (2012), 'Documents archéologiques et réseaux d'echanges en Méditerranée central (VIII–VII s. a.C.)', in L. Capdetrey and J. Zurbach (eds), *Mobilités grecques: mouvements, réseaux, contacts en Méditerranée, de l'époque archïque à l'époque hellénistique* (Paris: Diffusion De Boccard), pp. 179–198.

Tchernia, A. (2011), *Le Romains et le commerce* (Naples: Centre Jean Bérard).

Torelli, M. and Marroni, E. (eds) (2018), *Castrum Inui. Il santuario di Inuus alla foce del fosso dell'Incastro* (Rome: G. Bretschneider).

Vanotti, G. (1999), 'Erodoto e Roma', in P. Anello (ed), *Erodoto e l'Occidente* (Rome: G. Bretschneider), pp. 461–481.

Watson, J.S. (trans.) (1853), *Epitome of the Philippic History of Pompeius Trogus* (London: H.G. Bohn).

NOTES

1. This paper is part of a project funded by the EU: Horizon 2020 – MSCA – IF – 2017, No. 795214, at Paris, UMR 8546 CNRS / ENS – AOrOc (Archéologie & Philologie d> Orient et d> Occident). 'On the early Roman economy': Cifani (2020).
2. Tchernia (2011), pp. 1–17.
3. Montesquieu (1734); Mengotti (1803); Niebhur (1828–1832).
4. Mommsen (1888), pp. 41 and 413.
5. Pinza (1905).
6. *Castrum Inui*: Torelli and Marroni (2018). *Pyrgi*: Michetti and Belelli Marchesini (2018). *Gravisca*: Fiorini (2005).
7. Cifani (2020). On the Etruscan trade: Gras (1985). On Mediterranean interaction in the Archaic Period: Horden and Purcell (2000).
8. Arist. *Pol.* 7.6.2; Cic. *Rep.* 2.10.
9. Theophr. *Hist. Pl.* 5.8.1–5.8.3; Ps. Scylax V. See, also, Cassola (1962).
10. On *Caudicariae*, see Dell'Amico (2011); and for *penteconters*, Höckman (1995).
11. Arizza et al. (2013).
12. Cifani (2020), pp. 58–60.
13. Cic. *Rep.* 2.5: '*(Romulus) in ostio Tiberino, quem in locum multis post annis rex Ancus coloniam deduxit, urbem ipse conderet*'. See, also, Dion. Hal. 3.41.3. On Ancus Marcius: Liv. 1.33.9: '*in ore Tiberis Ostia urbs condita; salinae circa factae*'. On the literary tradition: Camous (2004).
14. Arnaud (2012).
15. State Hermitage Museum n. inv. B 2207; Depalmas (2005), p. 67 n. 36.
16. di Gennaro (2019).
17. Brocato et al. (2016).
18. Cifani (2020).
19. Just. *Epit.* 43.3.4. Translation by Watson (1853).
20. Vanotti (1999), pp. 463–464.
21. Translation from Hultsch and Shuckburgh (1889). For a critical analysis of the text: Scardigli (1991).
22. Mele (1979); Mele (1986); Bravo (1984); Nantet (2016), pp. 109–110.
23. *CIE* 8602.
24. Drakidès et al. (2010).
25. Nantet (2016), p. 108.
26. Parker (1992); Sourisseau (2012), p. 183, fig. 1.
27. Ampolo (1994); Krämer (2016). On the re-organisation of land frontiers in Central Italy: Cifani (2012).
28. Herod. 5.42; Cifani and Munzi (2003).
29. Hom. Od. 3.72 onwards; Thuc. 1.5.1. See the contribution by A Tarwacka later in this volume.
30. Gabrielsen (2013); Ferrer Albelda (2013).
31. Colonna (2006).

Chapter 3

Contingent Movement: Seafaring, Contracts and Law

Peter B Campbell

INTRODUCTION

By contrast to travel by road, which is relatively predictable, movement by sea is beset by uncertainty. As R Laurence has argued in connection with roads, movement has been under-theorised, with scholars often focusing on economy or speed.[1] This chapter argues likewise for movement by sea. Unlike movement on land, which is relatively direct and reproducible along roads or across landscapes, movement at sea is dependent upon external forces such as winds, currents and the sea state, the navigation of which requires constant situation-dependent decision-making. In the fields of archaeology and anthropology, the concept of contingency has been used to interpret routine creation and decision-making relating to seasonality in the agrarian countryside.[2] This chapter argues that contingency can also be used as a means to interpret ship and harbour activity. Contingency is not only descriptive of ship movement, but also a lens for examining the interconnectivity between the individuals, vessels, infrastructure and social mechanisms that comprised a maritime ecosystem for long-distance trade.

In Lucian's *Navigium* the author describes one of the great Roman grain carriers, the *Isis*, which had charted a course from Alexandria to Rome.[3] Lucian's tale, however, finds the vessel at Piraeus after it had been driven far off course.

'They set sail with a moderate wind from Pharus [Egypt], and sighted Acamas [Cyprus] on the seventh day. Then a west wind got up, and they were carried as far east as Sidon [Lebanon]. On their way thence they came in for a heavy gale, and the tenth day brought them through the Straits to the Chelidon Isles [Asia Minor]; and there they very nearly went to the bottom. I have sailed past the Chelidons myself, and I know the sort of seas you get there, especially if the wind is SW. by S.; it is just there, of course, that the division takes place between the Lycian and Pamphylian waters; and the surge caused by the numerous currents gets broken at the headland, whose rocks have been sharpened by the action of the water till they are like razors; the result is a stupendous crash of waters, the waves often rising to the very top of the crags. This was the kind of thing they found themselves in for, according to the master, – and on a pitch dark night! However, the Gods were moved by their distress, and showed them a fire that enabled them to identify the Lycian coast; and a bright star – either Castor or Pollux – appeared at the masthead, and guided the ship into the open sea on their left; just in time, for she was making straight for the cliff. Having once lost their proper course, they sailed on through the Aegean, bearing up against the Etesian winds, until they came to anchor in Piraeus yesterday, being the seventieth day of the voyage; you see how far they had been carried out of their way; whereas if they had taken Crete on their right, they would have doubled [Cape] Malea, and been at Rome by this time.[4]'

Unlike *periploi* and itineraries, which present idealised routes, Lucian's report accords with the reality of sea travel, in a manner that is consistent with first person accounts from the Bronze Age journey of Wenamun in *The Tale of the Shipwrecked Sailor*, to the accounts of the voyages made by Paul and Synesius in the Roman period.[5] Homer's *Odyssey* and Apollonius' *Argonautica* are also narratives whose plots are driven by the contingencies of sea travel. The *Isis*'s voyage started well, the vessel being carried to deep water and sighting Cyprus; however, a west wind took them the wrong direction, forcing them to the Levantine coast. In order to turn westwards, the ship had to sail north along the coast to Cilicia before heading west, facing a number of challenging circumstances close to shore, which required constant monitoring to avoid surge, currents and rocks. The crew had to work against the wind, beating to windward in an exhausting and difficult manoeuvre requiring constant adjustments. The final sentence indicates the ideal route: keep Crete and Cape Maleas to starboard. However, as is often the case at sea, the ideal route was unavailable to the vessel. As a result, the voyage is described as a constant negotiation with the sea that, in this case, the mariners were losing. It reveals how seafaring is both dependent upon, and a negotiation with, natural forces from instance-to-instance and how changes – wind direction and strength, storms, light levels and so forth – impact upon movement.

L Casson begins *Ancient Trade and Society* with an epiphany that he experienced while reading a book on the ancient economy.[6] A scholar had stated that a ship could sail from Alexandria to Puteoli in nine days, which is false for any sailing vessel. Casson realised that Pliny the Elder writes of sailing from Puteoli to Alexandria in nine days and that the scholar had assumed that the return journey would have taken a similar time. Ships, however, do not behave like vehicles on a road; the outward journey to Alexandria is quite different from the return. Rather than nine days from Alexandria to Puteoli, Casson suggested it should be thirty-nine days.[7] Sulpicius Severus records a 'prosperous voyage', indicating exceptional speed, of thirty days from Alexandria to Marseilles, which can be used as a benchmark for speed of travel from an eastern port to one in the west.[8]

In Casson's own words, the author in question did not fully appreciate 'the special way sailing craft behave'.[9] More generally, it is probably fair to say that scholars of the ancient world have traditionally had a form of *sea blindness*: a term that was coined to describe the public's inability to see their own large-scale connectivity to global maritime activity.[10] I would argue that this extends to scholarship on popular subjects such as connectivity, mobility and island studies, which do not fully engage with research into maritime activity. So far as maritime movement is concerned, simplistic models are still prevalent. Tools such as ORBIS that calculate travel time in the aggregate fail to distinguish sea movement from the steady travel rates on land.[11] The technical specifications of a vessel or the linear distance between two ports will not accurately convey the time of travel, as ships do not travel in straight lines or at steady speeds. Recently, a growth in studies of maritime trade and connectivity in the ancient economy has brought welcome external scholarship to the insular field of maritime archaeology; however, interpretations by non-maritime specialists are sometimes affected by an insufficient awareness of the realities of seafaring.[12] This awakening corresponds to a significant paradigm shift in the humanities, known as the 'blue humanities' or 'oceanic thought', which centres the sea as a means to examine broad social questions. This development offers promising engagement with maritime studies, though archaeology has yet to meaningfully contribute to the blue humanities.[13]

This chapter examines the special way that sailing craft behave and devises a term for it: contingent movement.[14] Lucian and Casson provide examples on which to build the concept of contingency in seafaring. To define it simply, contingent movement describes the way in which ships travel dependent on external forces and the inherent risks therein, a negotiation with the marine environment subject to chance and changing circumstances. Ships move in a special way because seafarers make decisions with each shift of the wind, changing current or passing headland. This sequence is known as 'contingent decision-making' by psychologists.[15] It is not uncommon for two ships that leave port at the same time for a common destination to experience different routes and travel times.[16] There is no road at sea, only starting and end points, and the path taken is conditional and changes with each voyage.

The contingency of movement at sea could lead to undesirable results, such as cargo spoiling, arrival during a market downturn, capture by pirates or shipwrecking. It establishes the rhythm of shore-based labour, where dockworkers, lightermen and ballasters are 'caught up in a world of contingent labor that shaped the communities built around the docks'.[17] The flow of work in ancient Portus and Ostia, for example, followed the rhythms of the sea and winds, which made for intense periods of seasonal labour that took place at certain times of day.[18] Disruptions in shipping would affect supply chains for food provisioning, building construction and more. Ships, harbours and canals were as important as the roads when it came to infrastructure for trade and communication. As with the road network, the maritime network facilitated mobility through its own nuanced context. Large-scale maritime infrastructure projects, beginning with the moles at Delos and Samos and culminating in the harbour facilities at Carthage, Alexandria and Portus, were designed to accommodate maritime contingency, just as roads were designed around cart movement.[19]

SEAFARING AS CONTINGENT MOVEMENT

To understand the contingency of movement at sea, it is necessary to have an awareness of the tension of forces that watercraft exist within, including displacement,

wind, currents and gravity.[20] Victor Hugo, after observing mariners for fifteen years
while exiled on the island of Guernsey, wrote:

> 'The sea, in conjunction with the wind, is a composite of forces. A ship is a composite
> of mechanisms. The sea's forces are mechanisms of infinite power; the ship's mecha-
> nisms are forces of limited power. Between these two organisms, one inexhaustible, the
> other intelligent, takes place the combat that is called navigation.'[21]

In another paper, I recently argued that the sea is a 'hyperobject', an entity of
vast scale and agency, and navigation, rather than being wayfinding as it is often
simplistically presented, is a negotiation with this hyperobject to derive movement
from forces quite different from those operating upon land-based movement.[22] As
Synesius wrote in the fourth century AD, movement at sea is contingent upon,
'those well-known chance events which no one . . . ever confronted at sea with
impunity'.[23]

   Since the advent of nautical archaeology in around 1960, the technical aspects
of ancient ships have become well understood.[24] Similarly, the modelling of the
marine environment is now advanced.[25] The latter forms part of the scholarship
that examines the maritime cultural landscape or seascape, the reconstruction of
the natural (for example, winds, water colour, islands and so forth) and cultural
features (for example, lighthouses, temples, cities) used by mariners to navigate
space and understand spatial positioning.[26] However, these well-researched areas
do not cover all aspects of seafaring. As J Leidwanger argues, while it is possible
to take into account winds, navigational conditions, ship performance and more,
relying on modelling or interpretations based on the aggregate '[fails] to capture
the varying ways in which winds – especially over smaller areas – could affect this
landscape and mariners' choices'.[27] A gap therefore exists between these aggregate
models and a ship's technical capability: that is, the lived experience of sailing.[28]
This gap can be filled by adopting the concept of contingent movement.

   The tension between natural forces and the ship is evident in the fact that
much of sea travel is indirect. Only when the wind is abaft, or from the stern,
does a vessel travel directly with the wind; the majority of sailing is conducted at
an angle to the wind. When tacking or beating against the wind, a vessel follows
a zig-zag pattern angled to the wind and the distance travelled is considerably
longer than the distance 'made good', or realised, between the departure and destination points.[29] Therefore, a 'favourable wind' allows for faster and more direct
travel, whereas a 'contrary wind' makes for slower and indirect travel.

   In addition to taking account of wind direction, it is important to address the
misconception that ancient mariners travelled along the coast and did not travel
at night.[30] Mariners travel where safest and often across open water, where there
is sea-room. Ancient sources make clear that the open water route from Rhodes
to Alexandria could be made year-round, even during winter when there was a
greater risk of storms.[31] Sailing near shore increases the risks of wrecking and
piracy, while putting into port at night increases financial expenditure. Ships only

entered a port while a voyage was ongoing for the purposes of trade, repair or shelter from severe gales, but seldom for any other reason.[32] Sailing at night is necessary when certain winds, which occur only during those hours, permit movement. These outdated ideas impose a false linear trajectory upon seafaring and ignore ancient sources to the contrary.[33]

The sea, therefore, does not provide limitless and unfettered travel in any direction *at all times*. Limits on free movement are the reason that resource-poor islands such as Delos, Fournoi, Malta and Menorca were political centres and strategic locations for navies and pirates.[34] In the 1920s, the Fascist Grand Council claimed that Italy was imprisoned and that 'the bars of this prison are Corsica, Tunisia, Malta and Cyprus'.[35] In a modern example, the blockage of the Suez Canal by the container ship *Ever Given* in 2021 is evidence of how movement is contingent even within the protected confines of a canal, due to windage impacting the vessel's steering.[36] In an ancient context, the prevailing winds are contrary to the harbour mouths of Alexandria and Portus, meaning that on most days departing ships would need the morning offshore wind in order to leave under sail, otherwise they would require towing.[37]

The benefit of sea travel is not that it is faster or safer than direct transport on land, but that large cargoes can be moved efficiently due to forces that are distinct from those on land.[38] The nature of water, specifically in terms of displacement, allows for cargo capacity that exceeds any method operating under the limits of gravity and friction on land. As Adam Smith stated, '[s]ix or eight men, therefore, by help of water-carriage, can carry and bring back in the same time the same quantity of goods between London and Edinburgh, as fifty broad-wheeled wagons, attended by a hundred men, and drawn by four hundred horses'.[39] A vessel classed as 'small' has a capacity of 10–20 tons, but the largest carts on land can only bear loads of only 1–2 tons.[40] Even in cases where transport by cart could potentially be faster, a cart's capacity is limited and the cost of transport is greater.[41] Another advantage of sea travel over land is that unlike beasts of burden, ships fitted with sails depend upon external forces for their propulsion and therefore do not tire. While not explicitly stated, it is the effect of displacement that lies behind R Duncan-Jones' Roman transport cost ratio between sea:river:land (1:4.9:28) and C Yeo's argument that grain from Egypt arriving by ship was cheaper than Italian grain transported by road.[42]

Though ancient sources do not provide precise routes for comparison, it is possible to map contingency using seventeenth century logbooks that record voyages from England to the American colonies. Figure 3.1 shows six westerly voyages recorded by Captain Edward Rhodes. This dataset is exceptional because the starting and end points (Plymouth and Chesapeake Bay), the captain (who was experienced with the route and sea conditions) and the vessel, all stay constant. The voyages, however, varied in duration from thirty-nine to eighty-one days.[43] While the ideal route would be a straight line, the logbook provides an insight into the forces that the ship contended with on each journey. Each turn or course correction was a decision prompted by a change in sea state, wind or currents,

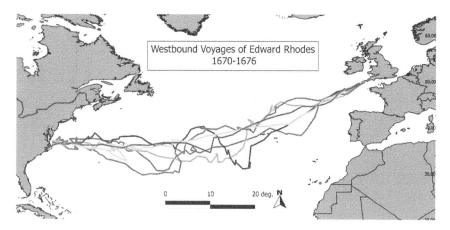

Figure 3.1 A map of westbound Atlantic voyages from Plymouth to Chesapeake Bay recorded in Edward Rhodes' logbook between 1670–1676 (Tucker (2017), figures 4–7).

with the aim of continuing in a westerly trajectory. The slowest time is more than double the fastest and the deviation from the median is as great as forty per cent. It is evident from ancient sailing times that a slow voyage could take twice as long as a fast one. Even so, the ability to move sizeable tonnage over long distances meant that variability in travel time was acceptable.

In research published by C Safadi and F Sturt, the concept of contingency is taken into account in the creation of maps that, rather than depict geography, illustrate the sailing environment based on conditions in specific times and places.[44] Figure 3.2 compares distances for ships sailing from Byblos on the same day: the left map showing a morning departure and the right a departure in the afternoon. Cyprus is a short jaunt for a vessel departing in the morning, but a long sail for one departing in the afternoon. It is significant that not only may travel time differ, but the route may change considerably as new metaphorical peaks and valleys open and close as conditions change. This could lead the afternoon vessel to travel on an entirely different route, just as the *Isis* was meant to pass south of Cyprus from Sidon but was rerouted north to Asia Minor.

The reason why navigation is a series of decisions made instance-to-instance based on local context is that the sea is in a constant state of change. Psychologist K Takemura argues that contingent decision-making is the most common kind of decision-making process.[45] It is decision-making where, 'outcomes lie out on distant branches that depend for their existence on a sequence of contingent decisions'.[46] On a ship, it is a moment-to-moment process of adjusting the vessel's interactions between buoyancy, sail area, centre of gravity and speed within a specific sea state. This has a cascading effect on the whole journey, as the episode concerning the *Isis* demonstrates (Figure 3.3). The sea state, time of day, type of cargo, experience of the crew and other factors impact upon the decisions made by human actors at certain points in a journey, so that no two journeys are ever identical. The author's

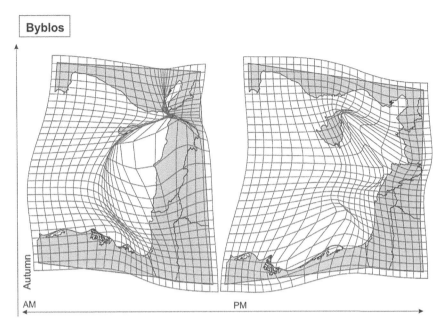

Figure 3.2 Map projections of the eastern Mediterranean based on sailing times from Byblos during the autumn, morning versus afternoon (Safadi and Sturt (2019), figure 6).

research in the Aegean examines how the navigational landscapes can constrain movement and cause wrecks, while modelling the built and natural environments at Portus shows how movement can change in short timeframes.[47]

This is not to over-emphasise the dangers: seafaring was generally quite safe in the past. The quantity of wrecks varies between 1–7.5 per cent per annum in periods for which there are records.[48] Based upon the interest rates in Athenian maritime contracts, E Cohen argues that participants perceived a low risk of loss on any given voyage.[49] Safety can be attributed to social aspects of seafaring, such as mariners' experience and decision-making, rather than improvements in technology that had limited impact in the Classical, Hellenistic and Roman periods.[50] Much of traditional maritime knowledge consists in anticipating changes through natural signs, whether it is an atmospheric pressure change or animal behaviour to indicate a coming front, 'catspaw' disturbance on the water's surface from katabatic downdrafts, or swell refraction indicating a distant island, to give a few examples.[51] A direct route at sea is not always a straight bearing between two points; taking a straight bearing to an island can result in a ship missing it by a wide margin due to currents.[52] A headland can be sanctuary one moment and a danger the next. Even at anchor a vessel requires decision-making to adjust to conditions, as illustrated by the 200 ships that sank in the harbour of Portus – which one might consider a protected space – during a storm.[53] The complexity of ship behaviour, the tension

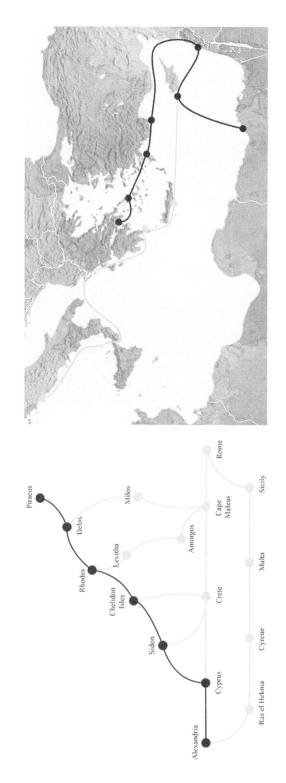

Figure 3.3 The contingent decision making of the *Isis* attempting to navigate from Alexandria to Rome. Figure by author, alternative routes interpreted based on common navigational routes.

between the vessel and the environment in order to navigate a route and the liminal state of the seascape are why contingency is a necessary framework to understand the special way sailing craft behave.

LAW, CONTRACTS AND CONTINGENT MOVEMENT

In the last section, I explained that navigational decision-making is contingent in the sense that the navigator's decisions are made in response to changes in the marine environment, such as weather conditions, the sea state, light levels and so forth. Another no less important factor in decision-making at sea concerns the institutional framework within which a voyage takes place. Maritime commercial enterprises were – and still are – complex affairs that frequently involved a multiplicity of contractual arrangements between numerous parties, including merchants, financiers, shipowners and carriers.[54] Since a number of chapters in this volume will address these relationships in some detail I will confine myself to a few brief examples of how the agreements entered into between various parties could influence navigational decision-making at sea.

One way in which merchants could fund the acquisition of cargo was to borrow money from a financier in the form of a maritime loan, the distinctive feature of which was that the debtor was only obliged to repay if the ship arrived safely at its destination.[55] Though the contents of only two maritime contracts of this kind have survived (at least, from the ancient period), both contain clauses that set out (for example) the general itinerary the vessel should take, the time limits for the voyage (and therefore the season it should travel in) and which harbours the borrower should use.[56] Similarly, in the papyri, the so-called 'navigation clauses' in Nilotic contracts of carriage specified the time of day during which sailing was permitted to take place, the berths in which the captain was allowed to anchor and so forth.[57] In general, the reason for the insertion of these clauses was to limit the parties' exposure to risk, for example, by specifying that the maximum duration of the voyage should coincide with the end of the traditional sailing season, or that sailing was only to take place during daylight. In other words, the parties to the enterprise frequently set limits upon the freedom of the pilot to navigate and therefore upon the range of choices available to them in the process of making contingent decisions. In both these kinds of contracts, the freedom of the pilot to navigate the vessel was therefore constrained by the tolerance of each of the parties to the contract for risk. The more risk averse the parties, the greater the restrictions placed upon navigation.[58]

The way in which the contractual limitations placed upon navigation influenced the decisions made by the pilot is not altogether straightforward. In the Roman period, it was common for shipowners to place the responsibility for the commercial operation of the vessel in the hands of a shipmaster (*magister navis*).[59] The navigation of the ship, meanwhile, was left to a pilot (*gubernator*),[60] who might either have been selected directly by the shipowner or (more likely) by the shipmaster who the shipowner had appointed.[61] In as far as contracts entered into by the shipmaster affected the decision-making of the pilot, this can only have been the case if these limitations were communicated to them by the shipmaster. However, assuming that both the shipmaster and the pilot worked to the same end, the limitations introduced by the contract would have comprised part of the institutional context within which navigational decision-making took place.[62]

At a broader level, the specific limitations introduced by the parties will only have exerted influence upon decision-making so far as their agreement was enforceable. Here, the broader legal framework becomes important: besides mechanisms for holding the parties accountable within trading communities (arbitration, ostracism and so forth), the enforceability of contracts in the courts was a significant factor. In fourth century BC Athens, the introduction of special maritime suits to expedite the hearing of commercial cases between both citizens and foreigners appears to have represented a major development[63]; and in Rome the incorporation of institutions of the *ius gentium* into Roman law may have had a similar effect.[64]

SHIPBOARD DECISION-MAKING

The evidence of shipboard decision-making in the ancient Mediterranean indicates a stark difference with the 'Age of Sail', which is commonly taken as a reference point for maritime hierarchies. In the latter period, a captain had complete command of a vessel and decision-making. This was not, however, the case for ancient Mediterranean seafaring. Due to the capital costs of the ship and cargo, which required investment from multiple stakeholders, making a decision was more complicated in antiquity.

This section seeks to understand shipboard decision-making as it relates to risk mitigation: that is, the individuals involved in making decisions on board and the sequence by which these were taken. Good examples of Takemura's concept of contingent decision-making may be found in the first-person accounts of voyages authored by Synesius and Paul, which depict the process as a discourse between the shipowner, captain, pilot, passengers and crew.[65] While the captain appears to have had the final decision, discussion among those with an interest in the success of the voyage was part of the process. It is also interesting to note that the individuals participating in the decision-making process were often of different social statuses: captains and crew could be enslaved, as could the representatives of moneylenders, while shipowners, merchants and passengers may have cut across different social strata.[66]

Synesius, sailing in the winter of AD 396, records a journey from Alexandria to Cyrene. The captain, Amarantus, was also the shipowner.[67] At the start of the journey, the vessel was towed out of Alexandria harbour after briefly running aground and passengers requested that Amarantus take a coastal route within sight of land, which the captain declined in favour of a deep-water route where large long-distance freighters were more commonly found.[68] The captain's decision proved correct when a storm struck and the ship had plenty of sea-room clear of the dangerous North African lee shore. Amarantus then tells Synesius:

> 'See what it is to be master of the art of navigation. I had long foreseen this storm, and that is why I sought the open. I can tack in now, since our sea-room allows us to add to the length of our tack. But such a course as the one I have taken would not have been possible had we hugged the shore, for in that case the ship would have dashed on the coast.'[69]

Later in the voyage, a different process is revealed. The ship arrives along the coast of North Africa and grounds on a reef. A local pilot joined the ship and the captain ceded control in order to guide the ship to a safe anchorage. Several other ships did the same and joined Synesius' vessel in the anchorage.[70] The sequence is an excellent example of contingency-based decision-making, in which the captain, and later pilot, direct the ship's course based on environmental conditions and knowledge of seamanship. Rather than following a direct line to the destination, the vessel travelled much farther north to pre-empt storms.

Paul's voyage from the Levant to Rome is another example of the contingency of decision-making at sea.[71] The route of the voyage is nearly identical to the one described by Lucian in connection with the *Isis*, sailing from Sidon to Rome, keeping Crete to starboard. A storm struck Paul's ship in the same open water region as Synesius, which led to concern among the crew that the vessel would run aground on the lee shore of North Africa. Paul records the discussion that was held while the ship was anchored in Crete. He voiced concern that the weather might turn due to the late time of year: 'but the centurion, instead of listening to what Paul said, followed the advice of the pilot and of the owner of the ship. Since the harbour was unsuitable to winter in, the majority decided that we should sail on'.[72] On this vessel, the owner and captain were separate individuals. They, along with the centurion, were part of the decision-making process and it appears that a majority was needed to act.

Later in the account, Paul provides one of the most important examples of contingent decision-making, in the episode known as the 'shipwreck'. In fact, it was a purposeful grounding. When the vessel arrived in Malta, the vessel was run ashore. This was a planned operation with care given to maximise the chances of survival for the crew and passengers. Soundings were taken to measure the depth of water and the cargo was jettisoned to lighten the ship. Upon sighting a small creek that would allow passengers access to land, rather than a scaling rocky coastline, the crew took in the anchors, pulled up the steering oars and put up the sail.[73] After grounding, individuals used boards as floatation devices to make it the rest of the way to shore and all survived. The jettison and intentional grounding were decisions made for the common good, sacrificing the ship and/or cargo to save the individuals on board.[74]

In Synesius' account, the captain made the final decision, while in Paul's it was the captain, shipowner and centurion together. However, it is significant

that these decisions were made following a discourse between the various stakeholders, revealing a more horizontal structure to the shipboard hierarchy than
was the case in later periods. Synesius makes it clear that Amarantus was pre-
occupied with repaying moneylenders, perhaps because his ship was the security on a loan.[75] Contracts relied upon witnesses and these accounts suggest
that stakeholder discussions were sometimes held for the purpose of meeting
contractual obligations and to provide for witnesses in the event that lawsuits
were initiated later. As opposed to the authority exercised by captains in later
centuries, it is clear that the division of the risk among stakeholders and the
notion of common good were practiced throughout the process of shipboard
decision-making.

Stakeholder decision-making could have a negative side. In 297 BC, Demetrios Poliorketes executed a captain and merchant for attempting to deliver grain
to Athens while it was under siege. The shared punishment was meted out by
Demetrios to both individuals because he recognised that they were both equally
responsible for the decision.[76]

CONCLUSION

In theorising 'the special way sailing craft behave' this chapter has used contingency as a lens through which to understand the impact of physical and social
factors upon navigational decision-making. In terms of physical factors, contingent movement describes the continuous process by which navigators respond
to changes in the marine environment when piloting a vessel. In terms of social
factors, contingent movement also takes account of the institutional environment within which navigational decision-making takes place. In this context, the
parties to an enterprise frequently agreed to place limits on aspects of the vessel's
navigation, which were intended to reduce the chance that the ship might be lost
to shipwreck or some other calamity. In combination with the legal framework
that made contracts such as these enforceable, social factors framed navigational
decision-making no less than the physical aspects experienced by navigators at
sea. Finally, the process of decision-making on merchant vessels in the ancient
world was not concentrated in the personality of the ship's captain, but rather
dispersed across a variety of actors, each of whom had an interest in the safe
conclusion of the voyage. This has implications for our understanding of the
contingency of movement at sea, which was responsive not only to natural conditions, but also to the institutional context within which maritime commercial
enterprises were conducted. The interruptions to the journeys of Odysseus, the
Argo and Paul are the contingencies that, taken as a whole, are not the exception
to sea travel, but the uncertainty that defines it. Nowhere in ancient itineraries
or the straight lines drawn on maps are found Calypso, Scylla, or Charybdis; however, the importance of these stories is not that sea monsters are real, but that the
trials of the sea can be overcome.

BIBLIOGRAPHY

Abulafia, D. (2011), *The Great Sea: A Human History of the Mediterranean* (London: Allen Lane).

Andreau, J. (1999), *Banking and Business in the Roman World* (Cambridge: Cambridge University Press).

Beresford, J. (2013), *The Ancient Sailing Season* (Leiden: Brill).

Blackman, D.J. (1982), 'Ancient Harbours in the Mediterranean, Part 1', *IJNA* 11(2), pp. 79–104.

Campbell, P.B. (2020), 'The Sea as a Hyperobject: Moving beyond Maritime Cultural Landscapes', *Journal of Eastern Mediterranean Archaeology Heritage Studies* 8(3), pp. 1–22.

Campbell, P.B. and Koutsouflakis, G. (2021), 'Aegean Navigation and the Shipwrecks of Fournoi: the Archipelago in Context', in S. Demesticha and L. Blue (eds), *Under the Mediterranean I: Studies in Maritime Archaeology* (Leiden: Sidestone Press), pp. 271–290.

Candy, P. (2020a), 'Limits of Juristic Argument in the Exercitorian Edict', in B. Spagnolo and J. Sampson (eds), *Principle and Pragmatism in Roman Law* (London: Hart Publishing), pp. 143–158.

Candy, P. (2020b), 'Parallel Developments in Roman Law and Maritime Trade during the Late Republic and Early Principate', *JRA* 33, pp. 53–72.

Carver, T.G. (1961), *Carriage by Sea* (London: Sweet & Maxwell).

Casson, L. (1984), *Ancient Trade and Society* (Detroit, IL: Wayne State University Press).

Casson, L. (1995), *Ships and Seamanship in the Ancient World*, 2nd edn (Baltimore: Johns Hopkins University Press).

Cohen, E. (2011), *Athenian Economy and Society: A Banking Perspective* (Princeton: Princeton University Press).

Duncan-Jones, R. (1974), *The Economy of the Roman Empire: Quantitative Studies* (Cambridge: Cambridge University Press).

Flinders Petrie, W.M. (1899), *Egyptian Tales: Translated from the Papyri*, 2nd edn (London: Methuen).

Frezza, P. (1949), *Ius Gentium* (Pisa: Nistri-Lischi).

Greeley, B. (2021), 'The Bank Effect and the Big Boat Blocking the Suez', *Financial Times*, 25 March.

Harris, E. (2018), 'Trials and Arbitrations in Classical Athens', in M. Bearzot, M. Canevaro, T. Giargiulo and E. Poddighe (eds), *Athenaion Politeiai tra storia, politica e sociologia: Aristotele e Pseudo-Senofonte* (Milan: LED), pp. 213–230.

Hoare, P. (2008), *Leviathan or, The Whale* (London: Fourth Estate).

Hodge, W.B. (1864), 'On Shipwrecks in the Royal Navy', *Journal of the Statistical Society of London* 27(2), pp. 234–244.

Hugo, V. [1866] (2002), *The Toilers of the Sea*, J. Hogarth (trans.) (New York: The Modern Library).

James, P. (2020), *Food Provisions for Ancient Rome: A Supply Chain Approach* (New York: Routledge).

Kahanov, Y. (2006), 'The Voyage of Synesius', *Journal of Navigation* 59(3), pp. 435–444.

Kaplan, M. and Kaplan, E. (2006), *Chances Are . . . Adventures in Probability* (New York: Penguin).

Keay, S., Campbell, P.B., Crawford, K. and Moreno Escobar, M.C. (2021), 'Space, Accessibility and Movement through the Portus Romae', in F. Vermeulen and A. Zuiderhoek (eds), *Space, Movement and the Economy in Roman Cities in Italy and Beyond* (New York: Routledge), pp. 375–417.

Laurence, R. (2002), *The Roads of Roman Italy: Mobility and Cultural Change* (New York: Routledge).

Leidwanger, J. (2020), *Roman Seas: A Maritime Archaeology of Eastern Mediterranean Economies* (Oxford: Oxford University Press).

Levinson, M. (2008), *The Box: How the Shipping Container Made the World Smaller* (Princeton: Princeton University Press).

Lindsay, W.S. (1876), *History of Merchant Shipping and Ancient Commerce*, Vol. 3 (London: Marston, Low and Searle).

Mentz, S. (2020), *Ocean* (London: Bloomsbury).

Meyer-Termeer, A.J.M. (1978), *Die Haftung der Schiffer im griechischen und römischen Recht* (Zutphen: Terra).

Morton, J. (2001), *The Role of the Physical Environment in Ancient Greek Seafaring* (Leiden: Brill).

Parker, A.J. (2012), 'Book review: Maritime Technology in the Ancient Economy: Ship-design and Navigation', *IJNA* 41, pp. 440–441.

Pomey, P., Kahanov, Y. and Rieth, E. (2012), 'Transition from Shell to Skeleton in Ancient Mediterranean Ship-Construction: Analysis, Problems and Future Research', *IJNA* 41, pp. 235–314.

Redford, D. (2014), 'The Royal Navy, Sea-blindness and British National Identity', in D. Redford (ed), *Maritime History and Identity: The Sea and Culture in the Modern World* (London and New York: I.B. Tauris), pp. 61–78.

Rich, S.A. and Campbell, P.B (eds) (forthcoming) *Contemporary Philosophy for Maritime Archaeology: Flat Ontologies, Oceanic Thought, and the Anthropocene* (Leiden: Sidestone).

Russell, B. (2013), *The Economics of the Roman Stone Trade* (Oxford: Oxford University Press).

Safadi, C. and Sturt, F. (2019), 'The Warped Sea of Sailing: Maritime Topographies of Space and Time for the Bronze Age Eastern Mediterranean', *Journal of Archaeological Science* 103, pp. 1–15.

Smith, A. (1776), *An Inquiry into the Nature and Causes of the Wealth of Nations* (London: W. Strahan and T. Cadell).

Sturt, F. (2005), 'Fishing for Meaning: Lived Space and the Early Neolithic of Orkney', in V. Cummings and A. Pannett (eds), *Set in Stone: New Approaches to Neolithic Monuments in Scotland* (Oxford: Oxbow), pp. 68–80.

Sutton, S.B. (2000), *Contingent Countryside: Settlement, Economy, and Land Use in the Southern Argolid Since 1700* (Stanford: Stanford University Press).

Takemura, K. (2001), 'Contingent Decision Making in the Social World: The "Mental Ruler" Model', in C.M. Allwood and M. Selart (eds), *Decision Making: Social and Creative Dimensions* (New York: Springer), pp. 153–173.

Tchernia, A. (1986), *Le Vin de l'Italie Romaine* (Rome: École française de Rome).

Tucker, S.A. (2017), *Smoke on the Water: An Historical Archaeological Assessment of Maritime Sources of Productivity Change in the Early English Tobacco Trade* (Department of Archaeology, University of Southampton).

Westerdahl, C. (1992), 'The Maritime Cultural Landscape', *IJNA* 21(1), pp. 5–14.

Whitewright, J. (2011), 'The Potential Performance of Ancient Mediterranean Sailing Rigs', *IJNA* 40(1), pp. 2–17.

Whitewright, J. (2018), 'Sailing and Sailing Rigs in the Ancient Mediterranean: Implications of Continuity, Variation and Change in Propulsion Technology', *IJNA* 47(1), pp. 28–44.

Yeo, C.A. (1946), 'Land and Sea Transportation in Imperial Italy', *TAPhA* 77(1), pp. 221–244.

NOTES

1. Laurence (2002). The author is grateful to Julian Whitewright and Ray Laurence for their advice on the chapter, as well as Crystal Safadi, Scott Tucker, Dan Diffendale and Emlyn Dodd for discussions. Thanks are to be given to the editors for the opportunity to contribute to the publication. Comments by the anonymous reviewers greatly improved the chapter. All errors are the author's own.
2. Sutton (2000).
3. Lucian's account is fictional, but Casson convincingly argues that it is based on first-hand knowledge: Casson (1995), p. 224.
4. Luc. *Nav.*, 7–9.
5. Flinders Petrie (1899), pp. 86–87; Papyrus Pushkin 120; *Acts* 27; Syn. *Ep.* 4. For an examination of Synesius' voyage, see Kahanov (2006).
6. Casson (1984), p. 15.
7. Casson (1984), p. 16.
8. Sulpicius Severus, *Dialogues*, 1.1.3; Whitewright (2011), p. 4.
9. Casson (1984), p. 16.
10. Sea blindness, coined by First Sea Lord Sir Jonathan Band, specifically refers to the public's inability to conceive of the centrality of maritime activity to their access to food and resources, and commerce and security: see Redford (2014).
11. ORBIS provides a twenty-one day estimate for a "fast" journey from Alexandria to Rome, which is faster than Sulpicius Severus "prosperous voyage" by thirty per cent: see, *https://orbis.stanford.edu/* (last accessed 29 September 2021).
12. Parker (2012), p. 441. In an effort to bridge the gap from the opposite shore, the author seeks to add nuance to seafaring with the aim of encouraging further interdisciplinary engagement.
13. Mentz (2020). For a forthcoming edited volume offering a contribution from maritime archaeology to the Blue Humanities, see Rich and Campbell (2021).

14. The author has chosen 'contingency' because it is the term used in maritime contracts and labour, e.g. Carver (1961), p. 777; Levinson (2008), p. 28. The term denotes the dependence on external factors, though in some sources the term 'conditional' is used synonymously: see, e.g. Kaplan and Kaplan (2006), p. 94.
15. Takemura (2001), p. 154.
16. Syn. *Ep.*, 4.29; Keay et al. (2021), p. 391.
17. Quote in Levinson (2008), p. 28. For dockwork dictated by diurnal winds in the Roman Period, see Keay et al. (2021), pp. 391–92. Levinson (2008), p. 28 details the bulk of dockwork focused on the mornings in Edinburgh, San Francisco, Marseille and elsewhere.
18. Keay et al. (2021), pp. 391–392. Note that the absence of wind can be as consequential as its presence.
19. Blackman (1982), p. 185.
20. Whitewright furthers Casson's criticism of a lack of understanding about navigation in his observation that the *Cambridge Economic History of the Greco-Roman World* contains only two paragraphs on ships: Whitewright (2018), p. 28.
21. Hugo (2002), p. 190.
22. Campbell (2020).
23. Syn. *Ep.*, 4.25.
24. For example, Pomey et al. (2012); Whitewright (2018).
25. For example, Safadi and Sturt (2019); Leidwanger (2020).
26. Westerdahl (1992).
27. Leidwanger (2020), pp. 67–68.
28. While individual journeys are non-replicable, research such as Safadi and Sturt (2019) has provided an excellent framework for examining the ranges of variability within regions.
29. Whitewright (2011).
30. Beresford (2013), p. 2.
31. *Dem.*, 56.30.
32. The treaty between Carthage and Rome dating to c. 509 BC shows that Roman vessels were not allowed entry into Carthaginian ports unless due to 'stress of weather or fear of an enemy': Polyb. 3.22. This hardly conforms with ships putting into harbour each night.
33. For example, Syn. *Ep.*, 4 for open water sailing; Plin. *HN.*, 2.48 for night sailing.
34. For the Aegean, see Campbell and Koutsouflakis (2021); for Malta and Menorca see Abulafia (2011).
35. Quoted in Abulafia (2011), p. 601.
36. The incident appears to be a combination of gusts, lulls, and the 'bank effect': Greeley (2021), p. 1.
37. For Portus see Keay et al. (2021); for Alexandria see Kahanov (2006). Rutilius (1.11) waited fifteen days in Portus in AD 416 for the contrary winds to shift before he could depart.
38. While sea travel is often faster there are certainly cases of it being slower, such as travel around peninsulas. The Diolkos, for example, expedited access to the Aegean/Gulf of Corinth, as sailing would be slower than the overland route.
39. Smith (1776), p. 22.
40. Russell (2013), p. 98.
41. James (2020), p. 28
42. Duncan-Jones (1974), pp. 366–396; Yeo (1946), pp. 241–242.

43. Tucker (2017), pp. 117, 145.
44. Safadi and Sturt (2019).
45. Takemura (2001), p. 154.
46. Kaplan and Kaplan (2006), p. 258.
47. Campbell and Koutsouflakis (2021); Keay et al. (2021).
48. Hodge (1864), p. 235; Lindsay (1876), p. 633; Tchernia (1986), pp. 85–87; Hoare (2008), p. 278.
49. Cohen (2011), p. 142.
50. Whitewright (2018), p. 42. Regarding experience, Apuleius states that a bad helmsman can destroy an otherwise excellent vessel: Apul. *Flor.* 23.
51. Morton (2001).
52. This is particularly evident in the example of the Orkneys as examined by Sturt (2005). Similarly, neither Bari and Antibari, nor Rhodes and Antirhodos, lie along the direct bearing opposite each other, but are the points of landfall for vessels sailing with the prevailing wind.
53. Tac. *Ann.* 15.18.2.
54. See, generally, Candy (2020b).
55. See the chapters by É Jakab and P Candy later in this volume.
56. Versions of these contracts are reported at Dem. 35.10 and D. 45.1.122.1 (Scaev. 28 *dig.*).
57. See, generally, Meyer-Termeer (1978), and Fiori's chapter in this volume.
58. Indeed, some papyri refer to the prohibition of 'navigating under bad weather conditions' SB.14.11552 = SB6,9212 (Oxyrhynchus, AD 221); P.Oxy.43. 3111 (AD257 Antinoopolis).
59. D. 14.1.1.2–3 (Ulp. 28 *ad ed.*); D. 20.4.6 pr (Ulp. 37 *ad ed.*); D. 4.9.1.6 (Ulp. 14 *ad ed.*).
60. D. 9.2.29.4 (Ulp. 18 *ad ed.*); D. 19.2.13.2 (Ulp. 32 *ad ed.*); D. 39.4.11.2 (Ulp. 5 *sent.*).
61. For the exercitorian edict, which made the person legally entitled to exploit the vessel (the *exercitor*) liable for contracts entered into by the shipmaster with third parties, see Candy (2020a).
62. Of course, one needs to consider the wrongful damage implied in the notion of *damnum iniuria datum*. Several legal texts indicate that a lack of knowledge and understanding of the range of variables involved in navigation (*peritia*), might be considered negligence, alongside the intentions of the parties concerned in the sea venture, to evaluate whether the loss could have been avoided or not, e.g. D. 9.2.29.3–5 (Ulp. 18 *ad ed.*).
63. See, e.g. Harris (2018).
64. See, e.g. Frezza (1949).
65. *Ep.*, 4; Acts 27.1–28.8.
66. Casson (1984), p. 30, see also Tarwacka's chapter in this volume.
67. *Ep.*, 4.15, 4.23.
68. *Ep.*, 4.8.
69. *Ep.*, 4.19.
70. *Ep.*, 4.28–29.
71. *Acts*, 27.1–28.8.
72. *Acts*, 27.9.
73. *Acts*, 27.38.
74. *Acts*, 27.39.
75. For example, Andreau (1999), p. 54.
76. Plut. *Demetr.* 33.3.

Chapter 4

Pirates' Captives in Light of Roman Law

Anna Tarwacka

INTRODUCTORY REMARKS

In the ancient Mediterranean world, sailors were threatened by many natural factors, such as sea storms and treacherous rocks.[1] However, danger coming from people, namely attacks by sea robbers,[2] should also be added to this list. They had been happening from time immemorial as a regular element of the reality of seafaring. Initially, attacks by pirates were not assessed entirely negatively since they were seen alongside other types of human activity at sea: trade and war.[3] Only with time did the term 'pirate' take on a clearly pejorative meaning.

In antiquity, piracy was understood as the practice of military activities using ships.[4] Pirate bands, however, had land bases, carrying out plundering attacks both at sea and on land. What was punishable was not only active participation in criminal activity but also membership in a criminal group. It should also be emphasised that pirates were distinguished from robbers whose activities were confined to the land.[5] It was only for the jurists of the classical period that this distinction ceased to be relevant, such that they often used uniform terminology to describe both sea and land robbers.[6]

The subject of maritime robbery has been discussed in literature since the time of Homer. Let us start with the myths. The best-known myth is the story of the kidnapping of Dionysus, whom the pirates expected to sell to earn profit as he was a handsome young man. The infuriated god made his persecutors mad and when they jumped into the sea, he turned them into dolphins. The steersman, who recognised the deity and tried to dissuade his companions from their plans of robbery, was the only person to be spared. Quoted by many authors,[7] the myth may shed some light on the treatment of pirate captives. The versions of the story vary: whereas sometimes Dionysus is abducted from a rock at other times he enters a Tyrrhenian ship as a passenger, and only on the high seas it turns out that the sailors do not intend to take him to Naxos but want to sell him into slavery. This may indicate that one of the ways pirates operated was to offer shipping services in order to bloodlessly obtain loot and prisoners.

In Ovid, it was Bacchus who complained about the heartlessness and cynicism of pirates, who broke their promises, and asked what the glory was in persecuting a younger person.[8] This complaint seems very genuine.

The poet Arion was also supposed to be a mythical abducted passenger.[9] The Corinthians who were transporting him decided to rob him of the prizes he had won in a music competition. Arion himself was to be killed as an unnecessary burden. He asked to be able to play the last tune and when he later threw himself into the sea, he was saved by a dolphin attracted by his music. In this story, there also appears a theme of dishonest carriers who turn out to be sea robbers.

As one can see, for those travelling by sea and being on the coast, abductions perpetrated by pirates always posed a serious problem. Captivity was the most frequent fate of prisoners.

It can be assumed that ancient societies tried to protect their citizens. These were most often measures of a military nature that were used to combat maritime robbery. However, there were also legal ways, such as treaties concluded between communities designed to prevent the other party from pirating[10] and abducting one's own citizens.[11] This category also includes all criminal regulations under which pirates and their supporters were subject to sanctions,[12] as well as decisions of officials who sought to ensure that sea robbers were captured and punished.[13]

However, it should be emphasised that, as a rule, capture by pirates led to a loss of freedom and captives were often sold as slaves, usually far from their place of origin. All legal regulations had only a limited, local scope of operation.

THE EVOLUTION OF PIRATE'S CAPTIVES PROTECTION IN ROMAN LAW

On the other hand, Rome gradually yet consistently developed congruous standards, ensuring legal protection for all victims of pirate attacks over time. The subject of the following discussion will be the evolution of legal thought in this area.

Initially, the Romans solved the problem on an ad hoc basis, using the method of bilateral treaties making provision for the safety of their citizens. This was the sentiment of the treaties concluded with Carthage establishing the zones in which it was forbidden to rob property and abduct people.[14] For Rome, these zones included the territory of the Republic and the states united with it in the form of *foedera*. According to the second treaty with Carthage concluded in 348 BC, people abducted in the territory of Latium, belonging to the community with which Rome made peace in the form of a written treaty, were kept as a part of loot by the Carthaginians but could not be brought to Roman ports.[15] If they were, any Roman could demand that the abducted person be released by performing the *manus iniectio*.[16] It seems that it is not about bringing the *legis actio per manus iniectionem*, as there are no grounds for it, and what is more, only a Roman citizen could be a party to the proceedings. It must therefore have been an out-of-court *manus iniectio*, aimed at questioning the right of a Punic to rule over the captured individual. This situation can be compared with the power of the *pater familias* to perform the *manus iniectio* over a person under their authority. In this case, the act of laying the hand would be of a public law character and the Roman who performed it would represent the interest of the state.

This clause in the treaty means that trafficking in people captured during pirate robberies was not prohibited because they became slaves. KW Welwei argued that the reason for agreements of this kind was to avoid selling slaves in their native lands, thus creating a system in which any slave came from afar, so that, their alienation from the society in which they ended up destroyed their morale and made them accept their fate.[17] This rule, however, did not require treaty regulations: after all, the Romans themselves sold insolvent debtors *trans Tiberim*, so that they would not be slaves in their own country.

Bilateral agreements between Rome and foreign communities were, in any case, the first step towards ensuring the security of Roman citizens. Such a solution resulted from the legal realities of that period: the principle of the personal nature of law meant that in relations with foreigners the Roman *ius civile* did not apply and it was necessary to regulate such connections by means of agreements.

The next stage in the evolution of law in the field of protecting pirate captives can be observed on the basis of Plautus's comedies, in which the theme of being abducted by sea robbers appears frequently. In the unpreserved play *Caecus vel praedones* there was even an assessment of sea robbers. Pirates do not spare anyone; that is who they are.[18]

The following fragment of the comedy *Curculio*, where Phaedromus wants to sue Therapontigonus, is a good example of a stage situation with a pirate abducting motif:

'Plaut. *Curc.* 620–621:
Qui scis mercari furtivas atque ingenuas virgines,
ambula in ius.
You who know that you trade in stolen and free-born virgins, go to court!'

The reason for performing the *in ius vocatio* was the purchase of abducted free-born girls. The kidnapped girls are referred to as the *furtivae*, or 'stolen ones'; a direct reference to theft. A similar pattern can be seen in the comedy *Poenulus*, where Agorastocles, who, like the girls, was captured by pirates and sold to a procurer (and adopted by him), demanded the *duplum pro furto*,[19] namely a double penalty typical for theft, here probably double amount of the price. From a legal point of view, it is difficult to properly analyse these references.

It would be easiest to start with the interpretation of pirates capturing a slave (in Roman legal terminology, a thing, or *res*) and, in this case, the nurse of the girls from the comedy *Poenulus*. It seems that she was treated as a stolen item (*res furtiva*) and therefore the merchant could not acquire her as property, even by usucaption. It can hence be concluded that items robbed by pirates were considered stolen, namely – unlike items taken from an enemy during a war – the current owner did not lose their right to them. By analogy, the buyer's rights to captured free persons were questioned by the jurists. Such reasoning meant that also in their case the acquisition of property by *usucapio* was not possible.

However, there is doubt about the buyer's legal interest. In the comedy *Poenulus*, the case of the procurer Lycus, who purchased two girls from a Sicilian robber,[20] is described:

'Plaut. *Poen.* 896–900:
SYNC. *Quia illas emit in Anactorio parvolas*
de praedone Siculo. MIL. *Quanti?* SYNC. *Duodeviginti minis,*
duas illas et Giddenenem nutricem earum tertiam.
et ille qui eas vendebat dixit se furtivas vendere:
ingenuas Carthagine aibat esse.
SYNC. Because he bought them at Anactorium when they were little from a Sicilian pirate. MIL. For how much? SYNC. Eighteen minas, the two of them and their nurse Giddenis as the third. And he who was selling them said they were sold as stolen and he declared that they were free-born from Carthage.'

The seller warned that both the girls and their nurse had been abducted, yet the buyer agreed to pay the price anyway (eighteen minas). Years later, the girls' father, Hanno, unexpectedly found them:

'Plaut. *Poen.* 1343–1348:
HAN. *In ius te voco.*
LYC. *Quid tibi mecum autem?* HAN. *Quia hasce aio liberas*
ingenuasque esse filias ambas meas;
eae sunt surruptae cum nutrice parvolae.
LYC. *Iam pridem equidem istuc scivi, et miratus fui,*
neminem venire qui istas adsereret manu.
HAN. I'm calling you to court. LYC. What do you want with me then? HAN. Because I declare both of those to be free-born and my daughters; they were kidnapped with their nurse when they were little. LYC. I had this known before and I wondered why nobody came to claim their freedom.'

Hanno performed the *in ius vocatio*, summoning the procurer to the magistrate. Lycus did not deny his claim, admitting the father was right. Ultimately, the trial did not take place. The procurer was informed by the seller of the status of the purchased individual and he therefore consciously bought free persons, thus risking a loss in the event of someone standing up for them as an *adsertor libertatis*. In this case, he had no claims against the seller.

On the other hand, the contract included in the comedy *Curculio* is very interesting. A stipulation (that is, the *repromissio*) was attached to the sales and purchase agreement:

'Plaut. *Curc.* 667–669:
Quia ille ita repromisit mihi:
si quisquam hanc liberali asseruisset manu,
sine controversia omne argentum reddere.
Because he promised me: if anyone claimed her freedom, he would give all the silver back without controversy.'

The seller promised to refund the entire price in the event that someone proved the freedom of the slave who was the subject of the contract. It therefore seems that the sales contract itself was invalid if it turned out that the commodity was a free person. However, since in such a case the interest of the buyer was not properly secured (after all, he was losing the possibility of using the complaint), the parties could apply additional security in the form of stipulation, which – as an abstract legal act – remained valid regardless of the circumstances.

Perhaps sellers had not always been willing to meet their buyers halfway.[21] Gellius described a custom according to which slaves who were not sold under guarantee were marked by wearing conical caps (*pillei – servi pilleati*).[22] *Pilleus* was first and foremost a symbol of freedom, which is why it can hypothesised that the custom was connected to people of questionable status, who, for example, could turn out to be free, like pirate captives.[23]

It is also worth mentioning that classical law adopted a solution more favourable to the buyer. The sales agreement of a free man remained valid as long as the buyer was not aware that the person they were to buy was not a slave.[24] This provided effective protection in all cases, even if the parties did not enter into any stipulations.

However, going back to the times of Plautus, it can be said that even then pirate captives were considered free people. It seems the legal basis was to consider the actions of sea robbers to be theft. This was probably due to the unequivocal classification of piracy as a form of lawlessness. In practice a person captured by pirates could count on regaining their freedom only when someone questioned the rights of the person who was in possession. Plautus wrote about the *manum adserere*, that is, about the procedure in which the *adsertor libertatis* asked for the recognition of a person treated as a slave as free (*causa liberalis*).

It can therefore be assumed that initially the protection of pirate prisoners was based on an analogy to the legal status of stolen items, which could not be usucapted and appropriated. Over time, however, this solution was improved and the key concept turned out to be a precise distinction between sea robbery and war. Thus, while the first ideas were based on private law standards, the further development of protection was based on the law of war (*ius belli*):

'Cic. *Off.* 3.29.107–108: *Nam pirata non est ex perduellium numero definitus, sed communis hostis omnium.*

Because a pirate is not defined within the group of state enemies but as the common foe of everyone.'

The basis of the new concept, fully expressed by Cicero, was the concept of the *iustum piumque bellum*, namely a war that was correctly declared against the people who were Rome's enemy (*hostis iustus atque legitimus, perduellis*). Pirates did not deserve to be called as such, since they did not constitute an organised community and therefore any conflict with them was not a war.[25] Cicero called sea robbers the common enemies of all,[26] thus opening the way for each community, and not only for victims, to pursue them. The consequence of such a theory was admitting *a contrario* that since pirate captives were not captured during war, they did not become slaves. Such opinions were also expressed by jurists of the classical period:

'D. 49.15.24 (Ulp. 1 *inst.*): *Hostes sunt, quibus bellum publice populus Romanus decrevit vel ipsi populo Romano: ceteri latrunculi vel praedones appellantur. et ideo qui a latronibus captus est, servus latronum non est.*

Enemies are those against whom the Roman people publicly declared war or they did so in respect to the Roman people. All the others are called bandits or pirates. And therefore anyone captured by bandits is not their slave.'

Ulpian stated that enemies are only those against whom the Roman people had declared war (and the other way round), while the rest were robbers and pirates.[27] Whomever, therefore, was captured by bandits did not become their slave.[28]

The reality, however, remained harsh for pirate prisoners. Capture meant humiliation, physical and mental suffering and sometimes even death. Moreover, the Romans provided much entertainment for pirates. Many captives demanded treatment consistent with their status[29]; then pirates dressed them in togas and, pretending to be humble, ordered them to leave the ship immediately . . . on the high seas.[30] Still, such episodes must have been infrequent because the death of a prisoner meant a financial loss.

'Strab. 14.3.2:
ἐν Σίδῃ γοῦν πόλει τῆς Παμφυλίας τὰ ναυπήγια συνίστατο τοῖς Κίλιξιν, ὑπὸ κή ρυκά τε ἐπώλουν ἐκεῖ τοὺς ἁλόντας ἐλευθέρους ὁμολογοῦντες.

In Side, a city in Pamphylia, the dockyards were available for the Cilicians so that they could auction the captives whom they acknowledged as free.'

Strabo reported that the Cilician pirates freely sold their captives in Side, Pamphylia (modern Turkey), openly admitting that they were free people.[31] A question thus arises about the practical application of the developed legal solutions.

First of all, it should be emphasised that pirate attacks had different purposes. The activities of sea robbers were initially limited to raiding ships and coastal dwellings in order to seize property and obtain people who were sold as slaves. With time, however, pirates began to take prisoners for ransom more and more often and with increasing audacity. Unlike the majority of captives intended for sale, these usually came from the upper classes and their capture was widely debated in society.

Two cases can therefore be distinguished: prisoners intended for sale, who were treated as slaves although the law guaranteed them to remain free; and those captured for ransom, who were held captive but with the prospect of being released in case of payment. Both of these situations should be analysed here.

THE DIFFERENCE BETWEEN THE FATE OF THE CAPTIVES INTENDED FOR SALE AND THOSE TAKEN FOR RANSOM

In the first case, captives were the subject of sales contracts. Different solutions were possible here depending on the awareness of the parties. In general, if the contract was valid, the seller was liable unless the parties expressly excluded it. A very interesting case of a pirate prisoner was described in a rhetorical exercise, being one of the declamations attributed to Quintilian:

'Ps.-Quint. *Decl. min.* 388 pr.: *Qui habebat matrem duxit uxorem, ex qua natum filium aviae nutriendum dedit. Moriens heredem filium fecit, substituit uxorem; dispensatorem suum manumitti iussit. Puer reductus ad matrem et ab ea in fundo maritimo, visis piratis, relictus non comparuit. Post paucos dies cadaver confusis lineamentis, quod filii putaretur, in idem litus eiectum mater ductis sepelivit exequiis. Dispensator manumissus ab ea, post aliquot annos negotiatum profectus, adulescentem, quem dominum diceret, apud venaliciarium repertum iudicio adserens evicit. Cum eo revertit in patriam. Puerum agnoscit avia, negat suum mater.*

He who had a mother married a wife, and he gave a son born from her to the grand-mother to raise. At his death he appointed the son his heir and his wife a substitute; he ordered his steward to be manumitted. The boy was brought back to his mother and, left by her at a seaside property after some pirates had been seen, he never reappeared. After a few days a dead body with blurred features which was believed to be the son's was thrown up by the sea and the mother buried it after having conducted the funeral ceremony. The steward manumitted by her, when he went on business after a few years, won a freedom case for a youth who he said was his master, found by the slave traders. He came back with him to his homeland. The grandmother recognised the boy, but the mother denies him to be hers.'

The case is quite complicated. The hero of the story was brought up by his grand-mother. The father made him his heir, while in his will he also included a pupil-lary substitution, calling his wife, namely the boy's mother, the heir in the second place (*heres substitutus*).[32] It seems that substitution was not included in the *tabulae secundae* but in the basic content of the will, as the woman apparently knew about it. While she was with her son at the seaside, a pirate ship appeared on the horizon and the mother ran away, abandoning the child. The boy went missing and a few days later was presumed dead after a body washed up by the sea was identified as his. However, the identification was not certain, as evidenced by the description: the facial features were obliterated, which must have made recog-nition difficult. Still, the mother inherited the property. She also manumitted a slave who was the administrator of the property, just as her husband wanted her to do – it was a *fideicommissum libertatis*. After a few years, during a business trip, the freedman found the boy with some slave traders, recognised him, released him through a court trial and then returned to his homeland. There the boy was rec-ognised by his grandmother but his mother claimed that he was not her son. The legal problem considered in the declamation was therefore the boy's claim for the inheritance from his father – *hereditatis petitio*.

In the content of the declamation, the fragment concerning the court proceedings on the basis of which the freedman won the boy's freedom is particularly interesting:

'Ps.-Quint. *Decl. min.* 388.6–7: *Cum forte videt puerum venalibus interpositum, simul et agnovit et agnitus est. 'Quis' inquit 'vobis narravit in quas terras delatus essem? Num avia vivit?' Itaque habuit puer adsertorem, adsertor sponsorem, peregrinus advocatos, cum ipse vultus causam ingenuitatis suae ageret. Filium istius quid aliud dicam quam agnoverunt? Nec mirum: nihil erat confusum. Fateor multum absentium quoque profuisse nomina, cum diceremus: 'habet matrem, habet aviam.' In una re, iudices, mentiti sumus: adfirmavimus enim futurum ut hunc mater agnosceret.*

When he accidentally sees the boy intended for sale he recognises him and is recognised at the same moment. The boy says: "Who told you on which land I was brought? Does grandmother live?" And so the boy had someone to claim his freedom, the claimant had his surety and the foreigner had his advocates, while the boy's very face proved (pleaded?) the case of his free-born status. What else can I say but that they acknowledged him as her son. No wonder: nothing was mistaken. I confess that the names of many of those absent were helpful, when we said: "He has got a mother, he has got a grandmother". In one thing, o judges, we lied: we confirmed that his mother would recognise him.'

According to the source text, the freedman played the role of the *adsertor libertatis* in the trial that took place. The proceedings thus took the form of the *causa liberalis*, in which it was possible to prove the boy's freedom. The relationship with his mother and grandmother was brought up but it also seems that the decisive argument was the fact the boy had been abducted by pirates. This is why he was legally a free person and, therefore, the *de libertate* proceedings were successful.

It is difficult to interpret the '*habuit puer adsertorem, adsertor sponsor, peregrinus advocatos*' excerpt. Who were the *sponsor* and the advocates? It seems to be a rhetorical trick: the orator tried to show that the boy's words about his mother and grandmother, as well as his face, indicating free birth, could convince those involved in the trial – in particular the judges – but perhaps also the audience, whose reactions, after all, frequently had an impact upon the verdict.

This interesting declamation seems to indicate in any case that the accidental recognition of a person captured by pirates resulted in the initiation of the *de libertate* procedure, in which the main difficulty was to present convincing evidence that the alleged slave was, in fact, a free person. The procedure used already in the times of Plautus became a standard in a world where it was becoming easier and easier to obtain legal protection due to the wider range of Roman rule and thus also the presence of magistrates with jurisdiction.

The other option used by pirates during raids was abducting prisoners in order to obtain a ransom.[33] Ordinary people were not the only victims of pirate attacks; sometimes they were famous personas. For instance, Antonia, Mark Antony's daughter, was captured, perhaps by way of revenge as her father led an anti-piracy campaign in Cilicia in 102 BC.[34] Clodius was also abducted and apparently had difficulty collecting the ransom.[35] In fact, magistrates like legates, quaestors and praetors could become prisoners too.[36] The praetors, moreover, were sometimes captured on land along with an escort of lictors.[37] Finally, one cannot forget about the most famous case, namely the kidnapping of Julius Caesar.[38]

Obviously, in this situation, the key issue was the question of paying the ransom to the pirates, which is very interesting from a legal point of view. Literary texts show that the moral and customary obligation to pay the ransom rested on the relatives of the abductee. This is attested to by fragments of works by Seneca the Elder and Quintilian, in which the theme of being captured by pirates appeared many times.[39] Relatives, most often fathers or sons of the victim, had to pay a ransom, which often required a journey to the 'lion's den' – *ire ad redemptionem*.[40] The text shows that it was not safe: the buyer risked being captured and sharing their fate with the person they wanted to buy out.[41] After all, they negotiated with criminals who were not bound by the norms of the *ius gentium*. In the absence of money for the ransom, a relative could also offer to be captured by the pirates in exchange for releasing the abductee (*vicariis manibus redimere*).[42]

However, failing to buy out a relative was treated as neglect of the *officium* unless it was due to poverty. Captives could get better treatment by informing the pirates they had relatives, as this gave hope for a ransom.[43] The lack of money could prove disastrous for the prisoner. Pirates used to kill such abductees, as shown by the numerous crosses they set up: *cruces eorum, qui non redimuntur*.[44]

When relatives were not present or were unable to collect enough money, somebody else could pay the ransom. This behaviour was considered virtuous.

Cicero distinguished two categories of generous people: the prodigal; and the noble.[45] The former spent money on fleeting pleasures, while the latter paid off their friends' debts, provided for their daughters' dowries or bought them out from pirates.[46] Squandering was universally condemned by the Romans, as it could lead to a reduction in their capacity to perform legal actions; on the other hand, generosity was viewed favourably.

However, there is a fundamental question regarding the possibility of recovering the money intended to buy somebody out from the hands of pirates. Naturally, there could be occasions when the benefactor did not ask for a refund, but surely such demands could sometimes be made. Here, it is difficult to use an analogy with the situation of the *redemptus ab hostibus*, because a person captured by enemies became a slave and, after being bought out, they were subject to the authority of the one who had provided the ransom until the debt was repaid. At the same time they could use the *ius postliminii* only after that. Similarly, a slave captured by enemies became the property of the one who had bought them out, and only after paying the ransom, they returned to the former owner. Meanwhile, those abducted by pirates remained free and therefore did not have to use the *ius postliminii*; and captured slaves remained the property of their masters and could not become the subject of usucaption since they were regarded as *res furtivae*. In the texts known to us, jurists did not deal with the problem of buying out prisoners from pirates but wrote instead about buying out property:

'D. 14.2.2.3 (Paul. 34 *ad ed.*): *Si navis a piratis redempta sit, Servius Ofilius Labeo omnesque conferre debere aiunt.*

If a ship is redeemed from pirates, Servius, Ofilius, and Labeo declare that everyone should contribute.

Paulus noted that in the event of a ship being bought out, everyone should contribute to the costs, as was the case with jettison, which was justified by acting in the interest of all.[47] Obviously, pirates seldom hijacked the ship itself and most often took prisoners, allowing them, as mentioned previously, to write to their relatives or send someone to collect funds for a ransom. It therefore seems that settlement with the ransom payer was obligatory. If one of the people travelling by ship paid, the settlement was probably in the form of legal recourse claims under the lease contract. However, in the case of a third party, it seems probable that it was possible to settle it on the basis of a loan agreement.

The already-quoted rhetorical declamations may provide some additional clues here. A fairy tale-like motif was described in *Declamatio minor* 343, where the father of an abducted girl promised her hand to whomever would buy the daughter out. In *Declamatio minor* 373, facing the indecisive attitude of his son from his first marriage, the second wife of the captured individual decided to open the grave of her predecessor to get hold of the jewels buried alongside the deceased in order to pay the ransom.[48]

A very interesting case is presented in *Declamatio minor* 257, in which a father abducted by pirates wrote to his son asking for a ransom. The son had no money so he agreed to marry the daughter of his father's wealthy enemy and, with his money (it is difficult to say whether it was a dowry or a donation), he bought his father out from the hands of sea robbers.[49] Upon his return, the father demanded that the son dismiss his wife.[50] The content of the declamation also mentions other methods of ransoming the captive: first, the aforementioned possibility of pirates accepting another prisoner in exchange for an abducted person (here, however, the robbers did not agree to such an exchange),[51] and secondly, taking out a loan.[52] Since the son remained under the father's authority, the latter possibility *de facto* entails burdening the father with the obligation under the *condictio certae creditae pecuniae de in rem verso*. The text of the declamation also mentions the *beneficium*, that is, paying of the ransom by the father-in-law. Nothing therefore indicates the emergence of a relationship similar to that between the benefactor and the *redemptus ab hostibus*, but it is possible to see here a confirmation of the contract node.

CONCLUSIONS

Summing up, one can trace the development of Roman legal regulations concerning the provisions affording protection to pirate prisoners. Initially, Rome tried to guarantee its citizens' security by concluding bilateral agreements with other communities. However, they had a limited territorial and subjective scope. With time (certainly at the end of the third century BC but perhaps even earlier), the status of people abducted by pirates began to be regulated, using the analogy to stolen items, which were not subject to usucaption or appropriation. Thanks to this analogy, it was recognised that the captured remained legally free, although in practice they were sold. If, therefore, someone (as the *adsertor libertatis*) proved in a trial that a person had been abducted by pirates, they were released. The next step was related to distinguishing pirates from enemies within the meaning of the law of war, which in turn led to the assumption that the prisoners of the former remained free and did not have to use the *ius postliminii*. In practice, it happened that some captives actually managed to be released by proving their status in court. Additionally, it also appears that a pirate prisoner for whom the ransom had been paid was not treated – unlike the *redemptus ab hostibus* – as a person with a status similar to that of a slave and dependent on the benefactor. Ransom debts were purely contractual.

BIBLIOGRAPHY

Amirante, L. (1957), 'Appunti per la storia della "redemptio ab hostibus"', *Labeo* 3, pp. 171–220.

Benincasa, Z. (2011), *'Periculi pretium'. Prawne aspekty ryzyka związanego z podróżami morskimi w starożytnym Rzymie (II w. p.n.e. – II w. n.e.)* (Warsaw: Liber).

Cassola, F. (1968), *I gruppi politici nel III secolo a.C.* (Rome: L'Erma di Bretschneider).

Casson, L. (1991), *The Ancient Mariners. Seafarers and Sea Fighters of the Mediterranean in Ancient Times* (Princeton: Princeton University Press).

Casson, L. (1994), *Travel in the Ancient World* (Baltimore: Johns Hopkins University Press).

De Souza, P. (1999), *Piracy in the Graeco – Roman World* (Cambridge: Cambridge University Press).

Ferrer Albelda, E. (2013), 'La piratería en los tratados entre Cartago e Roma', in A. Álvarez-Ossorio Rivas, E. Ferrer Albelda, and E. García Vargas (eds), *Piratería y seguridad marítima en el Mediterráneo Antiguo* (Seville: Secretariado de Publicaciones de la Universidad de Sevilla), pp. 95–125.

García Riaza, E. (2013), 'El tratamiento de los piratas en el ius belli romano-republicano', in A. Álvarez-Ossorio Rivas, E. Ferrer Albelda, and E. García Vargas (eds), *Piratería y seguridad marítima en el Mediterráneo Antiguo* (Seville: Secretariado de Publicaciones de la Universidad de Sevilla), pp. 127–143.

Grünewald T. (1999), *Räuber, Rebellen, Rivalen und Rächer. Studien zu 'latrones' im römischen Reich* (Stuttgart: Franz Steiner Verlag).

James, A.W. (1975), 'Dionysus and the Tyrrhenian Pirates', *Antichthon* 9, pp. 17–34.

Lentano, M. (2010), 'La figlia del pirata. Idee per un commento a Seneca, Controversiae I 6', *Annali Online di Lettere - Ferrara* 1, pp. 89–106.

López Barja de Quiroga, P. (2007), *Historia de la manumisión en Roma. De los orígenes a los Severos* (Madrid: Publicaciones Universidad Complutense).

Manfredini, A.D. (2010), 'Le *pilleus* libertatis (C.7.2.10 — C.7.6.1.5)', *RIDA* 57, pp. 247–263.

Metzger, E. (2010), 'Remarks on David Daube's Lectures on Sale, with Special Attention to the *liber homo* and *res extra commercium*', in E. Metzger (ed), *David Daube: A Centenary Celebration* (Glasgow: Traditio Iuris Romani), pp. 109–116.

Olson, S.D. (1988), 'Dionysus and the Pirates in Euripides' "Cyclops"', *Hermes* 116, pp. 502–504.

Ortu, R. (2010), '*Captus a piratis*: schiavitù di fatto?', *Rivista di diritto romano* 10, pp. 1–12.

Osgood, J. (2010), 'Caesar and The Pirates: or How to Make (and Break) an Ancient Life', *Greece and Rome* 57(2), pp. 319–336.

Pianezzola, E. (2004), 'Le parole dei pirati, schede lessicali', in L. Braccesi (ed), *La pirateria nell'Adriatico antico* (Rome: L'Erma di Bretschneider), pp. 11–19.

Rougé J. (1977), *Navi e navigazione nell'antichità*, R. Massari and A. Marazzi (trans.) (Firenze: Vallecchi Editore).

Tansey, P. (2010), 'Antonia and the Pirates', *CQ* 60(2), pp. 656–658.

Tarwacka, A. (2011), 'Causae communi libertatis inimicus. Verres and the right of provocatio in the provinces', *Revista General de Derecho Romano* 17, pp. 1–13.

Tarwacka, A. (2016), 'Piracy in Ancient Rome. The Crime and Its Punishment', in S. Nowicki (ed), *'They Called Me to Destroy the Wicked and the Evil'. Selected Essays on Crime and Punishment in Antiquity* (Münster: Ugarit Verlag), pp. 229–246.

Tarwacka, A. (2009), *Romans and Pirates. Legal Perspective* (Warsaw: Wydawnictwo Uniwersytetu Kardynała Stefana Wyszyńskiego).

Tarwacka, A. (2018a), 'Some Remarks on Piracy in Roman Law', *Annuaire de Droit Maritime et Océanique* 36, pp. 295–309.

Tarwacka, A. (2018b), 'The term "pirate" as a form of political invective in Republican Rome and its legal implications', in I.G. Mastrorosa (ed), *Latrocinium maris. Fenomenologia e repressione della pirateria nell'esperienza romana e oltre* (Rome: Aracne Editrice), pp. 53–70.

Tarwacka, A. (2019), 'Using lex Rhodia in the Case of a Pirate Attack', *Gdańskie Studia Prawnicze* 3, pp. 81–90.

Troster, M. (2009), 'Roman hegemony and non-state violence: a fresh look at Pompey's campaign against the pirates', *Greece and Rome* 56(1), pp. 14–33.

Ward, A.M. (1975), 'Caesar and the Pirates', *CP* 70, pp. 267–268.

Ward, A.M. (1977), 'Caesar and the Pirates II. The Elusive M. Iunius Iuncus and the Year 75/74', *AJAH* 2, pp. 26–36.

Welwei, K.W. (1950), 'Piraterie und Sklaverei in der frühen römischen Republik', in H. Bellen and H. Heinen (eds) *Fünfzig Jahre Forschungen zur Antiken Sklaverei an der Mainzer Akademie 1950–2000. Miscellanea zum Iubiläum* (Stuttgart: Steiner Verlag), pp. 73–81.

Wycisk, T. (2008), *Quidquid in foro fieri potest. Studien zum römischen Recht bei Quintilian* (Berlin: Duncker & Humblot).

Ziegler, K.H. (1980), 'Pirata communis hostis omnium', in M. Harder, G. Thielmann (eds), *De iustitia et iure. Festgabe für Ulrich von Lübtow zum 80. Geburtstag* (Berlin: Duncker & Humblot), pp. 93–103.

NOTES

I would like to thank Dagmara Łata for translating the chapter into English. The source text translations are my own.

1. Cf Casson (1994), pp. 149–150; Benincasa (2011), pp. 54–59. There are many literary texts that attest to the fear of going to sea. Cf *Anth. Pal.* 7.650; 7.532; 7.636; 13.27.

2. The considerations contained in this article are a continuation of the research presented in my monograph: Tarwacka (2009).

3. Cf Thuc. 1.4–1.5; Cassola (1968), p. 28; Rougé (1977), pp. 108–109; Casson (1991), p. 177; de Souza (1999), pp. 19–26.

4. Cf Sen. *Controv.*, 1.2.8; Flor. 1.41; Sen. *Ben.*, 5.14; Tarwacka (2009), pp. 17–21.

5. Cf Cass. Dio 36.20.3–4; de Souza (1999), pp. 9–13; Tarwacka (2009), pp. 17–21. Cf, however, Grünewald (1999), p. 7, who equated pirates with other bandits.

6. Cf, e.g., D. 47.9.3.2 (Ulp. 56 *ad ed.*); D. 48.19.28.10 (Call. 6 *cogn.*); D. 49.16.14 pr. (Paul. l.s. *de poen. milit.*); D. 50.16.118 (Pomp. 2 *ad Q. Muc.*).

7. Cf *Hom. Hymn. VII Dionys.* 32–54; Eur., *Cyc.* 11–20; Ov. *Met.* 605–92; Ps.-Apollod. *Bibl.* 3.37–8; Philostr. *Imag.* 1.19; Hyg. *Fab.* 134; *Poet. astr.* 2.17; Sen. *Oed.* 449–66. Cf James (1975), pp. 17–34; Olson (1988), pp. 502–504.

8. Ov. *Met.* 652–55: '*non haec mihi litora, nautae,/ promisistis" ait, "non haec mihi terra rogata est!/ quo merui poenam facto? quae gloria vestra est,/ si puerum iuvenes, si multi fallitis unum?*'

9. Cf Hdt. 1.23–24; Gell. *NA* 16.19; Luc. *Dial. D. marin.* 8; Hyg. *Fab.* 194.

10. Cf *SdA* III 482, as in de Souza (1999), p. 62.

11. Cf *SIG* 521, as in de Souza (1999), p. 61.

12. Cf *SEG* XXIV 154.19–23, as in de Souza (1999), p. 65.

13. Cf *IG* XII 3.1291, as in de Souza (1999), p. 53.

14. Cf Cassola (1968), p. 30; Welwei (2001) pp. 73–81; Ferrer Albelda (2013).

15. On this treaty, see the chapter by G Cifani earlier in this volume.

16. Polyb. 3.24. Polybius used a technical term 'ἐπιλάβηται', which corresponds to the Latin expression '*manus iniecerit*'.

17. Cf Welwei (2001), p. 79.

18. Plaut. apud Charis. 211: '*Ita sunt praedones: prorsum parcunt nemini*'.

19. Plaut. *Poen.* 1351.

20. On buying a girl from a pirate, see also Plaut. *Rud.* 40: '*eam de praedone vir mercatur pessumus*'.

21. For instance, in the comedy *Persa* one can find a situation in which the seller is not supposed to provide the buyer with a guarantee; Plaut. Pers. 524–25: '*ac suo periclo is emat qui eam mercabitur:/ mancipio neque promittet neque quisquam dabit*'.

22. Gell. *NA* 6.4.1–2: '*Pilleatos servos venum solitos ire, quorum nomine venditor nihil praestaret, Caelius Sabinus iurisperitus scriptum reliquit. Cuius rei causam esse ait, quod eiusmodi*

condicionis mancipia insignia esse in vendundo deberent, ut emptores errare et capi non possent, neque lex vendundi opperienda esset, sed oculis iam praeciperent, quodnam esset mancipiorum genus'. Cf Tarwacka (2018a), p. 305.

23. Cf TLL, s.v. *pilleum/pilleus*; López Barja de Quiroga (2007), pp. 40–43; Manfredini (2010), pp. 247–263.
24. D. 18.1.70 (Lic. Rufin. 8 reg.): '*Liberi hominis emptionem contrahi posse plerique existimaverunt, si modo inter ignorantes id fiat. quod idem placet etiam, si venditor sciat, emptor autem ignoret. quod si emptor sciens liberum esse emerit, nulla emptio contrahitur*'. Cf D. 18.1.4–6; Tarwacka (2009), pp. 117–118; Metzger (2010), pp. 109–116.
25. Cf Ziegler (1980), pp. 97–99; Tarwacka (2009), pp. 56–67; Ortu (2010), p. 3; García Riaza (2013).
26. Cicero had used this term before, but only here did he describe the legal consequences of classifying pirates in this way. Cf Cic. 2 *Verr.* 4.21; 5.76. Cf Tarwacka (2018b), pp. 53–70.
27. The terms *latro* and *praedo* could signify both land and sea robbers. Cf de Souza (1999), pp. 12–13; Pianezzola (2004), p. 11–12; Tarwacka (2009), pp. 17–21.
28. Similarly, D. 49.15.19.2 (Paul. 16 ad Sab.): '*A piratis aut latronibus capti liberi permanent*'.
29. The Romans were somewhat naive in the conviction that the declaration '*Civis Romanus sum!*' should guarantee their inviolability under all circumstances. They were convinced that everyone, even foreigners and bandits, would respect their *ius provocationis*. Cf Cic. 2 *Verr.* 5.167–8; Tarwacka (2011), pp. 1–13.
30. Cf Plut. *Vit. Pomp.* 24.
31. The scale of this practice probably decreased after Pompey's campaign in 67 BC, but such situations still happened locally. Cf Tarwacka (2009), pp. 43–55, along with the literature quoted there; also, Troster (2009), pp. 14–33.
32. Cf Wycisk (2008), pp. 170–171.
33. As a side note, it should be remembered that any failure to deliver a ransom promised to the pirates was not fraud: Cic. *Off.* 3.29.107: '*Ut, si praedonibus pactum pro capite pretium non attuleris, nulla fraus est, ne si iuratus quidem id non feceris*'. Cf Tarwacka (2009), p. 59. It seems, however, that sea robbers rather secured their interests and did not release prisoners before being paid a ransom.
34. Cf Cic. *Leg. Man.* 33; Plut. *Vit. Pomp.*, 24; Tansey (2010), pp. 656–658.
35. Cf Cic. *Har. resp.* 42; App. *B Civ.* 2.23.
36. Cf Cic. *Leg. Man.* 53.
37. Cf Plut. *Vit. Pomp.* 24.
38. Cf Ward (1975); Ward (1977); Osgood (2010); Tarwacka (2016), pp. 238–242.
39. Sen. *Controv.* 1.2; 1.6; 1.7; 3.3; 7.1; 7.4; Quint. *Decl. mai.* 5; 6. On the fragments of rhetorical works in which the subject of piracy appears, cf Lentano (2010).
40. Captives sent them a message asking for being bought out: *scribere de redemptione*. Cf Quint. *Decl. mai.* 5; 6.
41. Cf Sen. *Controv.*, 7.4.1. In *Controv.* 1.6.2., Seneca admitted that even the fathers of the abducted were afraid of meeting pirates: '*eo loco . . . in quem venire etiam patres timuerunt*'.
42. Cf Quint. *Decl. mai.* 6; Ps.-Quint. *Decl. min.*, 342.
43. Sen. *Controv.* 1.6.2: '*Ut dixi: "patrem habeo", inter bonos captivos sepositus sum*'.
44. Sen. *Controv.* 7.4.5.
45. Cic. *Off.* 2.55: '*Omnino duo sunt genera largorum, quorum alteri prodigi, alteri liberales; prodigi, qui epulis et viscerationibus et gladiatorum muneribus ludorum venationumque*

apparatu pecunias profundunt in eas res, quarum memoriam aut brevem aut nullam omnino sint relicturi, liberales autem, qui suis facultatibus aut captos a praedonibus redimunt, aut aes alienum suscipiunt amicorum aut in filiarum collocatione adiuvant aut opitulantur vel in re quaerenda vel augenda'.

46. The term *praedones* here means both land and sea robbers but most likely pirates, who posed a real threat in the time of Cicero. Cf Amirante (1957), p. 13.

47. Cf Tarwacka (2019), pp. 81–90.

48. The son then brought the *actio sepulchri violati* against his stepmother, for which his father disowned him after having returned from the pirates.

49. The legal problem here also concerns whether a union concluded without the father's consent counts as *iustum matrimonium*. Such a case for a person captured by enemies is described in D. 49.15.12.3 (Tryph. 4 *disp.*), where it is recognised that the father could neither authorise nor forbid the marriage. The grandson born out of this relationship came under the authority of the grandfather after his return. Despite different circumstances and the prisoner being of a different status, an analogy can be made here in terms of the *ratio* of such a solution given by the jurist: the compulsory situation (*necessitas*) and the public utility (*publica utilitas*) of marriage.

50. Ps.-Quint. *Decl. min.* 257 pr.: *'Qui habebat filium et divitem inimicum, captus a piratis, scripsit filio de redemptione. Ille cum pecuniam non haberet, offerente divite filiam suam, duxit eam in matrimonium et pecunia <eius> redemit patrem. Reversus ille imperat ut dimittat. Nolentem abdicat'.*

51. Ps.-Quint. *Decl. min.* 257.11.4–.6: *'Si piratae hoc mihi pollicerentur, ut vicarias pro patre manus acciperent, non recusarem catenas'.*

52. Ps.-Quint. *Decl. min.* 257.12.1: *'Si obligarer faenore, aes alienum tamen non timuissem ut redimerem patrem'.*

Chapter 5

The Personal Infrastructure of Maritime Trade[1]

Annalisa Marzano

In about 152 BC Marcus Minatius, an Italic banker of Oscan origin,[2] received an honorary decree on the island of Delos listing various honours granted to him by the 'association of the Worshippers of Poseidon from Berytus, the merchants, shippers and warehousemen'. Minatius had given substantial funds to complete the building of the Poseidoniastai and had promised that for the 'future . . . he will always be responsible for some good for the association'.[3] In return, the grateful members of the *collegium* granted him a statue, a crown and other honours. Several hundred years later, close contacts between prominent individuals active in the financial world and professional associations connected to trade were still the norm. Close to the heart of the empire, in the city of Ostia, Cn. Sentius Felix, an extremely well-connected and successful businessman and municipal magistrate, had complex links with trade, the municipal elite of Ostia and various professional associations. He had even adopted a member of a very prominent local family, Cn. Sentius Lucilius Gamala Clodianus, probably the natural son of P. Lucilius Gamala, the *duovir* of AD 71, and had been co-opted among the *decuriones*, holding the role of *quaestor* of the *aerarium* and *duovir*.[4] Of the various direct relationships he had with *collegia*, several stand out in the context of commerce: Cn. Sentius Felix had been co-opted for free among the traders from the Adriatic and the wine merchants of the *forum vinarium* and was furthermore the patron of the associations of the *praecones*, the *argentarii*, and the wine merchants of Rome.[5]

These two examples from opposite chronological moments – the mid-Republic and the mid-empire – and opposite geographic locations embody the central argument of this chapter: that, in the Roman world, successful trade, in particular transmarine trade, rested on a complex network of social interactions and personal contacts – what I refer to in the title of this chapter with the label 'personal infrastructure' – as much as on the physical infrastructure of ports, canals and roads and the legal and financial framework.

Recent studies on the Roman economy have recognised the importance of formal and informal social ties in the context of economic activity and trade, for instance as a way to find credit or form business partnerships with trustworthy people. However, this has not always been the case. The approach that dominated the field up to the twentieth century and which can be seen in the seminal works by M Rostovtzeff and T Frank,[6] used the available evidence to form a conceptual explanation of history in which human motivations were seen as universal constants. These studies did describe the actors of commerce as attested in the primary evidence available at the time – the freedmen, the servile commercial agents – but did not make any systematic attempt at reconstructing the exact roles these individuals played. Ties between commercial actors were examined only if formalised; interest was in the juridical tools used and in the broad comparison between the workings of the market and functioning of the economy compared to modern societies.

With Finley's *The Ancient Economy* (1973) and the 'primitivists' and 'modernists' that came after him, interest was in defining the *nature* of the ancient economy, not necessarily in exploring how private individuals and institutions operated in the context of trade. With the early 1980s, publications such as J D'Arms' *Commerce and Social Standing in Ancient Rome* (1981) started to bring into focus the human dimension of the individuals involved in trade, but the main subject was still the elite and their mentality. D'Arms was interested in aristocratic attitudes towards commerce and in the indirect role aristocrats had in commercial operations, due to tradition, convention and legislation.[7] Other types of interactions between individuals of very different social standing, and whether these were important to the very existence of trade, were not yet topics in the spotlight.

It has been only in the last ten years or so that specific social organisations typical of the Roman world have started to be studied as important structural components of the Roman economy at large and of trade specifically: the proper *collegia*, grouping individuals sharing the same profession but also groups defining themselves according to shared geographic and/or ethnic origins. The former had previously been understood as absolving important religious and social functions for their members; in essence, they would have been social clubs based on specific cults and rituals that, with their regular dinners, provisions for the burial of members and so forth, offered to middling members of society a shared identity and a minimum level of social assurances.[8] The latter, an example of which is the trading station of the Tyrians resident in Puteoli,[9] included individuals from a specific geographic origin, usually grouped together for cultic reasons, like the Poseidonastai from Berytus based in Delos mentioned above.

The fact that these foreign residents of important port towns like Puteoli and Ostia were connected to the world of trade had been already recognised, but recent studies have proposed that the actual *association* as a whole, and not just the individuals, played a role in ensuring commercial transactions. Among the studies that have changed the way in which we now consider *collegia* and other forms of associative order in the context of the ancient economy, we must start with the work by K Verboven.[10] In his 2007 study, Verboven was interested in how financial profits could be transformed into social prestige and in investigating the social conditions determining the efficiency of such strategies. The argument of the article is that status enhancement was not determined solely by patronage, luck or exceptional talent, but was 'institutionalised through the numerous voluntary associations (*collegia, corpora*) throughout the empire'.[11] Up to this point, with the economic relevance of the aristocracy's behavioural codes firmly in focus, analysis of the ways in which differences in sub-aristocratic status were construed, or of how they influenced decision-making by businessmen, remained undeveloped.

The other types of formal associations have been studied as facilitators of trading transactions are the resident aliens and translocal merchant associations, like the Tyrians of the Puteolan *statio*. Not only did these groups have cultic functions and cater to resident aliens, but they also provided services to visiting merchants and shippers.[12] The distinction between resident aliens and merchants was blurry in antiquity, since resident aliens themselves were often merchants and merchants' agents. A foreign *statio* in one of the Roman port-towns might have offered to traders a range of services, including performing sacrifices, laying contacts, obtaining introductions, finding lodgings and storing facilities and so forth. T Terpstra's research has taken these initial considerations and systematically analysed the role of these foreign associations using the framework of economic theory.[13] Moving away from the previous theories, with their focus on dependent labour as overseas business managers, Terpstra has argued that the key to understanding long-distance trade in the Roman empire was not the patron-client or the master-slave relationships, but the social links between the ethnic groups of foreign traders based overseas and the local communities they joined. These communities of long-term overseas residents participated in local life and established social bonds with the inhabitants of the towns they resided in. An endorsement or rejection of a newcomer trader from the same geographic region on the part of these associations overcame two basic problems of ancient trade. First, how to decide, in the case of commercial transactions, whom to trust; secondly, the fact that, despite the existence of detailed trade laws and contracts, the Roman state did not have effective means to enforce them. 'Misbehaving' traders could be 'punished' by excluding them from the services that the *statio* provided.[14]

Terpstra's model to explain the role of these associations in economic terms goes hand in hand with the hypotheses put forward by W Broekaert, who has emphasised how *collegia* and associations must have played several fundamental roles in respect to commerce.[15] First, there is the already-mentioned issue of the 'vetting' of newcomers and the peer pressure on acting in a trustworthy manner in trade dealings, in order not to be singled out by the group. Then, there is the case of associations that provided opportunities for interactions, for assessing someone and for finding suitable interlocutors to ask, for instance, for a loan or to form a business partnership.

Peace and political unity were crucial to prosperous maritime trade, and the emperor could symbolise this. Emblematic in this regard is the anecdote about how the Alexandrian traders hailed Augustus at the port of Puteoli after the conquest of Egypt, shouting: '*per illum se vivere, per illum navigare, libertate ac fortunis per illum frui*'.[16] But in the imperial period, at a lower level than the issues posed

by sea security and custom boundaries, trade flourished in many areas thanks to
the diffusion of associations, of business partnerships and the opportunities these
provided to find capital, to obtain information on goods and market demands and
so forth.[17]

THE COLLEGIA

Collegia were above all 'brotherhoods'; closed groups with a select number of members tied together in bonds of trust and solidarity. This community aspect rested
on three pillars: religious cult, commemoration and conviviality.[18] In the ancient
world, it was unthinkable that any community could exist without tutelary deities.
Collegia were always also cult associations; religious worship and the sharing of
cultic practices in the context of professional association was an important element
of social cohesion. The terms *schola, statio* and *templum* used in reference to associations overlap in meaning and were mostly chosen to stress either the profane or the
cultic aspects of a given association. Therefore, the question one should ask is not
'was this a religious association or not?' but, rather, 'what other purposes did the
association serve and how did its religious dimensions contribute to it?'.

By the start of the second century AD, professional associations had become
the prevalent type of *collegia* of the empire. Some of these *collegia* were explicitly
recognised as having public usefulness (*utilitas publica*) as, for example the *collegia fabrum*, and received various privileges from the state. A well-known case
concerns the shippers and boatmen operating on the Tiber who supplied the
capital and worked for the *annona*.[19] Associations of shippers and traders coming from particular regions or specialising in specific goods were rather common
throughout the Roman world in the imperial period. Concerns with maintaining
public order, which in the late Republic had determined the ban on *collegia* with
political functions, also remained high on the agenda in the imperial period and
it seems that *collegia* had to be authorised by either a senatorial or an imperial
decree, which would grant them the *ius coeundi*, the right to assemble.[20] However,
a senatorial decree probably dating to the first century AD, had allowed the existence of *collegia tenuiorum* – that is associations of common people – if they met
only once a month.[21] The *collegia tenuiorum*, which have been also referred to as
collegia funeraticia, because their primary function was understood as providing
members with funeral rites, may in fact have included a range of different *collegia*
that were authorised to legally exist under this senatorial decree.[22] Most *collegia*
of the imperial period had a rigid hierarchal organisation that mirrored the organisation of towns: the association's officers were elected and called *quinquennales,
curatores*, or *quaestores*, the council was made of *decuriones*, and eventual internal
subgroups of the association were organised in *centuriae* or *decuriae*. Just like the
town's *decuriones*, the *collegium*'s *decuriones* would issue decrees (*decreta*), while
the other members formed a *res publica*.[23]

As has been pointed out, by the late second century AD, the *ius coeundi* also
gave *collegia* important legal capacities, such as the right to hold common property,

have a common treasury, be represented by an agent and have the capacity to sue and be sued as a collective entity.[24] Furthermore, benefactors and patrons, whose donations were important in sustaining the associations, may have preferred *collegia* with the *ius coeundi* because making a donation in these cases was less problematic from a legal point of view.[25] The common property may well have included productive assets to the benefit of members, as for instance, the workshops donated to the associations of *centonarii* and *fabri* in the town of Brixia.[26] Similarly, shippers and traders may have collectively owned warehouses where members could store their goods, perhaps at attractive rates, although we do not have direct evidence for this.[27]

As far as associations of long-distance traders in the imperial era are concerned, recent work has stressed that key commercial nodes such as Ostia and Lyon had numerous strong and prestigious professional *collegia* that effectively dominated trade.[28] Below I discuss some of the financial benefits these associations may have offered, together with the case of *societates* or business partnerships, another important element supporting commerce in the Roman world.

FINDING CREDIT

Finding credit was a fundamental problem for middling individuals wanting to start a business. Seneca, in one of his *Epistles* (119.1), wrote that everyone aspiring to a career in business needed the services of financial agents and loan guarantors. Existing scholarly approaches to the issue of finding credit in the Roman world 'create a false impression of the allocation of credit (and capital goods) in the Roman economy, since they all operate on the (implicit) assumption that allocation took place within several specific social and commercial spheres, between which there existed few, if any interconnections'.[29] However, in the case of trade and commercial activity, there were multiple crossovers between social groups, not simply the case of loans given by former masters to their freedmen. Finding possible contacts for loans and financial support impinged on the same issue any commercial transaction faced: how to have *reliable* information on an individual. This is a sphere where *collegia* could be instrumental.

At the start of this chapter I referred to the example of the businessman and Ostia's magistrate, Cn. Sentius Felix, who had, among other co-optations, also been admitted into the ranks of the association of shippers of the Adriatic. As mentioned earlier, he was a very wealthy and well-connected businessman.[30] He must have had expertise in finance as well, since he had managed the city fund of Ostia and was also the elected patron of the association of bankers. Although we do not have hard proof of this, it is a reasonable inference that his links with the association of bankers, his personal wealth and financial expertise could have all concurred in offering opportunities for the members of the association of shippers to find credit if needed.

The *collegia* themselves must have acted as a means of finding credit and financial support. They could offer credit, or act as guarantors for loans, more often than we think, not simply by putting members in touch with each other and, arguably, allowing loans at low interest rates. Indeed, although surviving documentation in this respect for the western part of the Roman world is lacking, when looking at documentary evidence from Roman Egypt, we see that *collegia* could either act as guarantors for a member or make a short-term loan to a member from the *collegium*'s treasury.

An Egyptian papyrus containing the regulations of an association of tenant farmers working on an estate of the emperor Claudius mentions that the association could stand security for one of the members. It states: '[i]f any one of the undersigned men is held for debt for up to the amount of 100 *drachmai* in silver, security will be given for him for a period of sixty days by the association'.[31] The first century AD regulation of another, unidentified association, specifies that '[i]f anyone is given into custody for a private debt, let them [that is, the members of the association] go bail for him up to one hundred silver *drachmai* for thirty days'.[32]

Both Roman law and socio-economic history studies have put emphasis on how agency via dependent business managers allowed the creation of large commercial enterprises operating in different geographic territories while, at the same time, offering to aristocrats an indirect role in lucrative commercial operations. Freedmen were often put in the position of continuing in a specific trade they might have been involved with while slaves but this time for themselves, while also acting as agents of their former master. The use of dependent business agents is one of the possible answers to asymmetrical information and the fact that, in Roman law, a business partnership could be immediately dissolved by any one of the partners leaving, meant that often it was preferred to form *societates* with members of one's *familia*. This notwithstanding, partnerships among individuals of different families did take place. But can all cases be understood under this specific label? Do they all signify a *structured* relationship governed by law according to the praetorian remedy related to *institores*?

An example will elucidate the point I wish to make. Reused in the wall of a subsidiary building of a Roman fish-salting complex of the ancient town of Sexi (modern Almuñécar) in Spain, a marble pedestal bearing this inscription was discovered:

'C(*aio*) *Aemilio Ni/gro Annio Sen/ecae filio Arvaco / Galeria Sexitano / flamini divorum / Augustorum / provinciae Baeticae / amico rarissimo Ae/mili Ligurius et Itali/cus et Delius eximia / pro liber(alitate) posue/runt.*[33]

To Caius Aemilius Niger Annius Arvacus, son of Seneca, of the Galeria tribe and a citizen of Sexi, flamen of the cult to the deified emperors for the province of Baetica, a most rare friend, Aemilius Ligurius, Aemilius Italicus, and Aemilius Delius erected this in return for his extraordinary generosity.'

The recipient of the dedication, Caius Aemilius Niger Annius Arvacus from Sexi, was a distinguished individual, as signalled by the fact that he had held the position of *flamen* of the imperial cult for the entire province of Baetica. He was probably an equestrian.[34] The dedicants are three freedmen who had once been the slaves of an Aemilius, and who refer to our C. Aemilius Niger as '*amicus rarissimus*'. These are the uncontroversial facts reported in the text. However, how to interpret the relationship among these individuals signalled by such a dedication is open to different interpretations. For Étiénne, who published a new edition of the text in 1999,[35] this inscription is a private dedication by three *liberti* to their *patronus*, so to their former master. His name reveals that he was descendant from indigenous, Romanised stock, because the *cognomen* Arvacus can be connected to the *Arevaci*, the Celtic people who had settled in the Meseta Central of northern Hispania. That his family had prominence at local and provincial level is also indicated by the almost certain relationship of our recipient with the C. Annius Seneca, *duumvir* of Ilurco, who erected two dedications to the emperors Commodus and Marcus Aurelius. The location of the dedication in a fish-salting factory, although discovered reused in a wall, is taken as an indication that Aemilius Niger's wealth and influence largely derived from the exploitation of marine resources and the fish-salting industry. Further, Étiénne suggested that since Aemilius Niger had to reside in Corduba during his tenure of the flaminate, the three freedmen had been running his business in his absence with much zeal and profit.[36] The dedication from clients to patrons would have been presented in this text as an (unequal) friendship relation. Furthermore, the names of the freedmen, of clear geographic origin and pointing to Liguria, Italy and Delos, should be taken to suggest the extent of the geographic distribution of the fish-salted products of Aemilius Niger. In other words, these individuals would have once been slaves, or descendants of slaves, posted in these locations as commercial agents.

On the other hand, Pastor has argued that the expression '*amicus*' was not suitable for use on the part of freedmen of Aemilius Niger himself; if this were the case, they would have used '*patronus*' instead.[37] In his view, the inscription attests to an old friendship, based on distant family and business relationships in the Mediterranean area. Pastor does not elaborate on the possible reasons for the dedication. The text refers to *eximia liberalitas* so clearly Aemilius Niger did something to the benefit of the three *liberti*. If this had been a grateful dedication of an association, like the one from Delos with which I have opened this chapter, we could have thought of a largess, such as funds to build or maintain the seat of the association, or to offer a banquet or distribution of food on a festival date. But here we have only three individuals putting up the dedication, not a larger group. It is possible to offer an alternative explanation to the idea that the freedmen had been involved in running a fish-salting trade business on behalf of C. Aemilius Niger, a hypothesis that would better explain the choice of the term *amicus* rather than *patronus* and of the expression 'noteworthy generosity'. C. Aemilius Niger could have helped the freedmen in their commercial activity first and foremost by providing credit, the paramount need for starting and running a commercial activity; he might also have helped in fostering useful connections, increasing the 'social capital' of the three *liberti* and contributing to the establishment of their supply and distribution networks. As noted by Broekaert and Zuiderhoek:

> 'credit and loans were so ubiquitous in Roman economic life, that over time, business relationships established and maintained through moral reciprocal bonds connected many players in the field. This is a common trait of pre-industrial credit-markets, which relied to a great extent on personal ties and kinship, predominantly because of the absence of reliable and up-to-date information on the trustworthiness of potential business partners'.[38]

The three freedmen were possibly former slaves of a close relative of C. Aemilius Niger, and this existing social bond was at the base of the financial help Niger gave them. In this scenario, the freedmen were not running a business on behalf of the notable C. Aemilius Niger; they were helped by him and his *eximia liberalitas* to start an independent commercial activity.[39]

THE LOGISTICS OF TRADE

Networks and social ties were crucial when considering the logistics of trade and the intersection of the production side with the commercial distribution of the goods. *Societates* were often used as a way to bring together individuals who could offer different skills and means. In the second century AD, the merchant family of the Decimi Caecilii is a good example of the use of *societates* for this purpose. The Decimi Caecilii are one of the best-known Spanish merchant families thanks to abundant epigraphic data from amphorae and to monumental epigraphy from Spain, covering a chronological span that ranges from the second half of the first century to the mid-second century AD. Members of this family formed a *societas*, as indicated by the name in the plural, DD. Caecilii, attested in *tituli picti* on amphorae dating from the Flavians to the reign of Trajan. Many of the attestations come from Rome itself, but smaller urban centres like Pompeii also feature in the list.[40] Very often the name of the Caecilii appears in the *titulus* beta of the amphorae, which is understood as indicating the name of the merchants.[41] By the Hadrianic period, the Decimi Caecilii had established a business partnership with the wealthy landlord, municipal aristocrat and businessman L. Aelius Optatus, who had properties in Hispania at both Peñaflor and Astigi.[42] L. Aelius Optatus and his *familia* were involved in the production of both olive oil and amphorae, as indicated by the evidence offered by stamps and *tituli picti*.[43] The *societas* established between the Decimi Caecilii and L. Aelius Optatus specialised in the export of Spanish olive oil.

If we only had the evidence about the existence of this *societas* available, we would probably interpret it as a case of an elite landlord who was not interested in being directly involved in the commercialisation of his products and hence used the services of specialised traders. But L. Aelius Optatus and members of his *familia* are also attested, without any other names, on olive oil amphorae and are considered a prime example of a family who both produced *and* commercialised their olive oil. In other words, although there is no universal consensus on how to interpret the complex *tituli picti* on the Dressel 20 olive oil amphorae,[44] all indicators in the case of the Aelii Optati suggest a vertically integrated oil business that engaged with the different stages of production and distribution.[45]

Considering the direct involvement of the family in the commercialisation of their products, why did they also establish a *societas* with the Decimi Caecilii? As observed by Broekaert and Zuiderhoek,[46] Optatus was probably supplying both capital and the actual goods to this business partnership, while the Caecilii dealt with the transport and sale. Therefore, the advantage of a *societas* for Optatus would have been an easier way to sell his produce, while for the Caecilii it meant that they did not need to look for a supplier of olive oil, the product in which they specialised as traders. Furthermore, the *societas* offered a solution to a serious potential constraint in Roman business, the ready availability of capital resources. But how did the two sides decide to do business together? To choose to enter a *societas* together, they needed to trust each other; the two parties must have known each other already or, at least, must have known *about* each other and the respective business reputation.

There might be some additional motives, though. An inscription dating to the age of Hadrian mentions a member of the Decimi Caecilii, a D. Caecilius Abascantus who, in the text, defines himself as 'lictor curiatus' and 'diffusor olearius ex provincia Baetica'.[47] Years ago, MG Granino Cecere, considering the fact that we have clear attestations for a *corpus* of *negotiatores oleari ex provincia Baeticae*, suggested that the term 'diffusor olearius ex provincia Baetica' should indicate something other than a simple merchant in olive oil. She proposed that the term should be understood in relation to the technical meaning of the verb '*diffundere*', that is, to decant in amphorae, as is well attested to in literary sources discussing wine.[48] Therefore, she suggested that a *diffusor olearius* from Baetica was someone in charge of overseeing the transfer of the oil from the skins, used to transport it to the river ports of the Guadalquivir, into the Dressel 20 amphorae used in the transmarine journey to Rome. In this scenario, the *diffusor olearius'* role would have been to guarantee both quality and quantity of the goods. This role possibly had a privileged relationship with the *annona* and its officials, in a period, between the reigns of Hadrian and Marcus Aurelius, when the systematic oil distribution of Septimius Severus had not yet started.[49] The known *diffusores olearii* date precisely to the period comprising the reigns of Hadrian and Marcus Aurelius.[50] Christol has subsequently clarified that the post of *diffusor olearius ex Baetica* was a stage in the career of major *negotiatores*; they worked with the association of traders in olive oil and, through the *annona*, were responsible for issuing receipts of consignments and for supervising the distribution.[51] In other words, it is possible that the business partnership established between the Aelii Optati and the Decimi Caecilii had an additional reason to occur: the fact that a member of the Decimi Caecilii was a *diffusor*, and therefore in an official position that potentially allowed him to help in the olive oil trade that was now, in part, linked to the *annona*.

Be that as it may, it is undeniable that these two families must have known about each other well before deciding to enter a business partnership. Their social networks had been central in deciding about the creation of the *societas* and, in turn, the web of trade representatives located in Spain and in Ostia and Rome and the various social ties they entertained, including with high officials, formed the backbone of their maritime trade activity. How social bonds between different economic actors, framed within the context of professional associations, may have helped trade can be also postulated by bringing another example from Ostian epigraphy, the case of C. Septimius Quietus.

C. Septimius Quietus from Ostia was the assistant for an auctioneer who specialised in the sale of wine. He dedicated a statue to the tutelary deity of the association of wine traders, the *corpus splendidissimum importantium et negotiantium vinaroriorum.*[52] As has been observed, the dedication of this statue to be placed in the club house of the wine traders signifies not only that Quietus was well acquainted with the wine merchants operating locally, but also that he must have engaged in business with them routinely.[53] If these traders worked habitually with the same auctioneer and their personnel, they would have been able to receive information on regular buyers present at the market of Ostia; such links would have extended to bankers as well, since it was normal for bankers to be present at auctions.[54] Therefore, information on the reputation and trustworthiness of sellers and buyers could be exchanged. In sum, these kinds of social exchanges, masked behind what are, essentially, religious dedications, were a way to lower transaction costs and to identify trustworthy business interlocutors.

Information is a very basic and crucial asset for commerce. Availability of reliable information acquired via personal contacts is what, at times, should be assumed in order to explain certain events that are attested archaeologically. Take the case of the terra sigillata tableware that in the first century AD started to be produced around Tralles in Asia Minor: usually, these pottery shapes follow the ones of the Arretine sigillata, with some differences in detail, and presented bilingual stamps in Latin and Greek. Some of these stamps display the name of C. Sentius, a potter known from a workshop located in Arretium in the Augustan period and one subsequently active in Lyon.[55] Some pottery vessels are even stamped with the name '*aretina*', thus possibly branding for the literate consumers or wholesale buyers the items for which the producer knew there was demand. Pre-existing knowledge of this demand, probably coming from prior export links, must have been behind the decision of our Sentius and other craftsmen like him to expand manufacturing activity to the other side of the Mediterranean. He must have had local contacts that ensured that he would be able to produce and sell his tableware in the new location. It is possible that he had already been exporting his wares to the area and later, having realised that there was a commercial opportunity, and perhaps also for personal reasons, decided to either relocate or open a branch business entrusted to an agent. The key element in this example, however, is the fact that moving from one side of the Mediterranean to the other in order to start a business can be explained only if Sentius had already some existing contacts in Asia Minor and in the region of Tralles. Again, personal contacts and ties were at the core of commercial activities and trade.

SOCIAL CAPITAL, TRUST AND ENFORCEMENT OF CONTRACTS

An important function of professional associations and associations of alien residents and translocal businessmen was to forge and strengthen social relations between persons sharing the same background, customs and (mostly) profession. As mentioned above, associations were excellent places to forge social bonds that were also rather helpful to trade. Another role that has been suggested by Broekaert when considering the advantages that being a member of a *collegium* posed, is the possibility of gaining social capital. This includes not only the social respectability that membership of an association could offer but also opportunities for a more senior and respected member of the association to 'promote' others, giving them additional respectability, which could then in turn help in commercial activities and other relations.[56] As a concrete example of this scenario we can consider the case of P. Aufidius Fortis. In AD 146 Fortis, a grain merchant and municipal aristocrat, was elected *quinquennalis* for life by the association of grain importers based in Ostia. Two of his freedmen held the office of *quinquennalis* and *quaestor* in this same *collegium* and Broekaert argued that in this way their patron was increasing their social capital, a suggestion with which I wholly agree.

When it came to the enforcement of trade contracts, social pressure and – in the case of members of associations – the rules of the association itself could be powerful incentives to abide by the rules and behave honourably. Information on untrustworthy behaviour could easily be passed on via this social network and, from a business point of view, such a person could find themselves severely curtailed in their business dealings. There is evidence to suggest that there were occasions when traders used membership of an association, and the social contacts this brought, to enhance their business opportunities. For instance, in some cases the *collegia* seem to have been used in order to find good contracts and partnerships for the distribution of commercial goods; furthermore, it seems that *collegia* might have offered support to a member in case of business disputes and enforcement of contracts. Following Broekaert, I interpret in this sense the case of C. Apronius Raptor and M. Inthatius Vitalis. They were members of the association of wine merchants based at Lyon but belonged also to the association of shippers of the Saône[57]; they were eventually elected patrons of the association. It has been suggested that Raptor and Vitalis could have used their connection to the shippers of the Saône to prevent other merchants from acquiring means of transport, so that 'a wine merchant who was not willing to join the *corpus* in Lyon, could easily be hindered in successfully doing business in Gaul'.[58] To this example we can add the case of C. Sentius Regulianus, also from Lyon. He was a wine and oil merchant and also a shipper, who became a member of the association of oil merchants from Baetica and even held office in this association.[59]

These contacts offered information relevant to trade and an infrastructure of peer pressure and control that, in part, could compensate for the state's imperfect enforcement capability.

OFFICIALS, THE STATE AND PRIVATE TRADERS

So far, I have addressed the issue of personal bonds among individuals of various professions, framed by various forms of associative order or by the patron-client relationship. Another aspect that should be considered concerns the officials, the state and private traders. The issue is particularly relevant when examining trade flows directed to the city of Rome or to the army that was located in the northern provinces. It is known that the *annona* ended up subsidising, in one form or the other, private trade. We have evidence of wholesale traders paying homage to high-ranking officials, sometime indirectly by honouring their relatives. Were these homages indicators of something more than the expression of social subordination and recognition of distinction? In my view, the answer is yes. I wish to consider P. Clodius Athenio, a trader in salted products, most likely salted fish and *garum*, who died in Rome in the second century AD. He had been, as we learn from his funerary inscription, the high official (*quinquennalis*) of the *corpus negotiantium Malacitanorum*, which had headquarters in Ostia, just like many other associations of traders of the imperial era. An inscription discovered in Malaca itself shows not only that P. Clodius Athenio was a person of means but also that he had social connections in high circles. The text from Malaca is an honorific inscription to Valeria Lucilla, the wife of L. Valerius Proculus, praefect of the *annona* in AD 144. P. Clodius Athenio is recorded as having paid back the sum that the citizens, and presumably the decurions, had collected in order to erect a statue to Valeria, thus gaining considerable honour for himself for this generous act. According to Roman social norms, P. Clodius Athenio's intervention in the matter of the statue to be erected to Valeria Lucilla publicly signals that he was close to her and her husband L. Valerius Proculus. Personal ties like the ones indicated by this inscription may signal that there was a close involvement between the *annona* and traders from Baetica supplying Rome with foodstuffs such as salted fish and oil. While the state found ways to incentivise the service of traders and shippers to the *annona* of Rome,[60] it also gave incentives to take on board private cargoes, in effect subsidising private trade. Clodius Athenio's connections were not limited to the association of traders from Malaca to which he belonged and to high-ranking imperial officials. They extended also to other associations of traders: a fragmentary Greek inscription, also from Malaca, honoured as patron of an association of Syrians and Asians traders a *Klodios*, who was probably the same P. Clodius Athenio I have been discussing.[61]

He is certainly not the only example of someone involved in large-scale maritime trade who paid homage to the praefect of the *annona*. D. Caecilius Hospitalis was the *curator* of the association of traders in olive oil from Baetica. He was himself a trader in olive oil: his name, together with that of D. Caecilius Maternus, is recorded on olive oil amphorae discovered at Monte Testaccio and may have been involved in a *societas* attested in some *tituli picti,* which mentions the Decimi Caecilii, concerned with the production and trade of fish salt products such as the 'best of *garum*'.[62] This is the same *gens* that I have mentioned earlier in the chapter. D. Caecilius Hospitalis dedicated a statue to M. Petronius Honoratus, who was the prefect of the *annona* and the prefect of Egypt of AD 147.[63] The case of the *olearii ex Baetica* and the *annona* is, in a way, special and has a high profile, but I choose these two examples to make the point about the role played by connections between traders and imperial officials in the case of commerce. Successful social links with key officials, whether high- or low-ranking, were an important part of the 'personal infrastructure' of trade. Dedications from shippers and traders to lower-ranking imperial or local officials are a sign of relationships that often could include transactions related to trade. As remarked by J D'Arms many years ago, 'imperial administration and private *negotiatores* could be active simultaneously, with interests which overlap and converge'.[64]

However, *collegia* of shippers and traders seem not to have necessarily been present everywhere there was notable volume in trade. In a recent study, Verboven discusses the evidence from Ganuenta, in the territory of the Menapii, on the southern shore of the Scheldt estuary. The *civitas* of the Menapii belonged to Gallia Belgica, but the coast was part of a single military zone with that of Germania Inferior. Ganuenta was an important trading post, and altars to the goddess Nehalennia bearing dedicatory inscriptions attesting 200 names were discovered there. While many of these individuals were merchants and shippers, and some show a common identity (e.g. the *negotiatores Britanniciani*), Verboven points out that 'nothing in the inscriptions . . . suggests collective action by a formal association'.[65] Unlike Lyon, where many powerful associations were based, here the institutional set up was very different. The large presence of the army in the area, as pointed out by Verboven, must be one of the reasons for the difference but also, I suspect, the very low urbanisation rate of the region. *Collegia* are essentially an urban phenomenon.

CONCLUSIONS

The role social and personal networks had in the context of trade in antiquity should not be underestimated. The proliferation of associations in the imperial era was certainly a response to the way in which individuals tried to gain social respectability and created a system of social support, but they were also encouraged because of the various roles associations could have in facilitating commercial transactions. Professional associations could help in establishing new business contacts, in finding credit, in vetting someone's commercial trustworthiness, even in exercising peer pressure that could exclude others from operating on a particular market. In the empire, *collegia* that had received the *ius coeundi*, the right to assemble, could have a treasury and hold collective property; there are attestations of properties belonging to *collegia* that were relevant to the activities of the profession represented by the association, such as the workshops of the *fabri* and *centonari* of Brixia mentioned above. It is possible that some associations of shippers and traders owned storage facilities that their members could use. In some cases, it is possible to see the involvement of individuals in more than one association related to transmarine trade, and besides the social advantages and distinction that these multiple memberships brought, there must also have been advantages related to business activity. Accessing reliable information on the availability of goods, market conditions, prices and opportunities was, by itself, an important benefit the network provided by a *collegium* might offer. In the imperial period, *collegia* connected to transmarine trade, or individual members of such *collegia*, also show close links with state officials involved with the *annona* – from the praefect of the *annona* at the very top to lower ranking officials. While such connections are expressed through 'traditional' social frameworks patronage, public dedications and so forth – it cannot be doubted that these links centred around the trade and shipments of certain goods to Rome.

In addition to professional associations and ethnic groups attested to at major port towns, the various examples discussed above show also that *societates* or business partnerships were widespread in the Roman world and had an essential role in the trade and distribution of many different types of goods. While these business partnerships often arose from existing social bonds – with family members or with one's slaves and freedmen or, possibly, with members of the same *collegium* – the possibility to form and dissolve such partnerships *relatively* easily greatly aided trade. The extent of one's 'personal infrastructure', when combined with the physical and legal infrastructure available in the Roman world, could make a real difference.

BIBLIOGRAPHY

Andreau, J. (1987), *La vie financière dans le monde romain: les métiers de manieurs d'argent (4e siècle av. J.-C.-3e siècle ap. J.-C.)* (Rome: École Française de Rome).

Arnaud, P. (2016), 'Cities and Maritime Trade under the Roman Empire', in C. Schäfer (ed), *Connecting the Ancient World: Mediterranean Shipping, Maritime Networks and their Impact* (Rahden/Westf.: Marie Leidorf), pp. 117–174.

Aubert, J.J. (1999), 'La gestion des collegia: aspects juridiques, économiques et sociaux', CGG 10, pp. 49–69.

Broekaert, W. (2011), 'Partners in Business: Roman Merchants and the Potential Advantages of Being a "Collegiatus"', *Ancient Society* 41 (2011), pp. 221–256.

Broekaert, W. (2015), 'Sticky Fingers. The Investment Structure of the Spanish Oil Business', *Cahiers «Mondes anciens»* [Online] 7, URL: *http://journals.openedition.org/mondesanciens/1598* (last accessed 27 September 2021); DOI: 10.4000/mondesanciens.1598.

Broekaert, W. (2017), 'Conflicts, Contract Enforcement, and Business Communities in the Archives of the Sulpicii', in M. Flohr and A. Wilson (eds), *The Economy of Pompeii* (Oxford and New York: Oxford University Press), pp. 387–414.

Broekaert, W. and Zuiderhoek, A. (2015), 'Society, the market, or actually both? Networks and the allocation of credit and capital goods in the Roman economy', CGG 26, pp. 141–190.

Camodeca, G. (2006), 'Communità di 'peregrini' a Puteoli nei primi due secoli dell'impero'', in M. Bertinelli and A. Donati (eds), *Le vie della storia. Migrazioni di popoli, viaggi di individui, circolazione di idee nel Mediterraneo antico (Atti del II Incontro internazionale di Storia Antica, Genova 2004)* (Rome: Giorgio Bretschneider), pp. 269–287.

Carreras Monfort, C. and Funari, P.P. (2008), *Britania y el Mediterraneo. Estudios sobre el abastecimiento de aceite bético y africano en Britania* (Barcelona: Publicacions Universitat de Barcelona).

Ciambelli, S. (2016), 'Cnaeus Sentius Felix: la straordinaria ascesa di un mercante forestiero a Ostia tra I e II secolo d.C. (*CIL* XIV, 409)', *Storicamente* 12, DOI: 10.12977/stor644.

Chic García, G. (1992), 'Los Aelii en la Producción y Difusión del Aceite Bético', *MBAH* 11(2), pp. 1–22.

Christol, M. (2008), 'Annona Urbis: Remarques sur l'organisation du ravitaillement en huile de la ville de Rome au IIe siècle apr. J.-C.', in M.L. Caldelli, G.L. Gregori, and S. Orlandi (eds), *Epigrafia 2006: Atti della XIVe rencontre sur l'épigraphie in onore di Silvio Panciera* (Rome: Quasar), pp. 271–298.

D'Arms, J.H. (1974), 'Puteoli in the second century of the Roman Empire: a social and economic study', *JRS* 64, pp. 104–124.

D'Arms, J.H. (1981), *Commerce and Social Standing in Ancient Rome* (Cambridge, MA: Harvard University Press).

Étienne, R. (1999), 'Un nouveau prêtre provincial du culte impérial de Bétique', *Revue d'études antiques* 50, pp. 141–152.

Étienne, R. and Mayet, F. (2001), 'Les élites marchandes de la péninsule ibérique', in S. Demougin, M. Navarro Caballero, and F. Des Boscs-Plateaux (eds), *Élites Hispaniques* (Pessac: Ausonius), pp. 89–99.

García Morcillo, M. (2005), *Las ventas por subasta en el mundo romano. La esfera privada* (Barcelona: Publicacions i Edicions Universitat de Barcelona).

García Vargas, E. and Martínez Maganto, J. (2009), 'Fuentes de riqueza y promoción social de los "negotiantes salsarii" béticos en el alto imperio romano. Una aproximación diacrónica', *Aespa* 82, pp. 133–152.

Granino Cecere, M.G. (1994), 'D. Caecilius Abascantus, diffusor olearius ex provincia Baetica (*CIL* VI 1885)', in *Epigrafia della produzione e della distribuzione. Actes de la VIIe Rencontre franco-italienne sur l'épigraphie du monde romain (Rome, 5–6 juin 1992)* (Rome: École Française de Rome), pp. 705–719.

Liu, J. (2009), *Collegia Centonariorum: The Guilds of Textile Dealers in the Roman West* (Leiden: Brill).

Lowe, B. (2016), 'The trade in fish sauce and related products in the western Mediterranean', in T. Bekker-Nielsen and R. Gertwagen (eds), *The Inland Seas: Towards an Ecohistory of the Mediterranean and the Black Sea* (Stuttgart: Franz Steiner), pp. 215–235.

Manzini, I. (2014), 'I Lucilii Gamalae a Ostia', *MEFRA* 126 (online), URL: *http://journals.openedition.org/mefra/2225* (last accessed 27 September 2021); DOI: https://doi.org/10.4000/mefra.2225.

Meiggs, R. (1960), *Roman Ostia* (Oxford: Clarendon Press).

Pastor Muñoz, M. (2002), *Corpus de inscripciones latinas de Andalucía*, vol. 4 (Granada: Consejería de Cultura de la Junta de Andalucía, Dirección General de Bienes Culturales).

Remesal Rodríguez, J. (2004a), 'Las ánforas Dressel 20 y su sistema epigráfico', in Remesal Rodríguez (ed), *Epigrafía Anfórica. Proyecto Amphorae* (Barcelona: Publicacions i Edicions Universitat de Barcelona), pp. 127–148.

Remesal Rodríguez, J. (2004b), 'Promoción social en el mundo romano a través del comercio', in F. Marco Simón, F. Pina Polo, and J. Remesal Rodríguez (eds), *Vivir en tierra extraña: emigración e integración cultural en el mundo antiguo (Collecció Instrumenta 16)* (Barcelona: Universitat de Barcelona), pp. 125–136.

Remesal Rodríguez, J. (2019), 'Monte Testaccio (Rome, Italy)', in C. Smith (ed), *Encyclopedia of Global Archaeology* (Cham: Springer).

Rougé, J. (1966) *Recherches sur l'organisation du commerce maritime en Méditerranée sous l'Empire romain* (Paris: S.E.V.P.E.N.).

Sánches León, M.L. (1978), *Economía de la Hispania Meridional durante la dinastía de los Antoninos* (Salamanca: Universidad de Salamanca).

Sirks, B. (1991), *Food for Rome: The Legal Structure of the Transportation and Processing of Supplies for the Imperial Distributions in Rome and Constantinople* (Amsterdam: J.C. Gieben).

Soricelli, G. (2007) 'Comunità orientali a Puteoli', in R. Compatangelo-Soussignan and C.G. Schwentzel (eds), *Étrangers dans la cité romaine* (Rennes: Presses universitaires de Rennes), pp. 129–144.

Tchernia, A. (1964), 'Amphores et marques d'amphores de Bétique à Poempei et à Stabies', *MEFRA* 76, pp. 437–439.

Tchernia, A. (2016) *The Romans and Trade*, J. Grieve and E. Minchin (trans.) (Oxford: Oxford University Press).

Terpstra, T. (2013), *Trading Communities in the Roman World: A Micro-Economic and Institutional Perspective* (Leiden: Brill).

Thouvenot, E. (1952), 'Una familia de negociantes en aceite establecida en la Bética an el siglo II: los Aelii Optati', *Aespa* 25, pp. 225–231.

Tod, M. (1934), 'Greek Inscriptions at Cairness House', *The Journal of Hellenic Studies* 54, pp. 140–162.

Tran, N. (2006), *Les membres des associations romaines. Le rang social des collegiati en Italie et en Gaules sous le Haut-Empire* (Rome: École Française de Rome).

Tran, N. (2020), 'Boatmen and their Corpora in the Great Ports of the Roman West (Second to Third Centuries AD)', in P. Arnaud and S. Keay (eds), *Roman Port Societies. The Evidence from Inscriptions* (Cambridge: Cambridge University Press), pp. 85–106.

Verboven, K. (2007), 'The associative order. Status and ethos among Roman businessmen in late republic and early empire', *Athenaeum* 95, pp. 861–893.

Verboven, K. (2011), 'Introduction: Professional Collegia: Guilds or Social Clubs?', *Ancient Society* 41, pp. 187–195.

Verboven, K. (2019), 'Associations, Roman', in T. Whitmarsh (ed), *The Oxford Classical Dictionary* (Oxford: Oxford University Press).

Verboven, K. (2017), 'Guilds and the Organisation of Urban Populations During the Principate', in K. Verboven and C. Laes (eds), *Work, Labour, and Professions in the Roman World* (Leiden: Brill), pp. 173–202.

Verboven, K. (2020), 'The Structure of Mercantile Communities in the Roman World. How Open Were Roman Trade Networks?', in P. Arnaud and S. Keay (eds), *Roman Port Societies. The Evidence from Inscriptions* (Cambridge: Cambridge University Press), pp. 326–366.

Wilson, A.J.N. (1966), *Emigration from Italy in the Republican Age of Rome* (Manchester: Manchester University Press).

Zabehlicky-Scheffenegger, S. (2003), 'C. Sentius and his Commercial Connections', in C. Abadie-Reynal (ed), *Les céramiques en Anatolie aux époques hellénistiques et romaines. Actes de la Table Ronde d'Istanbul, 23–24 mai 1996* (Istanbul: Institut Français d'Études Anatoliennes-Georges Dumézil), pp. 117–119.

NOTES

1. I wish to thank Emilia Mataix Ferrándiz and Peter Candy for inviting me to give a keynote address at the very successful and stimulating conference they organised in Helsinki in 2019 and for subsequently asking me to contribute to this volume. I am very grateful to Koen Verboven and Nicolas Tran for sharing with me their chapters (2020) in advance of publication.
2. Wilson (1966), p. 119.
3. IDélos 1520; Tod (1934) for the first commentary on the text.
4. *CIL* XIV 409 = *ILS* 6146; Meiggs (1960), pp. 200–201. On the *Lucilii Gamalae*, see Manzini (2014). An inscription of AD 135 attests Cn. Sentius Lucilius Gamala Clodianus as the patron of a local *collegium*, possibly the association of the *lenuncularii traiectus Luculli*: *CIL* XIV 5374.
5. Tran (2006), pp. 68–69; Ciambelli (2016).
6. Rostovtzeff (1926); Frank (1920); *Id.* (1938).
7. For example, the *plebiscitum Claudianum* of 218 BC: Livy 21.63.3.
8. Verboven (2011).
9. *IG* XIV 830 = *OGIS* 59.
10. Verboven (2007); *Id.* (2017); *Id.* (2020).
11. Verboven (2007), p. 861.
12. Arnaud (2016), pp. 154–155.
13. Terpstra (2013).
14. See Verboven (2020), pp. 350–352 for critical remarks about Terpstra's reconstruction; *inter alia*, Verboven points out that 'pure reputation-based enforcement systems only worked within closed groups' and that 'at least in the case of the *peregrini* we cannot take it for granted that they were members of a single, close-knit merchant society'.
15. For example, Broekaert (2011); *Id.* (2017).

16. *Suet.* Aug. 98: 'they lived thanks to him, they sailed thanks to him, they enjoyed their liberty and fortunes thanks to him'. On foreign communities in Puteoli: Camodeca (2006); Soricelli (2007).
17. For the discussion of case studies which show important regional differences in the spread of professional associations, see Verboven (2020).
18. Aubert (1999).
19. Asc. *Corn.* p. 67 C; D. 50.6.6.12 (Call. 1 *de cogn.*); the *collegia fabrum, centonariorum* and *dendrophorum* are referred to in some inscriptions as the *tria collegia principalia* (e.g. *CIL* V 7881); Sirks (1991); Tran (2020).
20. D. 47.22.3.1 (Marcian. 2 *iudic publ.*); Cf *CIL* VI 2193; Plin. *Pan.* 54. Liu (2009), pp.103–108.
21. D. 47.22.1 (Marcian. 3 *inst.*); Verboven (2015).
22. Verboven (2015).
23. Verboven (2015); see, e.g. *CIL* III 7485; VI 6320.
24. D. 3.4.1 pr.–2 (Gai. 3 *ad ed. provinc.*); the right to own property, receive legacies as a collective and so forth, was extended to all *collegia* who had the *ius coeundi* no later than Marcus Aurelius' reign: Liu (2009), p. 106.
25. Liu (2009), p. 107.
26. *CIL* V 4488.
27. The availability in port towns like Puteoli of private warehouses in which traders could rent storage spaces is inferred, for example, from documents in the financial archive of the Sulpicii; some mention *horrea* located on the *praedia* of Domitia Lepida, in which one could rent numbered storage stalls. *TPSulp.* 46 tab. III.5 pag. and *TPSulp.* 79 (both dating to March in AD 40) mention a 'grain stall number 26' in which 20,000 *modii* of Alexandrian grain had been stored for 100 sesterces a month. Verboven (2020), p. 348 reminds us of an anecdote in Aelian's work *On Animals* (13.6) about a giant octopus feeding on salted fish stored in a house along the shore in Puteoli by a group of Spanish merchants. Leaving aside the fictional nature of the giant octopus, the detail of Spanish traders storing their imported goods in a private house is a likely scenario from 'real' life and suggests that merchants had available to them a range of options to store their goods. The story does not specify whether the traders were business partners or *collegiati* or none of the above. On these tablets see, further, the chapter by É Jakab later in this volume.
28. Tran (2020); Verboven (2020).
29. Broekaert and Zuiderhoek (2015), p. 144.
30. Ship-owning could be part of a diversified wealth investment and besides freedmen the municipal elites often were involved in shipping: Arnaud (2016), p. 143.
31. P. Mich. V 244.
32. P. Mich. V 243.
33. AE 1995, 845 = AE 1999, 898.
34. García Vargas and Martínez Maganto (2009), p. 137.
35. Étiénne (1999).
36. A hypothesis advanced again in Étienne and Mayet (2001), p. 98.
37. Pastor (2002), pp. 226–228, no. 169.
38. Broekaert and Zuiderhoek (2015), p. 177.
39. Tchernia (2016), p. 37.
40. Tchernia (1964).
41. Remesal Rodríguez (2004a), pp. 128–134; Dressel had thought that the *titulus beta* indicated the producers: Remesal Rodríguez (2019), p. 4. See, also, the chapter by E Mataix Ferrándiz in this volume.

42. Sanchez Leon (1978), p. 262; Thevenot (1952); Chic García (1992).
43. The amphora stamp 'L·AE·OP·COL', suggests that he produced his own amphorae: Broekaert (2011), p. 239; Broekaert (2015).
44. Remesal Rodríguez (2004a). See, also, the chapter by E Mataix Ferrándiz later in this volume.
45. Sanchez Leon (1978), pp. 262–263; amphorae with the name of L. Aelius Optatus are known from Monte Testaccio in Rome, Autun, Saint-Satur and Vindolanda: CIL XV 3993; Carreras Monfort and Funari (1998), pp. 35–36; Broekaert (2015).
46. Broekaert and Zuiderhoek (2015), p. 173.
47. CIL VI 1885: *Memoriae / Caeciliae Helladis / uxoriis karissimae / D. Caecilius Abascantus / lictor curiatus /diffusor olearius ex / provincia Baetica / fecit sibi et libertis [l]ibertabusque sui[s]/posterisque eoru[m]*.
48. Granino Cecere (1994), p. 718.
49. Granino Cecere (1994), p. 718.
50. Granino Cecere (1994), p. 719 also observes that the special relationship between oil merchants and the *annona*, with the institution of the *diffusores*, could have been caused by Hadrian's attention to the trade and distribution of olive oil, as indicated by the *lex olearia* of Athens (IG II^2 1100) and the *rescriptum sacrum de re olearia* from Castulo, in Spain, of which only the title is known: AE 1958, 9. See also E Mataix Ferrándiz in this volume.
51. Christol (2008), p. 292.
52. AE 1955, 165.
53. Broekaert and Zuiderhoek (2015).
54. On auctions and bankers see Andreau (1987), pp. 148–155; 171–172; García Morcillo (2005).
55. Zabehlicky-Scheffenegger (2003).
56. Broekaert (2011).
57. Broekaert (2011), p. 242.
58. Broekaert (2011); see, also, considerations in Verboven (2020).
59. CIL VI 29722.
60. Arnaud (2016).
61. IG XIV 2540.
62. See Lowe (2016), p. 228.
63. CIL VI 1625b.
64. D'Arms (1981), p. 151.
65. Verboven (2020), p. 356.

Chapter 6

On Dressel 20 and Beyond: Management, Punishment and Protection in the Context of Roman Imperial Oil Distribution

Emilia Mataix Ferrándiz

INTRODUCTION

Every scholar dealing with the subject of the Roman economy must confront the issue of the Roman *annona* at some point. Following the same logical path, many of the scholars studying the *annona* should equally face the problems related to Dressel 20 amphorae, those recognisable containers bearing a characteristic epigraphic record.[1] One of the most discussed issues concerning this vessel regards its level of entanglement within an imperial bureau of collection and distribution, which, in fact, varied as much as the political organisation of Rome. There are certain similarities in the way that different products supplied and controlled by the Roman state were managed. The lease of quarries, mines and estates was equally managed through *locationes conductiones*, or letting and hiring contracts, that established the terms of the agreement between the empire (represented by its magistrates) and the lessees.[2] In that sense, the activities derived from oil supply administration – as well as of mining and quarrying – were intended to keep imperial involvement to a minimum without renouncing control of these ventures.[3]

The main aim of this chapter is to address the changing epigraphy of Dressel 20 as an artefact reflecting the inner organisation of state supply. Bearing in mind the similarities in the organisation of the activities related to public supply, Dressel 20 epigraphy will be compared and related to the epigraphic record of other supplies controlled by the Roman state such as marble. As will be seen throughout this work, the different nuances of public supply management will be perceived in their epigraphic record when these objects are considered as being part of one specific commercial cycle of distribution. In addition, I would like to explore in more detail what sort of protection and legal remedies could have been used by the imperial administration by comparing different texts and materials.[4] I will argue that the changing epigraphic record of Dressel 20 witnesses the variations taking place in the management of the *annona*. However, the correctness of this interpretation brings more problems than it solves and it is still unclear whether the individuals working for the *annona* benefitted from any legal protection; who was responsible for these tasks; how the issues arising from the activities related to state supply would have been addressed; or who was in charge of solving these sorts of controversies. To answer questions such as these the only option available is to contrast different sources to gain an insight into the criminal repression and protection of those subjects working for the Roman state. Unfortunately, there are not many texts that reflect these sorts of issues, and the two inscriptions that I have chosen to draw a comparison from correspond to different chronological periods and businesses, even if they are related to state-managed activities. The first deals with the protection of the *conductores* in charge of taking care of the imperial flocks, and the second is the inscription recording the complaint of the shipmasters of Arles, dealing with the damages suffered due to the use of faulty measures. Both sources will provide hints about how these activities were managed and carried out, thus helping us to better understand the framework within which Dressel 20s were distributed.

THE CHANGES IN THE EPIGRAPHY OF DRESSEL 20 AMPHORAE

Let me first start by presenting the issues concerning the changes in the epigraphic apparatus of Dressel 20. These oil containers were produced along the Guadalquivir valley (province of *Baetica*, Hispania), the part of the southern territory of Hispania designated by the Greek and Latin authors under the name *Turdetania*.[5]

   The study of the epigraphic record of the artefacts involved in public supply reveal certain specificities in the *formula* written on the objects, as happens in the case of Dressel 20 amphorae (Figure 6.1). This image displays the epigraphic

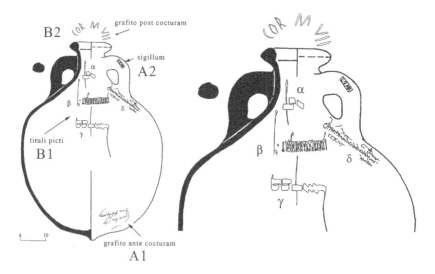

Figure 6.1 Dressel 20 epigraphic apparatus. Image courtesy of Dr. Piero Berni Millet.

apparatus of these containers, of which the inscriptions that interest us are mainly β (merchant name) and δ (fiscal formula). Both inscriptions were written on the container before reaching Rome and most probably in the same kiln or estate where the oil was packaged.[6] These writings should be considered in relation to another, and while the β refers to the merchant responsible for the oil, the δ inscription indicates who is in charge of controlling and registering the cargoes of oil sent to Rome. However, behind inscription β we should see two possible characters: the merchant, who is obliged, as in a sale or a lease of services contract, to provide a final product (for example, the oil), and the lessor. However, not all merchants were also shipmasters[7] and in many cases the job of transporting goods was entrusted to professional shippers.[8]

Table 6.1 shows that inscription β does not vary until the reign of Septimius Severus, when the names were replaced with the formula *Dominorum Nostrorum [. . .] Augustorum*. The name of the *Augusti* (in brackets) changed depending on the period, with *Severi et Antonini* used between AD 198 and 205

Table 6.1 Chart summary of the evolution of inscription β.

Era (AD)	Emperor	Text of the *scriptum*	Example(s)
1–100	Julio-Claudian/ Flavian Dynasty	*Q, Conniveriveraci*	CIL XV 3652
100–198	Antonine Dynasty	*Ocra Odesti et Cassi Olavsti*	CIL XV 3972
198–205	Septimius Severus / Caracalla	*Dominorum Nostrorum [] Augustorum Severi et Antonini*	Rodríguez Almeida: (1972), pp. 35–37; Id. (1979), p. 3, 4ª; Id. (1989), p. 6
205–217	Septimius Severus / Caracalla/ Geta	*Dominorum Nostrorum [] Augustorum Severi Antonini et Getae*	Rodríguez Almeida: (1972), pp. 33–34; Id. (1979), 5, 6, 9, 10–14; Id. (1989), pp. 7, 16
217–222	Macrinus / Elagabalus	*Fisci Rationis Patrimoni Provinciae Baeticae*	CIL XV 4111; 4114; 4116
217–222	Macrinus / Elagabalus	*Fisci Rationis Patrimoni Provinciae Tarraconensis*	CIL XV 4135–7
222–235	Severus Alexander	*Fisci Rationis Patrimoni provinciae Baetica* + names private merchants	Remesal and Aguilera (2010), pp. 27–158

and *Severi Antonini et Getae* from AD 205. Around AD 217, the inscription is replaced by *Fisci Rationis Patrimoni Provinciae Baeticae* or *Provinciae Tarraconensis*, which remained in use until about the middle of the third century AD. During the reign of Severus Alexander (AD 222–235), the names of private merchants reappeared in inscription β together with the inscription *Fisci Rationis Patrimoni Provinciae Baeticae*.

During the brief period of the reign of *Macrinus*, the β inscription changes again to indicate *fisci rationi patrimoni provinciae* [*Baetica* or *Tarraconensis*]. In the reign of Alexander Severus, the names of the merchants appear once again next to the fiscal inscription.

Following Table 6.2, inscription δ appears as quite simple until the reign of Hadrian, when it starts including an R/, the name of the city and the name of an *acceptor*, the person in charge of supervising the oil cargoes.[9] The simplicity of the δ inscriptions until the Severans indicates that the management of the collection and shipment was left primarily in the hands of private actors, who sometimes constituted large families of merchants who created partnerships or even employed agents to facilitate the oil distribution.[10]

In fact, the high level of state involvement in the *annona* supply stimulated parallel commercial practices rather than suppressing them with the demands of imperial redistribution: a behavioural pattern that lasted into the late antique period. A recent discovery in Arles of a jar of olives mentioning the famous oil merchant DD Caecilii contains writing in the same calligraphic style as that used on inscriptions α, β and γ on Dressel 20 amphorae.[11] This assertion underlines how peculiar the calligraphy of the Dressel 20 inscriptions was and also that a merchant as important as DD Caecilii was distributing products on behalf of the state and for his own sake using the same labelling instruments.[12]

Therefore, from this account we can raise several questions upon which the epigraphic texts analysed in the next sections can shed some light. These are: (a) who was liable and, at the same time subject to, protection, for the transport of oil amphorae according to the different changes in inscription β?; (b) what is the role of the emperor and the bureau *a rationibus* in all this?[13] And of the *fiscus*?; (c) what

Table 6.2 Chart summary of the evolution of inscription δ.

Era (AD)	Emperor	Structure inscription	Example(s)
1–100	August to Hadrian	Name + a + number (pounds)	Colls *et al.* (1977), p. 66; *CIL* XV 3642
117–138	Hadrian	R/ + city of *Baetica* + name + acc + name	*CIL* XV 4091
149–193	Antoninus Pius	R/ + city of *Baetica* + name + acc + name + Consular date	*CIL* XV 3957; 3995

is the relation between *fiscus* and *patrimonium?*; (d) what is the meaning of the R/ from the inscription δ? And how can it be interpreted in relation to inscription β?; and, (e) what sort of procedure could have been used in case of issues arising from distribution? The next sections will be dedicated to summarising and contextualising the two inscriptions that provide some hints about the liabilities of people involved in public supply. Both texts had general appeal, which looked either to protect the tasks performed by the *conductores* or to avoid fraud in the various stages of maritime transport.

INSCRIPTIONS REFLECTING ISSUES CONCERNING PUBLIC SUPPLY

Monumental inscription found in Saepinum (Italy) dating AD 169–172[14]

The *Saepinum* (modern Altilia, near Sepino) inscription consists of an *epistula* dealing with the abuses suffered by the *conductores* of the Imperial flocks working in the area located south of the modern Campobasso in south central Italy.[15] The inscription was placed by the ancient gate of the city, visible to the public,[16] and it is composed of three parts written chronologically in the reverse order in which they occurred. In modern terms, what we see is a letter with two attachments. In its text we can find, at the end, a report from the imperial freedman Septimianus to his hierarchical superior, the freedman *procurator a rationibus* named Cosmus, about the ill-treatment suffered by the *conductores* of the flocks by the local magistrates and the *stationarii*.[17] Second, there is a petition form the *procurator a rationibus* to the prefects of the *praetorium* to which the report of Septimianus had been added as an attachment. At the end of the inscription, there is a letter of *admonitio* from these prefects to the magistrates of *Saepinum* threatening them with sanctions based on the petition from Cosmus and the report of Septimianus. This inscription gives an outline of the duties of the bureau *a rationibus* and the prefects for the safeguarding of a public task that will provide clues to the responsibilities of this bureau in matters concerning oil supply (given that the Dressel 20 inscriptions indicate their involvement in this activity). The inscription reads[18]:

'I. *Bassaeus Rufus et Macrin(i)us Vindex magg(istratibus)* / *Saepinat(ibus) salutem* / *exemplum epistulae scriptae nobis a Cosmo Aug(usti) lib(erto)* / *a rationibus cum his quae iuncta erant subiecimus et admonem/us abstineatis iniuri(i)s faciendis conductoribus gregum oviarico/rum cum magna fisci iniuria ne necesse sit [et] recognosci de hoc* / *et in factum si ita res fuerit [ut oportet(?)] vindicari* /

Bassaeus Rufus and *Macrinius Vindex* to the magistrates of *Saepinum*, greetings. A copy of the letter written to us by *Cosmus*, freedman of the Emperor *a rationibus*, we have subjoined with that letter which had been added and we admonish you that you abstain from committing outrages on the contractors for the sheep flocks causing great harm to the *fiscus*, then it may be necessary that to carry out a judicial investigation about this and that there should be a legal claim on the facts arising from the event, if the matter should be so.

II. *Cosmi Aug(usti) lib(erti) a rationibus scriptae ad Bass(a)eum Rufum et ad / Macrin(i)um Vindic(em) pr(aefectos) pr(aetorio) e(minentissimos) v(iros) exemplum epistul(ae) scriptae mih(i) / a Septimiano co<n=L>liberto et adiutore meo subieci et peto tanti / faciatis sc(r) ibere magg(istratibus) Saepin(atibus) et Bovian(ensibus) uti desinant iniuriam / conductoribus gregum oviaricorum qui sunt {sunt} sub cura mea facere / ut be(ne)ficio vestro ratio fisci indemnis sit*

Written by *Cosmus*, freedman of the Emperor *a rationibus*, to the most eminent *Basseus Rufus* and to *Macrinius Vindex*, praetorian prefects. A copy of a letter written to me by *Septimianus*, my fellow freedman and helper, I have subjoined, and I ask that you consider it so important to write to the magistrates of *Saepinum* and *Bovianum*, that they cease to commit outrages upon the contractors for the sheep flocks that are under my supervision, so that by your help the *fiscus* may be unharmed.

III. *Script(ae) a Septimiano ad Co/smum conductores gregum oviaricorum qui sunt sub cura tua in re pr(a)esenti / subinde mihi quererentur per itinera callium frequenter iniuria(m) / se accipere a stationari(i)s et magg(istratibus) Saepino(!) et Boviano(!) eo quod in tra(n)situ / iumenta et pastores quos conductos habent dicentes fugitivos esse et / iumenta abactia habere et sub hac specie oves quoque dominicae / di[ffu]giant in illo tumultu necesse habeamus etiam scribere quietius ag/erent ne res dominica detrimentum pateretur et cum in eadem contumacia / perseverent dicentes non curaturos se neque meas litteras neque si tu eis / scrips[isses] litter[a]s t[e] rogo domin<e=I> si tibi videbitur indices Bass(a)eo Rufo / et Macrin(i)o Vindici pr(aefectis) pr(aetorio) e(minentissimis) v(iris) ut epistulas emittant ad eosdem magg(istratus) et stati/onarios [3] ta<m=N>diu t[eme]re(?) [ir]ritum(?) factum est*

[Text] written by *Septimianus* to *Cosmus*. Since the contractors for the sheep flocks that are under your supervision were repeatedly complaining to me on the spot that along the roads they frequently receive outrageous treatment from the *stationarii* and the magistrates at *Saepinum* and *Bovianum* on this account, because they (hold?) in transit the animal flocks and the shepherds that they have hired, saying that they are runaway slaves and have animals [from the flocks] that have been stolen, and because under this pretext the Emperor's sheep also have perished in that event, we held necessary also to write that they should act more peacefully, lest the Emperor's affairs suffer loss; and since they persist in the said obstinate disobedience, saying that they will not be concerned either about my letter or if you yourself should write to them that the situation should not occur at all, I ask, my lord, if it seems best to you, that you inform the most eminent *Basseus Rufus* and *Macrinius* Vindex, the praetorian prefects, that they send letters to the said magistrates and *stationarii* . . . it has happened.'

The *Saepinum* inscription, from early in Marcus Aurelius' reign,[19] offers the first hard evidence for the prefects' independent police authority in Italy (where there was no provincial governor).[20] The letter indicates the term *iniuria*, in the generic and objective sense of *quod non iure fit*.[21] It preserves shepherds' complaints of mistreatment at the hands of local officials and *stationarii*[22] and a menacing letter from the praetorian prefects to the magistrates of *Saepinum*, urging that the abuses be stopped, especially since some of the affected flocks belonged to the emperor. The mention of *oves quoque dominicae* and to *ne res dominica detrimentum pateretur* (§3. l.6), point to the ownership of the emperor of some of the flocks (bearing in mind the use of *quoque*) and that others would have been owned privately. The standard view of the inscription is that the responsibility of the *a rationibus* over the *conductores* was because these were the contractors for the Imperial flocks. In its turn, the damage caused to the *fiscus* arose because of loss inflicted on the Imperial possessions, either because some sheep were actually lost[23] or because the contractors were unlikely to be willing to pay as much as they had in the past.[24] Two main issues arise from this part: the still problematic distinction between *fiscus* and *patrimonium* and the role of the *a rationibus* in the whole issue. Both points relate to the epigraphy of the Dressel 20 amphorae because their inscriptions make reference to these officers *a rationibus*, as well as to *fiscus* and *patrimonium* and offer similar problems.

It follows from the standard view of the *Saepinum* inscription that the contracts for the Imperial flocks were the responsibility of the *a rationibus*.[25] Contrasting the opinion of scholars such as Laffi[26] or Millar,[27] M Corbier[28] thinks that this inscription does not deal with the management of the *patrimonium*, but to the fact that the *a rationibus* was involved in looking after the *conductores gregum oviaricum* in the context of a general responsibility for the processes of transhumance, as she appreciates by reading the expression *sub cura tua* (§3. l.2) in the inscription.[29]

I think that Corbier is right, and that if we compare this activity with the supply of Dressel 20, it is possible to see that public and privately owned oil cargoes were shipped simultaneously and that the involvement in public supply boosted the private businesses of many oil merchants such as the Caecilii. In that sense, it does not seem strange that the flocks were mixed and that the *a rationibus* oversaw the security of all of them, to protect the activity in its entirety. Indeed, Corbier makes it clear that:

> 'as far as the Saepinum affair is concerned, we should surely see it as involving the *Fiscus* as the recipient of dues for pasturage; even if the inscription includes no explicit reference to fees for pasture rights, since the abuses in question do not bear directly on these, these fees are the key to the understanding of the inscription; for any damage inflicted on the *conductores* reduces their ability to pay and hence the value of their obligations to the *Fiscus*'.[30]

If we think of oil distribution as an activity linked to the *fiscus*, as it was because of the income that the Roman state received from the oil estates, it makes sense to understand that the office *a rationibus* would be in charge of the smoothness of the conduct of publicly related activities.[31]

The inscription also highlights that the *patrimonium* was no longer an autonomous entity and it may even be argued that the *fiscus* encompassed the *patrimonium*.

In a 1966 article, PA Brunt indicated that the obscurity that he found in his sources was not merely to be attributed to their vagueness.[32] Soon (though after Augustus) it ceased to be clear which funds were public and which were private, and even if jurists had been able to make a sharp distinction in principle, the amalgamation of imperial and public funds in administration and the secrecy of the accounts divested the distinction of any practical importance.[33] In addition, E Lo Cascio[34] indicates that this mixture on the ownership of the flocks, and the fact that these are all under the supervision of the *a rationibus* shows that there was no juridical distinction between *fiscus* and *patrimonium* and that there would not be a *patrimonium fisci* different from the *patrimonium caesaris*.

Monumental inscription found at Beirut from the navicularii from Arles dating AD 198–203

CIL III 14165 (=*ILS* 6987) constitutes one of the two columns of a singular bronze inscription,[35] which was found in Beirut[36] and refers to a joint complaint raised by the *navicularii* of Arles. The chronology has been set around AD 198–203 by reconstructing the charge of the *Claudius Iulianus* (the *praefectus annonae*) mentioned in the inscription.[37] The writing displays a complaint from the *navicularii* of Arles to the *praefectus annonae* because the authorities did not properly survey their distribution operations, causing them to sustain a loss.[38] This inscription appears as a disposition oriented to protect these subjects working for the public supply of Rome and working for the bureau *a rationibus*, which will help us to interpret the changes in Dressel 20's inscription δ. The inscription reads:

'[---I] IVLIANVS NAVICVLARIIS / [MAR]INIS ARELATENSIBVS QVINQVE/ [C]ORPORVM SALVTEM/ [QV]ID LECTO DECRETO VESTRO SCRIPSERIM/ [[---]] PROC. AVGG.E.V. SVBI/ CI IVSSI OPTO FELICISSIMI BENE VALEATIS / E.E./ EXEMPLVM DECRETI NAVICVLARIORVM MA. RINORVM ARELATEN-SIVM QVINQVE COR/ PORVM ITEM EORVM QVAE APVT ME ACTA/ SVNT SVBIECI ET CVM EADEM QUERELLA LA/ TIVS PROCEDAT CETERIS ETIAM INPLORANTI / BVS AVXILIVM AEQVITATIS CVM QVADAM DE / NVNTIA-TIONE CESSATVRI PROPEDIEM OBSEQVI / SI PERMANEAT INIVRIA PETO VT TAM INDEMNI / TATI RATIONIS QVAM SECVRITATI HOMINVM / QVI ANNONAE DESERVIVNT CONSVLATVR / INPRIMI CHARACTERE REGV-LAS FERREAS ET / ADPLICARI ROSECVTORES EX OFFICIO TVO IV / BEAS QVI IN VRBE ONDVS QVOD SVSCE / PERINT TRADANT

Claudius Iulianus Naviculariis from the marine navicularii from Arles, who are part of the five corporations, greetings. After having read your decree, I have written to [here a name, deleted] procurator of the two emperors, eminent man, the letter of which one copy is attached. I wish you good luck and good health. [copy of the letter] You will find here attached a copy of the decree of the marine navicularii from Arles, who are part of the five corporations, as well as items of the case instructed before me. And because the first complaint lasted longer than the others and that the other (navicularii) are also complaining about the protection of my arbitration, threatening to stop their services, if we keep on causing injury to them, I ask you – for assuring that the ratio does not suffer any prejudice and that the men who work for providing food do not suffer any prosecutions – to give the order of stamping the metallic measuring tools and appoint some men for the safeguard under your services, that will return to Rome the weight (of the cargo) that they had received.'

The inscription reads '*inprimi charactere regulas ferreas et / adplicari prosecutores ex officio tuo iu/beas qui in urbe pondus quo susce/perint tradant*'. The authorities had to ensure that the weights used conformed to official standards to assure the accuracy of these operations.[39] These standard tools, called *sekomata* or *tabulae ponderariae* played a crucial role in controlling different types of merchandise and provided information about how these procedures of monitoring and control of the cargoes were performed, sometimes even in inscriptions written on them.[40] In fact, one Digest text indicates that Trajan even established an edict punishing cases of using false measures with the penalties of the *Lex Cornelia de falsis*.[41] These *regulas ferreas* related to the official standards that should be used when measuring the grain loaded. If we bear in mind that the shipmasters would have been paid for the amount of grain they were transporting, that explains perfectly why they felt mistreated when the use of these fake standards caused them to be paid less. The cargoes arriving at a port, either destined for retail trade or public use, had to be examined. The inscription suggests the presence of some subjects in charge of receiving cargoes on behalf of the *praefectura annonae*, thus having a role between transport and storage of goods.[42] At every stage of this process there might have been officials and overseers who monitored the exchanges, compared the commodity to official weights and measures,[43] collected taxes and ensured that none of the cargo had disappeared in the course of the sea voyage.[44] For that reason, the shipmasters demanded that the procurator take appropriate measures (*regulas ferreas*) relating to the integrity of the accounts register to ensure that the shippers working for the *annona* received what was due to them. The identification of these subjects as *ratio* and the need of keeping an accurate quantification and accounting for the merchandise can be related to the Dressel 20, especially in what I identify as a general change in the management of the oil distribution, which is reflected in inscription δ. This identification as *ratio* is used during the Severan period, which I think demonstrates the efficiency of the Hadrianic reform that introduced the *ratio* as the identification for several of the bodies working for the public supply.

INQUIRING INTO THE SOURCES

Both inscriptions constitute epistles that can be construed as *admonitiones*, which is to say warnings or preventive policing measures: the prefects limit themselves to turning to the magistrates for a simple injunction to provoke a change in conduct. These epistles advised those addressed that otherwise they would be subject to investigation and prosecution, but previous cases of injustice would be left unpunished. The *conductores* complained to the magistrates and to the *stationarii* because they were not properly controlling activities and performing their duties; however, the complaint was not about the controls themselves, because Roman law did not assume the possibility of an *iniuria* in the exercise of public authority.[45] The case is similar to the complaint that can be found in *CIL* III 14165. To sum up other important details: on the one hand, we have the *praefectus of the praetorium* protecting the *ratio*, and on the other hand we find that the *a rationibus* is in charge of the *conductores* who work for a *fiscus-patrimonium*.

DRESSEL 20 STRIKES AGAIN

As can be appreciated by looking at Table 6.1 above, the simplicity of the β inscriptions until the Severans indicates that the management of the collection and shipment was left primarily in the hands of private actors. The continuity of inscriptions β and δ during the Julio-Claudian and Flavian dynasties indicates that the distribution of oil was a large part of the business for Spanish merchants at that time. However, oil distribution had not yet reached its peak, as is revealed by the existence of several shipwrecks with mixed cargoes dated to the first century AD,[46] compared to the increase of single oil cargoes during the Antonine period.[47] One clear example of this phenomenon is the Port-Vendres wreck, which held a mixed cargo of Dressel 20, ingots and other sorts of vessels.[48]

So, looking at inscription β (Table 6.2), it is possible to appreciate that until the reign of the Severans private merchants were supplying Rome with oil and, looking at the δ inscription, that these private merchants, until the reign of Hadrian, were controlled by some official unrelated to the *ratio*, or at least not identified as such in the inscriptions. The δ inscription is quite simple, indicating names that do not even seem to have servile features and just acknowledging the weight of the oil. These private merchants might have been working for the public supply, by placing their services for hire. I think that we need to turn to the conclusions of PJ du Plessis when studying several *leges* concerning public works (for example, the *lex Irnitana*; *lex Ursonensis*), who indicates that these reflect that the relations between the government and individuals was not directly protected by laws.[49] Although this opinion seems to indicate that a contractor would have been exposed to corrupt magistrates, there are indications that certain safeguards existed from which the contractor could have benefitted indirectly.

In that sense, inscription δ changes during the reign of Hadrian, when it starts including an R/, the name of the city and the name of an *acceptor*, a person in charge of supervising the oil cargoes. That points to the fact that the control of these cargoes was managed by subjects working for the Roman state, but not organised in a particular way until the reign of Hadrian. The R/ also appears inscribed on other types of artefacts, such as marble,[50] the late ostraca from the *Îlot de l'Amirauté* at Carthage,[51] or some amphorae (AD 75–125) found in the Pecio Gandolfo in Almería (Spain).[52] In the case of the Dressel 20, the R/ has been interpreted in different ways, such as *recognitum*,[53] *recensitum*,[54] or *ratio*.[55] It is clear that R/ does not need to mean the same in every case, especially for the example of the ostraca of the *Ilôt de l'Amirauté*, because these are records written when the oil arrived at the port of Carthage and not inscriptions written on the containers before setting sail, as was the case of Dressel 20. Looking at the sort of objects on which this R/ is inscribed and their context, it is possible to see that it corresponds to a mark of registration for public consumption. In my view, the R/ might refer to *ratio*, and this could be linked to a reorganisation of the distribution of Baetican oil that took place during Hadrian's reign that could itself be linked to other changes in the administration of transport for other goods such as marble.

This argument is based on the changes in the R/ inscription during Hadrian's reign (AD 117–138), which can be compared with the epigraphic formula on marble (Table 6.3, appendix) from Chemtou (Numidia), Phrygia or Ostia from that same period. In addition, the marble that displays these inscriptions are of the kind *Giallo antico* and *pavonazzetto*, which were used for luxury buildings that were generally destined for public imperial buildings or to wealthy customers with a taste for luxury goods.[56] These writings indicate that the R/ inscription referred to the fact that an imperial official in charge of a *ratio* collected the product. The inscribed blocks would represent the material that the contractors were contractually obliged to produce, under contract that would then have been credited to their account (*ratio*). I would like to recall the model of distribution described by Russell, in which the complex inscriptions present on marble blocks constitute *formulae* that allowed officials to track the blocks until they reached their destination.[57] In that respect, it is interesting to see that in the case of Ostia, all the marbles bear that R/ in the inscription, so that the *ratio* took care of the distribution of these marbles the whole time. Differently, the inscriptions coming from Phrygia start including the R/ after AD 136 and those from Chemtou after AD 137. The Phrygian inscriptions reflecting the organisation of the marble quarries did not reflect changes in the last decades of the first century, or in the first decades of the second, but they did in the last years of Hadrian.[58] The latter would indicate a change not in the ownership of these quarries, but in the distribution model during Hadrian's reign.[59]

In addition, one inscription recently discovered in modern Turkey (Table 6.4, appendix) adds weight to this hypothesis. The writing refers to the permission given by Hadrian to the Milesians to form an association of shippers. This inscription was found at the east side in the area of the suspected eastern port of the city.[60] The conjecture of the archaeologists is that the stele was fitted into the wall of the gatehouse itself in such a manner that the writing was at eye level for passers-by. So it was wise to use such a significant location, not far from where the headquarters of the association of the Milesian shipowners lay.[61] Thus perhaps the creation of this association can be linked with that reorganisation of the distribution by Hadrian and, consequently, to the R/ included in the inscription.[62] It seems to be good evidence that Miletus acted as an entrepôt for the shipment of marble from the imperially owned quarries in inland Asia Minor, especially those of Phrygia that provided the luxurious marble known as *pavonazzetto*. These operations could have been overseen by a *procurator a marmoribus,* as was a certain Chresimus (under Domitian and Nerva), attested in Asia Minor, at Tralles, Mylasa, Ephesus, and Miletus.[63] None of these sites are particularly close to the imperial quarries in Phrygia, but it is possible that this official was tasked with overseeing transport rather than quarrying.[64]

Comparing the marble marks to the Dressel 20 inscriptions (Tables 6.1–6.2), we can see that they indicate a reorganisation of the oil transport carried out under Hadrian, seeking to guarantee that the supply for public consumption was going to be managed by a group of contractors identified under a *ratio.* These are not the only inscriptions that seem to point to a reorganisation of transportation of goods related to public supply and control of these ventures. In fact, during the same period (AD 125–128),[65] one Athenian oil law[66] indicated that the subjects exporting oil should complete a declaration indicating to whom they were selling it and where the ship would be moored, which indicates a high level of control. The aim of the law was to prevent the export of all the oil: it is necessary to ensure a sufficient supply for internal consumption. However, even if the aims of this law targeted a concrete area, it can be indicative of the emperor's interest in systematising oil supply. Perhaps the change in the Dressel 20 inscriptions can also be associated with this policy of Hadrian, to systematise the shipping of Baetican oil to Rome.[67]

Another inscription that can tell us something about the tight control on oil supply of the Antonine emperor was found at Cástulo, near Linares in southeastern *Tarraconensis,* reading '*RESCRIPTVM SACRVM DE RE OLEARIA*'[68] and associated with Hadrian. The inscription was published for the first time by D'Ors and Contreras, who related the emperor's reply to the oil farmer and reflected in this *rescriptum* to the protective measures established in the oil law of Athens (*IG* II[2] 1100). D'Ors's suggestion was that Hadrian considered the Athenian law as a general precept applicable to the whole Empire, an opinion followed by Sáez Fernández and Lomas.[69] In addition, G Chic García[70] argues that the rescript was born from a complaint raised by the landowners, by which they asked for the application of the *Lex olearia Hadrianea* in their states. The latter would have ensured that at least one part from their production would be acquired, ensuring their income and also the *annona* supply.[71] Another interpretation argues that the emperor, replying to an oil farmer, established that the farmer's land contributed to the *annona* supply and, with that publicly stated, the farmer's land would be protected from the abuses of the oil collectors, who were subjects of a public contract.[72] One final interpretation of this inscription is that the oil farmers from Cástulo had to pay an extra fee for the transport of their oil as far as *Corduba,* where the shipyards and the amphora kilns were located, and this was the reason they complained to the emperor in order to obtain a solution to that unequal treatment.[73] However, it is impossible to confirm these hypotheses and, therefore, these need further revision, even though the document probably demonstrates the interest of Hadrian in agrarian policies linked with oil.

Thus, I maintain that the R/ could indicate that Hadrian began collecting oil using procurators in charge of a *ratio* and that the notation would relate to administrative issues of the goods arriving in Rome. Finally, the addition of a consular date by Antoninus Pius (Table 6.2) was probably a way of completing Hadrian's reform, providing further details for the registration process. Relating this inscription to the one of *Saepinum*, the latter shows that some flocks were owned privately and they call for protection from the *procurator a rationibus*. By comparing both sources, I think that what we can see is that being inserted in this cycle of distribution probably provided greater protection from the bureau *a rationibus* to the subjects because it was in the interest of the state to keep this flow of supply working smoothly. In addition, if we look at both the *Saepinum* and Arles inscriptions, we can see that the fact of managing that supply with that body of people will provide them with the possibility of being protected, in the first instance, by the magistrates in charge of the *a rationibus*, but even being able to reach the higher hierarchy. The latter is shown by the fact that in both inscriptions, the case reaches the *praefectus praetorium* or the *praefectus annonae*, who would have been in charge of these issues since this magistrate was in charge of food supply, and some texts indicate that they had *iurisdictio*.[74] The fact of being managed by this office could have provided these contractors with extra protection, even if they were individually liable for the transport, something that we do not know whether they benefitted from previously.

A different image can be appreciated in the inscriptions belonging to the Severan era (Table 6.2), when as can be acknowledged in inscription β, the names of individuals started being replaced by the names of the emperors. Some scholars have used the *Historia Augusta* (hereinafter, HA) to say that Severus, after having put an end to Clodius Albinus' rebellion, confiscated the estates of the allies of his enemy in Gaul and Spain and incorporated them into the *aerarium*, thus acquiring nor only large sums of money, but also oil-producing farms, especially in Baetica.[75] Centralisation of the administration was one of the most characteristic features of Severus and Caracalla's reforms and may have coincided with the separation of the *fiscus* and the personal *patrimonium* of the emperor.[76] In addition, Severus consolidated the *fiscus* to the detriment of the *aerarium*, thus strengthening the figure of the *princeps* (holder of the *fiscus*) at the cost of the *populus* (holder of the *aerarium*) in contracts employed to gather goods for public supply.[77] E Rodríguez Almeida argued that the change in the *tituli* could be connected to the high expenses for maintaining the shipping carried out on behalf of the *annona* and the profits made by the oil merchants, which made the emperor decide to deal directly with the *navicularii* and eliminate the merchants.[78] This would have meant a complete reorganisation of the oil supply. This theory was further elaborated by J Remesal Rodríguez, who claimed that the Severans not only radically transformed the organisation of oil imports, but also effectively controlled a major part of the trade.[79] W Broekaert challenged these ideas, arguing that the emperors included their names in order to stimulate merchants and skippers to bring oil to Rome by paying transport costs and taking responsibility for shipping the cargoes.[80]

I think that the change in inscription β under Severus needs to be linked with one text of the HA,[81] which refers to the free provision of oil granted by the emperor. The inclusion of their name in the amphoras' epigraphic *apparatus* could imply that the emperors were paying for the oil and its transport to stimulate the *annona* transport of this product to Rome.[82] Despite the fact that many scholars have pointed to *Severus* as the emperor boosting the oil supply on the basis of that same passage of the HA,[83] oil supply reached a peak under the Antonines, as can be seen in the archaeological evidence preserved at the Monte Testaccio.[84] Indeed, the HA fragment does not directly mention anything that can be linked to a confiscation of land in Baetica and, in fact, it says that the assets of the executed people were auctioned off. Besides, even if the emperor owned these estates, it is well known that the owner-emperor was absent from them and that his main aim was to receive a permanent income from the estates.[85] The only element that can point to the direct management of three concrete estates (called *ceparia*, *barba* and *grumese*),[86] around AD 197, is that these carry stamps bearing the inscription AVGNNN (*augustorum nostrorum triorum*) instead of the potter's name. P Berni Millet provides the most convincing theory about these stamps, emphasising that marking was more common on amphorae involved in public supply, because the demand and the control over these containers was very strict.[87] However, that will just tell us about the production of the container, not about the whole cycles of distribution and transport. Moreover, under Severus, *arca* is mentioned in the δ inscription in relation to other details and its use continues into the following periods. The mention of *arca* could be related to the place where the money to finance the shipping of oil was kept.[88] Thus, for the Severan era, the relationship between R/ and *arca* completed the formula written on the amphorae, indicating the subjects in charge of the distribution of oil and the institutional unit financing it.

The mentions of *pondo* and *actus* appear after the reign of Septimius Severus, which can be linked with the fact that if the HA is true, it reflects then a tighter control on the collection of that oil. That can be linked to the fact that Severus included oil in the *annona* supply, even if it was not under him that oil distribution found its highest peak. In addition, it is well known that the inscription found in Beirut, describing an issue of the *navicularii* of Arles concerning weights and dated in the Severan period, indicates the constant care that should be taken by the authorities when measuring goods in order to pay the amount that is due to the people working on that supply. During the reign of Severus, the names following the inscription reflecting the act of weighing were mentioned before those reflecting features that are more servile. Perhaps that is why these inscriptions also include the word *actus*, indicating the records generated by these members of the imperial bureau (who probably oversaw weights and measures). Therefore, in this period, if the emperors are undertaking that liability, that would provide enough protection to the contractors whose liability would otherwise have been assumed by them. However, in the names written in inscription β we need to distinguish two people: the merchant supplying the oil and the shipper in charge of the transport, whose agency in this case can be recognised in the inscription of Arles and also as being part of the *ratio* reflected in inscription δ. Therefore, these subjects can apply for that protection on the basis of two claims: not just because they act using a collective action,[89] but also because they belonged to that *ratio* that needed to keep performing its tasks in order to keep distribution flowing.

During the brief period of the reign of Macrinus, the β inscription changes again to indicate *fisci rationi patrimoni provinciae* [*Baetica* or *Tarraconensis*], which needs to be read in relation to the *acta* mentioned in inscription δ. Macrinus was an *advocatus fisci*,[90] and it would not be surprising then that he created these two divisions of the *fiscus* in order to supply oil to the empire, which highlights the different financial units through which this transport was financed.[91] This change may reflect two things: that the *fiscus* was undertaking liability for the oil being gathered and that, effectively, as mentioned for the inscription of Saepinum and as suggested by Lo Cascio, there was no juridical distinction between *fiscus* and *patrimonium*.[92] The presence of the R/ in inscription δ might indicate the presence of the *rationalis* in charge of controlling these cargoes.[93] Thus, the government would have still been responsible for the gathering and transport, precluding liability for the contractors in these cases.

Finally, during the reign of Alexander Severus, inscription β changes again, probably indicating a joint venture between the Roman government and the merchants who, even if they had to participate in the risks of the venture, were exempted from the *aurum negotiatorium* according to the HA.[94] This is probably the reason why we can find both names written together on the container. Following Broekaert's interpretation,[95] it looks like this might have been a joint venture between the *fiscus* and the privates and bearing in mind that the inscription still mentions the R/ (*ratio*), these subjects could have asked for the protection of that body in case of need. Therefore, in case of trouble, the private owners would not have evaded liability but shared it with the *fiscus*. In that way, subjects may work individually and not be part of the *ratio*, as happened with the *navicularii* of Arles. That would be a way of including more people, encouraging them to work for the *annona* and providing them with adequate protection.

What sort of procedure would they have been granted in case of trouble? Both inscriptions constitute *admonitiones* (warnings), but the first column of the Beirut inscription does not refer to any procedure, because it reflects a collective claim by the body of *navicularii*. In the Saepinum inscription, the use of *cognosci de hoc* makes sense only if the purpose of the action expressed was precisely the ascertainment of the crime and not its repression through a criminal trial, even if that was probably the case.[96] In that inscription, *vindicari* also alludes to a general and not to a specific legal notion.[97] *Factum*, instead, refers to actions of this kind presided over by the magistrates. However, this mention is unique in monumental epigraphy; I have not found any other reference to *in factum* in any other epigraphic record. In the formula *in factum*, the *intentio* mentions the fact from which the plaintiff draws their claim and the judge is authorised to condemn the defendant if the fact in question is proved. It is quite usual to find the use of actions of this sort for criminal proceedings, as it would be in the case of attempting a crime against the state, and this case would not be an exception.[98] However, I do not think that here we are talking about *actiones in factum* that would refer us to the formulary procedure, and these *praefecti* would apply the *cognitio extra ordinem* within the scope of their competence. Both inscriptions constitute disciplinary measures that would be the first step taken to ask for protection in public distribution and that had the the violation continued, these subjects could have then opted for going to court.

CONCLUSION

I suggest that the subjects working inside a *ratio* would have enjoyed a higher level of protection since they were part of that group in charge of keeping public supply flowing, and they could have made claims on that basis. In the end, being associated with a *ratio* would have been beneficial for the people working for the public food supply in order to ensure their protection, but this detailed formulaic apparatus of the Dressel 20 would also have been of great help to keep accountability and serve as proof in case something went wrong. As in the case of the inscription of Arles, the magistrate mentioned the use of *regulas ferreas* as the tools to ensure that the right quantification, the epigraphic apparatus of this container would also have ensured the performance of the people working for this supply, helped grant their protection and not just manifest their liability. Indeed, abstract systems such as this accounting acted sometimes to depersonalise relationships, but sometimes repersonalised them, that is, allowing novel personal investments and trust that would not have been possible otherwise.

BIBLIOGRAPHY

Aguilera Martín, A. and Berni Millet, P. (1998), 'Las cifras hispánicas', in *Calligraphia et tipographia. Arithmetica et numerica. Chronologia* (Barcelona: Universitat de Barcelona), pp. 257–282.

Aguilera Martín, A. (1999), 'Los *tituli picti* del monte Testaccio. El control fiscal del aceite bético' (Department of Ancient History, Universidad de Barcelona).

Aguilera Martín, A. (2001), 'Los tituli picti D del convento Astigitano en el primer tercio del s. III d.C.', in *Congreso Internacional Ex Baetica Amphorae. Conservas, aceite y vino de la Bética en el Imperio Romano. Sevilla-Écija, 17–20 de diciembre de 1998, 4, Écija 2001* (Écija: editorial gráficas sol), pp. 1231–1240.

Aguilera Martín, A. (2007), 'Evolución de los *tituli picti* de las ánforas Dressel 20 entre mediados del Siglo I y Mediados del s. III', in *XII Congressus Internationalis Inscriptiones Graecae et Latinae* (Barcelona: Institut d'estudis catalans), pp. 15–22.

Aguilera Martín, A. (2012), 'La Normalisation de l'épigraphie amphorique: Les *tituli picti* des amphores Dressel 20', in M.E. Fuchs, R. Sylvestre, and C. Schmidt Heidenreich (eds), *Inscriptions mineures: noveautés et reflexions, Actes du premier colloque ductus (19–20 Juin 2008, Université de Lausanne)* (Bern: Peter Lang), pp. 135–143.

Aliquot, J. and Badawi, M. (2013), 'Trois Poids Romains de Gabala (Syrie)', *ZPE* 184, pp. 202–204.

Aubert, J.J. (2003), *Tâches publiques et entreprise privée dans le monde romain* (Geneva: Droz).

Barea Bautista, J.S., Barea Bautista J.L., Solís Siles, J. and Moros Díaz, J. (2008), *Figlina Scaliensa: un centro productor de ánforas Dressel 20 de la Bética* (Barcelona: Universitat de Barcelona).

Baccini Leotardi, P. (ed) (1979), *Scavi di Ostia: Marmi di cava rinvenuti a Ostia e considerazioni sul commercio dei marmi in età romana, a cura di P. Baccini Leotardi* (Rome: Ist. Poligrafico dello Stato).

Barot J. (1905), 'Les naviculaires d'Arles à Beyrouth', *RA* 61, pp. 262–273.

Berni Millet, P. (2008), *Epigrafía anfórica de la Bética. Nuevas formas de análisis* (Barcelona: Universidad de Barcelona).

Berni Millet, P. and Gorostidi, D. (2013), 'Iulius Valerianus et C. Iulius Iulianus. Mercatores del aceite Bético en un *signaculum* de plomo para ánforas Dressel 20´, *JRA* 26, pp. 167–189.

Blanco Freijeiro, A. (1962), 'El aceite en los albores de la Historia de España', *Oretania* 10, pp. 138–148.

Blázquez Martínez, J.M. and Remesal Rodríguez, J. (eds) (1983), *Producción y comercio del aceite en la antigüedad. II Congreso Internacional* (Madrid: Universidad Complutense de Madrid).

Boulvert, G. (1970), *Esclaves et affranchis impériaux sous Haut-Empire: Rôle politique et administrative* (Naples: Jovene).

Broekaert, W. (2008), 'Roman economic policies during the third century AD: the evidence of the *tituli picti* on oil amphorae', *Ancient Society* 38, pp. 197–219.

Broekaert, W. (2008), '*Creatio ex nihilo?* The origin of the *corpora naviculariorum* reconsidered', *Latomus* 67, pp. 692–706.

Broekaert, W. (2011), 'Partners in business. Roman merchants and the potential advantages of being a *collegiatus*', *Ancient Society* 41, pp. 221–256.

Broekaert, W. (2012), 'Welcome to the family! Marriage as a business strategy in the Roman economy', *MBAH* 30, pp. 41–65.

Broekaert, W. (2013), *Navicularii et Negotiantes: a Prosopographical Study of Roman Merchants and Shippers* (Leidorf: Pharos).

Broekaert, W. (2016), 'Freedmen and Agency in Roman Business', in A. Wilson and M. Flohr (eds), *Urban Craftsmen and Traders in the Roman World* (Oxford: Oxford University Press), pp. 222–253.

Brunt, P.A. (1966), 'The "Fiscus" and Its Development', *JRS* 56, pp. 75–91.

Burdese, A. (1975), 'Sull'origine dell'*advocatus fisci*', in *studi E. Guicciardi* (Padova: Cedam), pp. 3–24.

Casson, L. (1965), 'Harbour and River Boats of Ancient Rome', *JRS* 55, pp. 31–39.

Chankowski, V. and Hasenohr, C. (2015), 'Étalons et tables de mesure à Délos Hellénistique: Évolutions et ruptures', in C. Saliou and N. Monteix (eds), *La mesure dans l'Antiquité*, *DHA Suppl.* 12, pp. 21–39.

Chic García, G. (1979), 'El intervencionismo estatal en los campos de la producción y la distribución durante la época de los antoninos', *Memorias de Historia Antigua* 3, pp. 125–137.

Chic García, G. (2002), '*Degustatio o recognitio*', in L. Rivet and M. Sciallano (eds), *Vivre, produire et échanger: reflets méditerranéens. Mélanges offerts à Bernard Liou* (Montagnac: Monique Mergoil), pp. 335–342.

Christol, M. and Drew-Bear, A. (1986), 'Documents latins de Phrygie', *Tyche* 1, pp. 41–87.

Christol, M. and Drew-Bear, A. (1987), 'Inscriptions de Dokimeion', *Anatolia Antiqua* 1, pp. 83–137.

Colls, D., Etienne, R., Lequement, R., Liou, B. and Mayet, F. (1977), 'L'épave Port-Vendres II et Le commerce de la Bétique à l'époque de Claude', *Archaeonautica* 1, pp. 3–145.

Corbier, M. (1983), '*Fiscus* and *Patrimonium*: The Saepinum Inscription and Transhumance in the Abruzzi', *JRS* 73, pp. 126–131.

Corbier, M. (2006), 'Les mesures et les hommes: les naviculaires d'Arles et leurs "règles de fer"', in *Donner à voir, donner à lire: mémoire et communication dans la Rome ancienne* (Paris: CNRS), pp. 233–256.

Coriat, J.P. (1997), *La technique législative des Sévères et les méthodes de création du droit impérial à la fin du Principat* (Paris: De Boccard).

Corritore, R.P., Marin, B. and Virlouvet, C. (2016), 'Fonctionnement administratif et économique', in C. Virlouvet and B. Marin (eds), *Entrepôts et trafics annonaires en Méditerranée: antiquité-temps modernes* (Rome: École française de Rome), pp. 173–197.

Cottier, M. et al. (2008), *The Customs Law of Asia* (Oxford: Oxford University Press).

Cursi, M.F. (2002), *Iniuria cum damno. Antigiuridicità e colpevolezza nella storia del danno aquiliano* (Milan: Giuffrè).

D'Ors, A. (1963), 'El conjunto epigráfico del museo de Linares, portada-epígrafe de un rescripto imperial sobre hacienda olivera', *Oretania* 5, pp. 84–86.

D'Ors, A., and Contreras, R. (1956), 'Nuevas inscripciones romanas de Castulo', *Aespa* 29, pp. 126–127.

De Martino, F. (1975), *Storia della costituzione romana* (Milan: Giuffrè).

De Salvo, L. (1992), *Economia privata e pubblici servizi nell'impero romano: i corpora naviculariorum* (Messina: Samperi).

Dalla Rosa, A. (2016), 'From Exploitation to Integration: Imperial Quarries, Estates and Freedmen, and the Integration of Rural Phrygia', *Studi Ellenistici* 30, pp. 305–330.

Dalla Rosa, A. (Forthcoming), 'Hadrian, middlemen and the exploitation of imperial domains', in P. Erdkamp and K. Verboven (eds), *Law and Economic Performance in the Roman World* (Leiden: Brill).

Dalla Rosa, A. (Forthcoming), 'Adriano e lo sfruttamento delle cave di Dokimeion. Una rilettura dei cambiamenti nelle sigle di cava del 136/137 d.C.', in H. González Bordas (ed), *Adriano y la gestión de la propiedad imperial en el occidente romano. Aproximación a las fuentes epigráficas* (Alcalá de Henares: Editorial Universidad de Alcalá).

Djaoui, D. (2011), 'Découverte d'un double sceau en bois a date consulaire (épave de Tiboulen de Maire, Marseille). Étude préliminaire', *SFECAG Actes du Congres d'Arles* (Paris: Decitre), pp. 625–633.

Djaoui, D. (2014), 'Découverte d'un pot mentionnant la société des DD Caecilii dans un contexte portuaire situé entre 50–140 av. J-C', *Colloque International de La SECAH, Ex Officina Hispana* (Porto: Faculdade de Letras da Universidade do Porto), pp. 693–710.

Dressel, H. (1891), *Corpus Inscriptionum Latinarum. Vol. XV. Inscriptiones Urbis Romae instrumentum domesticum* (Berlin: G. Reimerum).

Drew-Bear, T. (1994) 'Nouvelles inscriptions de Dokimeion', *MEFRA* 106(2), pp. 747–844.

du Plessis, P.J. (2004), 'The protection of the contractor in public works contracts in the Roman Republic and Early Empire', *JLH* 25(3), pp. 287–314.

Eck, W. (2012), 'Administration and Jurisdiction in Rome and in the Provinces', in M. Van Ackeren (ed), *A Companion to Marcus Aurelius* (Oxford: Wiley–Blackwell), pp. 185–199.

Ehrhardt, N. and Günther, W. (2013), 'Hadrian, Milet und die Milet. Zu einem neugefundenen kaiserlichen Schreiben', *Chiron* 43, pp. 199–220.

Fant, J.C. (1998), 'The Roman Emperors in the Marble Business: Capitalists, Middlemen or Philantropists?', in N. Herz and M. Waelkens (eds), *Classical Marble Geochemistry, Technology, Trade* (Dordrecht: NATO ASI Series, Series E: Applied Sciences), pp. 147–158.

Fant, J.C. (1989), *Cavum Antrum Phrygiae. The Organization and Operations of the Roman Imperial Marble Quarries in Phrygia* (Oxford: British Archaeological Reports).

Faoro, D. (ed) (2018), *L'amministrazione dell'Italia romana. Dal I secolo a.C. al III secolo d.C. Fondamenti* (Florence: Mondadori).

Fuhrmann, C.J. (2012), *Policing the Roman Empire: Soldiers, Administration, and Public Order* (Oxford: Oxford University Press).

Gatier, P.L. (2014), 'Poids et vie civique du Proche-Orient hellénistique et romain', *DHA Suppl.* 12, pp. 125–162 in C. Saliou and N. Monteix (eds), *La mesure dans l'Antiquité*.

Giangrieco Pessi, M.V. (1988), *Situazione economico-sociale e politica finanziaria sotto i severi* (Naples: Edizioni Scientifiche Italiane).

Gisbert Santonja, J.A. (2008), 'Puerto y fondeaderos de Dénia en la Antigüedad clásica: evidencias de comercio y distribución de vino y aceite en Dianium y su *territorium*', in J. Pérez Ballester and G. Pascual Berlanga (eds), *Comercio, redistribución y fondeaderos: la navegación a vela en el Mediterráneo: [V Jornadas de Arqueología Subacuática: actas]* (Valencia: Universidad de Valencia), pp. 247–267.

Grenier, A. (1905), 'La transhumance des troupeaux en Italie et son rôle dans l'histoire romaine', *MEFRA* 25, pp. 307–312.

Haensch, R., and Weiss, P. (2005), 'Gewichte mit Nennung von Statthaltern von Pontus et Bithynia', *Chiron* 35, pp. 443–498.

Haensch, R., and Weiss, P. (2007), 'Statthaltergewichte aus Pontus et Bithynia. Neue Exemplare und neue Erkenntnisse', *Chiron* 37, pp. 183–218.

Harter-Uibopuu, K. (2008), 'Hadrian and the Athenian oil law', in O.M. Van Nijf and R. Alston (eds), *Feeding the ancient Greek city* (Leuven: Peeters), pp. 127–141.

Hauken, T. (1998), *Petition and response: An epigraphic study of petitions to Roman Emperors* (Bergen: The Norwegian Institute at Athens).

Héron de Villefosse, A. (1914), 'Deux armateurs narbonnais. Sextus Fadius Secundus Musa et P. Olitus Apolonius', *Mémoires de la Société des Antiquaires de France* 74, pp. 153–180.

Hirt, A.M. (2010), *Imperial Mines and Quarries in the Roman World: Organizational Aspects 27 BC–AD 235* (Oxford: Oxford University Press).

Hirt, A.M. (2015), 'Mines and Economic Integration of Provincial 'Frontiers' in the Roman Principate', in S.T. Roselaar (ed), *Processes of Cultural Change and Integration in the Roman World* (New York: Brill), pp. 201–221.

Hirt, A.M. (2017), 'The Marble Hall of Furius Aptus: Phrygian Marble in Rome and Ephesus', *CGG* 28, pp. 231–248.

Holland, L. (2009), *Weights and Weight-like Objects from Caesarea Maritima* (Haifa: Hadera).

Jones, A.H.M. (1950), 'The *Aerarium* and the *Fiscus*', *JRS* 40, pp. 22–29.

Kaser, M./Hackl, K. (1996), *Das römische Zivilprozessrecht* (Munich: Beck).

Kehoe, D.P. (1988), *The Economics of Agriculture on Roman Imperial Estates in North Africa* (Göttingen: Vandenhoeck and Ruprecht).

Kłodziński, K. (2018), 'The *collegium* (or *officium*) *rationalium*. The controversy over the reform of central financial administration in the 2nd half of the 2nd c. A.D.', *Pallas* 107, pp. 291–310.

Laffi, U. (1965), 'L'iscrizione di Sepino (*CIL* IX, 2438) Relativa ai contrasti fra le autorità municipali e i "conductores" delle greggi imperiali con l'intervento dei prefetti del pretorio', *Studi Classici e Orientali* 14, pp. 177–200.

Lambrini, P. (1993), 'In tema di "*advocatus fisci*" nell'ordinamento romano', *SDHI* 59, pp. 325–336.

Liou, B. and Tchernia, A. (1994), 'L'interprétation des inscriptions sur les amphores Dressel 20', in *Epigrafia della produzione e della distribuzione. Actes de la VIIè Rencontre franco-italienne sur l'épigraphie du monde romain organisée par l'Université de Roma-La Sapienza et l'École française de Rome, sous le patronage de l'Association internationale d'épigraphie grecque et latine. Rome, 5–6 juin 1992* (Rome: École française de Rome), pp. 133–156.

Liou, B. and Rodriguez Almeida, E. (2000), 'Les inscriptions peintes des amphores du Pecio Gandolfo', *MEFRA* 112:1, pp. 7–25.

Lo Cascio, E. (1971), 'Patrimonium, *ratio privata, res privata*', *Istituto italiano per gli studi storici* 3, pp. 55–212.

Lo Cascio, E. (1985–1990), 'I 'greges oviarici' dell'iscrizione di Sepino (*CIL* IX 2438) e la transumanza in età imperiale', *Abruzzo* 23/28, pp. 557–569 = Id. (2000), *Il princeps e il suo impero: studi di storia amministrativa e finanziaria romana* (Bari: Edipuglia), pp. 151–161.

Long, L. (2017), 'Extracting economics from Roman marble quarries', *Economic History Review* 70(1), pp. 52–78.

Manacorda, D. (1977), 'Il kalendarium Vegetianum e le anfore della Betica', *MEFRA* 89(1), pp. 313–332.

Maiuro, M. (2012), *Res Caesaris. Ricerche sulla proprietà imperiale nel Principato* (Bari: Edipuglia).

Martín, F. (1994), 'Las constituciones imperiales de Hispania', in J. González (ed), *Roma y las provincias: realidad administrativa e ideología imperial* (Madrid: Ediciones Clásicas), pp. 169–188.

Martin, F. (2001), 'De re olearia: la ley ateniense de Adriano y el rescripto de Cástulo', in J.M. Blázquez Martínez and J. Remesal Rodríguez (eds), *Estudios sobre el Monte Testaccio II* (Barcelona: Universidad de Barcelona), pp. 475–486.

Mentxaka, R. (2001), 'Algunas consideraciones en torno a las concesiones administrativas y sus garantías: capítulos 63–65 de la *Lex Malacitana*', *Mainaké* 32, pp. 71–96.

Millar, F. (1963), 'The *Fiscus* in the first two Centuries', *JRS* 53, pp. 29–42.

Mommsen, Th. (1996), *A History of Rome Under the Emperors* (London: Routledge).

Mouritsen, H. (2011), *The Freedman in the Roman World* (Cambridge: Cambridge University Press).

Orestano, R. (1968), *Il problema delle "persone giuridiche" in diritto romano* (Torino: Giappichelli).

Ozcáriz Gil, P. (2013), *Administración de la provincia Hispania citerior durante el Alto Imperio romano* (Barcelona: Universidad de Barcelona).

Parker, A.J. (1992), *Ancient shipwrecks of the Mediterranean and the Roman Provinces* (Oxford: British Archaeological Reports).

Paschalidis, P. (2008), 'What Did Iniuria in the Lex Aquilia Actually Mean?', *RIDA* 55, pp. 321–363.

Passerini, A. (1939), *Le Coorti Pretorie* (Rome: Studi pubblicati dal R. Istituto Italiano per la Storia Antica).

Pensabene, P. (1994), *Le vie del marmo: i blocchi di cava di Roma e di Ostia: il fenomeno del Marmo nella Roma Antica* (Rome: Soprintendenza archeologica di Ostia).

Pensabene, P. and Gasparini, E. (2015), 'Marble Quarries: Ancient Imperial Administration and Modern Scientific Analyses', in E.A. Friedland, M. Grunow Sobocinski, and E.K. Gazda (eds), *The Oxford Handbook of Roman Sculpture* (Oxford: Oxford University Press), pp. 94–106.

Peña, J.T. (1998), 'The Mobilization of State Olive Oil in Roman Africa: the Evidence of the 4th Century Ostraca from Carthage', in J.H. Humphrey (ed), *The Carthage papers. The early colony's economy, water supply, a public bath, and* the mobilization of state olive oil, *JRA Suppl.* 28 (Oxford: British Archaeological Reports), pp. 116–238.

Piganiol, A. (1956), 'La Politique agraire d´Hadrien', in *Les empereurs romains d'Espagne. Madrid-Italica, 31 mars-6 avril 1964* (Paris: CNRS), pp. 135–146.

Pons Pujol, Ll. (2009), *La economía de la Mauretania Tingitana (s. I-III d. C.): aceite, vino y salazones* (Barcelona: Universidad de Barcelona).

Poole, R.S. (1873), *A Catalogue of the Greek Coins in the British Museum* (London: British Museum).

Puliatti, S. (1992), *Il "de iure fisci" di Callistrato e il processo penale in eta Severiana* (Milan: Giuffrè).

Purpura, G. (ed) (2012), *Revisione ed integrazione dei fontes iuris romani anteiustiniani (FIRA) Studi Preparatori, I. Leges* (Turin: Giappicchelli).

Remesal Rodríguez, J. (1983), 'Ölproduktion und Ölhandel in der Baetica', *MBAH* 2, pp. 91–111.

Remesal Rodríguez, J. (1989), 'Tres nuevos centros productores de ánforas Dressel 20 y 23. Los sellos de Lvcivs Fabivs Cilo', *Ariadna* 6, pp. 121–153.

Remesal Rodríguez, J. (1991), 'Sextus Iulius Possessor en la Bética', *Gerión* 3, pp. 281–296.

Remesal Rodríguez, J. (1996), '*Mummius Secundinus*. El *Kalendarium Vegetianum* y las confiscaciones de Severo en la Bética (HA Severus 12–13)', *Gerión* 14, pp. 195–221.

Remesal Rodríguez, J. and Aguilera Martín, A. (2010), 'Los *tituli picti*', in J.M. Blázquez Martínez and J. Remesal Rodríguez (eds), *Estudios sobre el Monte Testaccio (Roma) V, Collecció instrumenta 35, Corpus international des timbres amphoriques 17* (Barcelona: Universidad de Barcelona), pp. 41–166.

Ricci, C. (2018), *Security in Roman Times, Rome, Italy and the Emperors* (London: Routledge).

Rizzi, M. (2012), '"*Si Quis Mensuras Conduxerit*": Note Su D. 19,2,13,8', *Zeszyty Prawnicze* 12(2), pp. 181–198.

Rizzi, M. (2016), *Legislazione di Mercato ad Atene attraverso la documentazione epigrafica* (Canterano: Aracne).

Rodríguez Almeida, E. (1972), *Novedades de epigrafia anforaria del monte Testaccio* (Rome: école française de Rome), pp. 107–241.

Rodríguez-Almeida, E. (1979), 'Monte Testaccio: i mercatores dell'olio della Betica', *MEFRA* 91(2), pp. 873–975.

Rodríguez Almeida E. (1980), 'El Monte Testaccio, hoy: nuevos testimonios epigráficos', *Producción y comercio del aceite en la Antigüedad, I* (Madrid: Universidad Complutense de Madrid), pp. 57–102.

Rodríguez-Almeida, E. (1989), *Los tituli picti de las anforas olearias de la Bética. Tituli picti de los Severos y la Ratio fisci* (Madrid: Universidad complutense de Madrid).

Rodríguez Almeida, E. (1993), 'Graffiti e produzione anforaria della Baetica', in W.V. Harris (ed), *The Inscribed Economy. Production and distribution in the Roman Empire in the light of instrumentum domesticum. The proceedings of a conference held at the American Academy in Rome 1992, JRA Suppl.* 6 (Oxford: British Archaeological Reports), pp. 95–106.

Rovira Guardiola, R. (2007), 'El archivo Sulpicio y los tituli picti b: circulación de comerciantes en el Mediterráneo', in M. Mayer i Olivé, G. Baratta, and A. Guzmán Almagro (eds), *Provinciae Imperii Romani inscriptionibus descriptae* (Barcelona: Universidad de Barcelona), pp. 1263–1268.

Russell, B. (2014), *The Economics of the Roman Stone Trade* (Oxford: Oxford University Press).

Sáez Fernández, P. and Lomas F.J. (1981), 'El *Kalendarium Vegetianum*, la Annona y el comercio del aceite', *Mélanges de la Casa de Velázquez* 17, pp. 55–84.

Salway, B. (2019), '*Navicularii, naucleroi*, and the Roman state', *Gdanskie Studia Prawnicze* 3(3), pp. 41–54.

Sánchez-Moreno Ellart, C. (2015), 'Zur Gerichtsbarkeit des Praefectus annonae in D. 14.5.8 (Paul 1 decr.)', in S. Panzram, W. Riess, and Chr. Schäfer (eds), *Menschen und Orte der Antike: Festschrift für Helmut Halfmann zum 65. Geburtstag* (Trier: Pharos), pp. 361–372.

Sirks, A.J.B. (1992), *Food for Rome: the Legal Structure of the Transportation and Processing of Supplies for the Imperial Distributions in Rome and Constantinople* (Amsterdam: J.C. Gieben).

Taglietti, F. (1994), 'Un inedito bollo laterizio ostiense ed il commercio dell'olio betico', in *Epigrafia della produzione e della distribuzione. Actes de la VIIe rencontre franco-italienne sur l'épigraphie du monde romain (Rome, 5–6 juin 1992)* (Rome: École française de Rome), pp. 157–193.

Terpstra, T. (2013), *Trading communities in the Roman World: A Micro-Economic and Institutional perspective* (Leiden: Brill).

Terpstra, T. (2019), *Trade in the ancient Mediterranean: Private Order and Public Institutions* (Princeton, NJ: Princeton University Press).

Tran, N. (2011), 'Les Collèges professionnels Romains: '"clubs" ou "corporations"?' L'exemple de la vallée du Rhône et de CIL XII 1797 (Tournon-Sur-Rhône. Ardèche)', *Ancient Society* 41, pp. 197–219.

Trisciuglio, A. (1998), *Sarta tecta, ultrotributa, opus publicum faciendum locare sugli appalti relativi alle opere pubbliche nell'età repubblicana e augustea* (Naples: Jovene).

Vera, D. (2006), 'Un'iscrizione sulle distribuzioni pubbliche di vino a Roma (CIL VI, 1785=31931)', in M. Silvestrini, T. Spagnuolo Vigorita, and G. Volpe (eds), *Studi in onore di Francesco Grelle* (Bari: Edipuglia), pp. 303–317.

Verboven, K. (2011), 'Introduction: professional *collegia*: guilds or social clubs?', *Ancient Society* 41, pp. 187–195.

Virlouvet, C. (2004), 'Les naviculaires d'Arles. À propos de l'inscription de Beyrouth', *MEFRA* 116(2), pp. 327–370.

Watson, A. (1985–1998), *The Digest of Justinian* (4 vols.) (Pennsylvania: University of Pennsylvania Press).

Weaver, P.R.C. (1972), *Familia Caesaris. A Social Study of the Imperial Freedmen and Slaves* (Cambridge: Cambridge University Press).

Wickert, L. and Mommsen, Th. (1959), *Eine Biographie. Band I: Lehrjahre (1817–1844)* (Frankfurt: Vittorio Klostermann).

NOTES

1. This paper was presented at two symposia and has benefitted from the comments and suggestions of their participants, which have improved this piece immeasurably. The first one was an Ancient Law in Context meeting ('Crime and Punishment'), which took place in Edinburgh on 15 April 2019. I would like to thank Prof. Paul J du Plessis and Prof. Ulrike Roth for their invitation. The second symposium was held in Helsinki on the 29 October 2019, under the title 'Law and Imperial Power: Agents of Transformation of the Territorial and Urban Landscapes in Roman Hispania'. Here, I would like to thank Dr Anthony Álvarez Melero, Dr Diego Romero Vera and Dr Antonio López García for their invitation. Any errors that remain are, of course, my own responsibility. There is a large bibliography on Dressel 20, but in general, see: Rodríguez Almeida (1979); Remesal Rodríguez (1983); Liou and Tchernia (1994); Rodríguez Almeida (1993); Berni Millet (2008).
2. On the use of letting and hiring in public supply, see: Trisciuoglio (1998); Aubert (2003); du Plessis (2004). On the particular conditions established in these sorts of contracts, see one very interesting case in Mentxaka (2001), pp. 72 and 96.
3. A comparative study of mines and quarries has been carried out by Hirt (2010), p. 368; *Id.* (2015), pp. 210–211, also Russell (2013); and Pensabene and Gasparini (2015), pp. 100–101.
4. Even if this paper is the first that compares Dressel 20 to other inscriptions, we are not the first to compare publicly related affairs, as can be seen in Millar (1963), pp. 29–42, concerning the *fiscus*.
5. On the different locations of the kilns producing these containers, see Blázquez Martínez and Remesal Rodríguez (1983); Remesal Rodríguez (1983); *Id.* (1989); Berni Millet (2008); Barea Bautista et al. (2008). Note also the project Oleastro, from the Casa de Velázquez (Madrid), which explores the production of these containers in Turdetania (*https://www.casadevelazquez.org/es/investigacion/excavaciones-arqueologicas/oleastro/presentation/objectifs/* (last accessed 2 October 2021)). A general account on these amphorae have been compiled at: *http://amphorae.icac.cat/amphora/dressel-20-baetica-coast* (last accessed 2 October 2021).
6. Aguilera Martín and Berni Millet (1998); Aguilera Martín (2001); *Id.* (2007); *Id.* (2012).
7. Broekaert (2008) presumes that the merchant acquiring the oil was also the shipper transporting it to Rome, based on a paper by A. Héron de Villefosse (1914), but not all merchants had the economic capacity to be shippers as well. Proof of this is found in the texts of the Digest which indicated the exemptions established for subjects performing different roles in public distribution. See D. 50.6.6 (Call. 1 *de cogn.*) §3 (*Negotiatores olearii* and *navicularii*); §5 (*navicularii*); §6 (*Negotiatores olearii* and *navicularii*); §8 (*navicularii*); §9 (*navicularii*); D. 50.4.5 (Scaev. 1 *reg.*), including *navicularii* and *mercatores olearii*; D. 50.5.3 (Scaev. 3 *reg.*), including *navicularii*.
8. Some of the better-known books for the study of the *navicularii* are De Salvo (1992) and Sirks (1992), which were published in the same year but provide very different accounts, the one by Sirks providing a more accurate description of the functions of these bodies, even if he relies too heavily on their state involvement, which has been accurately discussed by Broekaert (2008), pp. 692–706.
9. Aguilera Martín (2001), pp. 1234–1236.
10. For the case of the Dressel 20, these issues have been explored in detail by Broekaert (2012), pp. 41–65 and (2016), pp. 222–253.

11. The inscription was originally published by Djaoui (2014), pp. 693–710.
12. On DD Caecilii, see Broekaert (2013), pp. 330–334.
13. Briefly, *ratio* indicates the bureau in charge of administering the different fiscal products. See De Martino (1975), p. 900.
14. *CIL* IX 2438= JRS-1983-126 = AE 1983, 00331 = AE 2006, 00134 = AE 2007, 00267. Some comments on the inscription can be found in Passerini (1939); Laffi (1965); Corbier (1983); Faoro (2018), pp. 144–145.
15. A picture of its current location can be found in the Eagle epigraphic database, see: *https://www.europeana.eu/es/item/2058806/EDR__4d37a14269eefe79a78451aea4a8 4cb9__artifact__cho* (last accessed 4 October 2021).
16. Even though Mommsen, when he first recognised the inscription in 1846 while compiling volume IX of the *Corpus Inscriptionum Latinarum*, said that '*a ita minutis litteris scriptum et aetate exesum muscoque et squalore foedatum [titulum vidi], denique loco vade incommodo collocatum, ut legere non posset, neque ectypon quod confeci quidquam mihi mostravit praeter fines vv. 8–14. 20–22*', as referred to in Wickert (1959), pp. 164–170.
17. On the role of the freedman *a rationibus*, see Boulvert (1970), pp. 97–106; Weaver (1972), pp. 259–266; Mouritsen (2011), pp. 101–104.
18. Translation by Corbier (1983), p. 127, with amendments by the author.
19. The dating of the inscription is based on the mention of the two *praefecti praetorio* of Marcus Aurelius, *Bassaeus Rufus* and *Macrinius Vindex*, though cf Eck (2012), p. 197.
20. Fuhrmann (2012), p. 138. Besides, it is clear that in the lower Empire these two prefects would have had assumed jurisdictional competences in the procedure of appeals as representatives of the Emperor, but it is unclear what would have been their role in appeals in this period: Kaser/Hackl (1996), pp. 464 and 533. In any case, they are always responsible in the *cognitio extra ordinem* and never by the procedure *per formulam*, see: D. 12.1.40 (Paul. 3 *quaest.*); D. 14.3.2 (Gai. 9 *ad ed. Prov.*); D. 22.1.3.3. (Pap. 20 *quaest.*).
21. D. 9.2.5.1 (Ulp. 18 *ad ed.*). The doctrine is divided into what concerns Ulpian's texts on the one hand, by people who consider the objective value of *iniuria* (bearing in mind the first part of the definition), and others who consider the influence of *culpa* in conduct involving *iniuria*. The bibliography on *iniuria* is enormous, so I will avoid quoting all of it, but only refer to Cursi (2002), pp. 21–22 nt. 77; cap. II, § 1.2 and cap. III, § 2; and Paschalidis (2008), p. 332, both of whom provide an overview of bibliography on the topic.
22. The inscription may allude to praetorian *stationarii* in rural Italy, as Fuhrmann (2012), p. 132 nt. 39 and 213. For her part, Ricci (2018), pp. 324–326, affirms that these *stationarii* were soldiers made available by the central power to guard a strategic point in the region with a dual purpose. On the one hand, they had to ensure the proper conduct of the operations associated with transhumance and on the other, prevent the banditry of other goods and animals.
23. Laffi (1965), p. 192.
24. Passerini (1939), pp. 253–254.
25. At the beginning of the century, Grenier (1905), pp. 307–312 argued that the *conductores* were for flocks of diverse ownership and that they were under the *cura* of the bureau *a rationibus*, and that the fees that they paid for pasture rights accrued to the fiscus.
26. Laffi (1965), pp. 187–188.
27. Millar (1963), p. 31.

28. Corbier (1983), pp. 130–131.
29. There is another possibility that needs to be considered, and I have to thank Prof. Rosa Mentxaka for her suggestion, even if unfortunately we do not have enough evidence to assert that 'could we suppose that the praetorian prefects act on appeal? We could suppose that the municipal magistrates had known about it initially at the request of the *conductores* and that by not getting satisfied by the answer, they appealed to the prefects?'.
30. Corbier (1983), p. 131.
31. Indeed, it seems that Severus strengthened the role of the *fiscus* in his reign in order to help boost the oil supply, since he included olive oil in the *annona*, as mentioned in the *Hist. Aug. Sept. Sev.* 18.3.
32. Brunt (1966), pp. 75–91.
33. *Contra*, Millar (1963), p. 42, who thinks that during Severus' reign, there was a division between *patrimonium* and *res privata* (*Hist. Aug. Sept. Sev.* 12.3).
34. Lo Cascio (1971), pp. 83–90; *Id.* (1985–1990), p. 567.
35. The second column cannot be reconstructed.
36. The hypotheses explaining the location of the inscription vary, with some people like Corbier (2006), p. 238 indicating that the inscription was set there either because the *navicularii* were conducting activities in that area, or because this decretal was set up there to be considered as an example. However, I am more convinced by the hypothesis that the bronze plaque was brought there by the crusades (according to Virlouvet (2004), p. 352), and that it was originally displayed in the south of France.
37. Barot (1905), pp. 262–273; Virlouvet (2004), p. 331.
38. The word used in the inscription is *iniuria* which translates as 'damage'.
39. Standardisation of weights and measures was established in the decree from Athens found in *IG II²* 1013 (second century BC). It established penalties for sellers and customers when official standard measures were not employed. In the case of Rome, the importance of standards appears in the *lex Silia de ponderibus publicis* (287–218 BC), which specifies the penalties imposed upon magistrates who forged fake weights or measures (Festus, 288 L).
40. Thus both in Greece and Rome, these weights and measures were standards, used as a matrix for shaping other measuring tools, and thus they were kept in protected spaces such as temples, as can be seen in Chankowski and Hasenohr (2015), pp. 33 and 37; *CIL* XI 6727.1; *ILS* 8627). The practice of using official standards to shape measuring tools was also used in other areas of the eastern Mediterranean, such as Pontus and Bithynia, as pointed out by Haensch and Weiss (2005); (2007); and for Syria, see Aliquot and Badawi (2013); Gatier (2014); and for Caesarea Maritima, Holland (2009).
41. D. 47.11.6.1 (Ulp. 8 *de off. proc.*):

    '*Onerant annonam etiam staterae adulterinae, de quibus divus Traianus edictum proposuit, quo edicto poenam legis Corneliae in eos statuit, perinde ac si lege testamentaria, quod testamentum falsum scripsisset signasset recitasset, damnatus esset*'. 'The price of corn is also affected by false measures, concerning which the deified Trajan issued an edict whereby he imposed upon those who used them the penalty of the *lex Cornelia*, just as if, under the statute on wills, a person were condemned because he wrote, sealed or read aloud a will which was false' (trans. Watson (1985), Vol. 4, p. 298). See also Rizzi (2012), pp. 181–198.

42. Corritore et al. (2016), p. 170.
43. *Mon. Eph.* 45–47 = § 18, Cottier et al. (2008), pp. 42–43.
44. Casson (1965), p. 35.
45. D. 47.10.13.1 (Ulp. 57 *ad ed.*).
46. For example, Lavezzi A (AD 25–50); Port-Vendres 2 (AD 42–48); Chiessi (AD 60–85); Sud-Lavezzi 2 (AD 10–30); Ponte d'Oro (AD 10–50); Sud-Perduto 2 (AD 1–15). For a general account on Mediterranean shipwrecks, see Parker (1992) or its compilation at the OxRep Database: (*http://oxrep.classics.ox.ac.uk/databases/shipwrecks_database/* (last accessed 4 October 2021)). Moreover, *TPSulp.* 78 = *TP* 13 refers to the slave of a certain P. Attius Severus who engaged a loan in connection with a transport contract: see Rovira (2007), p. 1264; Broekaert (2012), p. 321; also, the chapter by P Candy later in this volume.
47. Broekaert (2008), p. 611, figure 11.
48. Colls et al. (1977).
49. du Plessis (2004), p. 305.
50. Christol and Drew-Bear (1986), pp. 41–87; *Id.* (1987), pp. 83–137; Drew-Bear (1996), pp. 747–752; Russell (2014), p. 46.
51. Peña (1998), pp. 123–130.
52. Liou and Rodríguez Almeida (2000), pp. 19, figure 7 and 22, figure 10.
53. Dressel (1891); *CIL* XV 562.
54. Rodríguez Almeida (1972), p. 126; based on *CIL* II 1180, which reads:

'*Sex(to) Iulio Sex(ti) f(ilio) Quir(ina) Possessori / praef(ecto) coh(ortis) III Gallor(um) praeposito nume/ri Syror(um) sagittarior(um) item alae primae Hispa/norum curatori civitatis Romulensium Mal/vensium tribuno mi[l(itum) leg(ionis)] XII Fulminat[ae] / curatori coloniae Arcensium adlecto / in decurias ab Optimis Maximisque / Imp(eratoribus) Antonino et Vero Augg(ustis) adiu/tori Ulpii Saturnini praef(ecti) annon(ae) / ad oleum Afrum et Hispanum recen/sendum item solamina transfe/renda item vecturas navicula/riis exsolvendas proc(uratori) Augg(ustorum) ad / ripam Baetis scapharii Hispalen/ses ob innocentiam iusti-tiam/que eius singularem.*

Concerning the career of *Sextus Iulius Possessor*, see Remesal Rodríguez (1991), pp. 281–296.
55. Chic García (2002), p. 340.
56. Hirt (2017), pp. 231–238 has rightly pointed out that the acquisition of the Simithus and Dokimeion quarries and the spectacular intensification of production at these sites was at the time an important weapon in the competition for prestige and power.
57. A model that has been further developed by Long (2017), pp. 52–78.
58. Fant (1989), p. 127 nt. 40; Hirt (2010), pp. 328–331.
59. Della Rosa has elaborated on this question in two forthcoming papers, and concretely in Della Rosa (2020), p. 5, but he previously provided a more general overview on the administration of the Phrygian quarries in Della Rosa (2016), pp. 305–330. *Contra,* Fant (1988), pp. 151–152.
60. Salway (2019), p. 43: 'the significance of the location is explained by the fact that this gateway would originally have opened onto the quayside of the east harbour of ancient Miletus, facing the estuary of the river Meander and sheltered from the open sea of the Aegean by the promontory that survives as the now landlocked Humeitepe'.
61. Erhardt and Gunther (2013), p. 199; Salway (2019), p. 50.

62. Also suggested by Salway (2019), pp. 49–50.
63. Russell (2014), p. 43.
64. Russell (2014); Hirt (2010), pp. 115–117; the relevant inscriptions are *CIL* III 7146; *AE* 1988, 1028 = *SEG* XXXVIII 1073; IK 13, 856 (Ephesos); Milet, inv. no. 288.
65. The date of this law is not completely clear, though Harter-Uibopuu (2008), p. 127 and Chaniotis and Pleket (*SEG*) date it to AD, pp. 124–125.
66. *IG* II² 1100 = *SEG* 15, 108; Silver (2001), pp. 8–15; Harter-Uibopuu (2008), pp. 127–141; Purpura (2012), p. 599.
67. See also Chic García (1979), p. 132.
68. *AE* 1958, 9 = *AE* 2001, 128 = *AE* 2001, 181.
69. Sáez Fernández and Lomas (1981), pp. 67–70.
70. Chic García (1979), pp. 132–134.
71. On the Athenian law, see also Blanco Freijeiro (1962), pp. 138–148. It was recently analysed by Martin (1994), pp. 182–186 and (2001), pp. 475–486, who doubts that the Athens law had a universal character and proposes dating the *rescriptum* to the Hadrianic era or to before the Flavians. Other authors who share the opinion that this inscription belongs to Hadrian's reign are Piganiol (1956), p. 143; Pons Pujol (2009), p. 76 and Ozcariz Gil (2013), p. 36. Expressing their doubts concerning its relationship to the Athenian law, however, are Purpura (2012), p. 603 and Rizzi (2016), pp. 122–123.
72. These rescripts were labelled as *rescrits gracieux* by Coriat (1997), pp. 474–502, indicating that they could grant protection from military and financial abuse. See, also, Hauken (1998), p. 304 and *Hist. Aug. Hadrian* 22.8. For the protection of tax farmers, D. 39.4.1 pr. (Ulp. 55 *ad ed.*). Also on the protection of tax farmers, see D. 39.4.9.2 (Paul. 5 *sent.*); D. 49.14.3.6 (Call. 3 *de iure fisci*).
73. Aguilera Martín (1999), pp. 165–166.
74. Sánchez-Moreno Ellart (2015), pp. 361–376, in relation to D. 14.5.8 (Paul. 1 *decr.*). Otherwise, Höbenreich (1997), p. 55 mentions that this *iurisdictio* would be granted to these magistrates in processes *extra ordinem*.
75. *Hist. Aug. Sept. Sev.* 12.1–4.
76. *Hist. Aug. Sept. Sev.* 12.3; Jones (1950), p. 28; Giangreco Pessi (1988), pp. 80 and 152.
77. Orestano (1968), pp. 234–235 and 262; Puliatti (1992), pp. 106–110.
78. Rodríguez Almeida (1980), pp. 277–290; *Id.* (1989), p. 36.
79. Remesal Rodríguez (1983), pp. 91–111; *Id.* (1996), pp. 195–221.
80. Broekaert (2008), pp. 201–209; *Id.* (2011), pp. 591–623.
81. *Hist. Aug. Sept. Sev.* 18.3.
82. The practice of financing supply and transport has been attested to previously, first during the Hannibalic wars (Livy, 23.48.4; 49.4) and subsequently during Claudius' reign (Suet. *Claud.* 18.2; 19.1), when a famine seized Rome. This detail is also mentioned by Broekaert (2008), p. 201–206.
83. Broekaert (2008), p. 201–206.
84. For the evidence of Monte Testaccio, see *http://ceipac.ub.edu/MOSTRA/u_expo.htm* (last accessed 4 October 2021). However, the interest of Severus in the food supply of Rome is confirmed by the coinage, which featured an anthropomorphised figure of the *annona* from AD 194–201 and AD 206–207, for which see Poole (1873), pp. 98, 100, 103, and 106.
85. As happened in similarly managed estates such as the case of North Africa, as pointed out by Kehoe (1988), p. 125; or Maiuro (2012), p. 183, for the case of Italy.
86. These *figlinae* were associated with the *Kalendarium vegetianum* (a financial institution from the Empire to fund agrarian activities): Manacorda (1977), pp. 315–316; Sáez Fernández and Lomas (1981), p. 77; Remesal Rodríguez (1996), p. 201.

87. Berni (2008), pp. 33–38. In relation to that tight control of *annona*-related cargoes, there are some circular seals that have been identified as oil stopper seals. They provide the name of a *societas*, Berni and Gorostidi (2013), pp. 185–187; consular date, Taglietti (1994), p. 191; Djaoui (2011), pp. 625–633; or the name of a merchant, Gisbert Santonja (2008), pp. 247–267; *CIL* II 14 2308 = *IRAT* 34. They cover a chronological period from AD 50 to AD 200. Berni and Gorostidi indicate the importance of these seals as providing proof to ensure the quality of the product, while Taglietti highlights the importance of the seals in the process of distribution and storage. Finally, Djaoui affirms that they were used to mark stoppers of containers destined for the *annona*, to be recognised at the *statio* as goods exempt from taxes.

88. Several legal texts (e.g. D. 18.1.71 (Papir. 1. *const.*); D. 35.2.30.4 (Maec. 8 *fid.*); C. 2.7.26.4) mention *arca* as an object where money was kept, sometimes located in temples. In CTh. 14.6.3, the term *arca vinaria* appears, referring to the administrative unit in charge of the payment for the supply of wine in Aurelian's era, see Vera (2006), p. 305.

89. In his latest work, Terpstra (2019), pp. 125–167, highlights the importance of collective action as a warranty to enforce a contract and he uses the example of the Sulpicii archive to indicate that the names of the subjects signing the contract and their status contribute to allowing that enforcement. Even though I do not think that his conclusion can be drawn with respect to all kinds of contracts (in fact, the ones that he uses as examples in his chapter are formal contracts that imply the transmission of property), it is true that in this case the fact that the *navicularii* acted as a whole entity to claim might have helped being heard by the authorities. The advantages of being part of a *collegium* for the protection of their members has been the object of studies by Broekaert (2011); Tran (2011); and Terpstra (2013), pp. 95–125. See, also, the chapter by A Marzano earlier in this volume.

90. *Hist. Aug. Sept. Sev.* pp. 44–46. On the role of the *advocatus fisci*, see Burdese (1975), pp. 3–24; Lambrini (1993), pp. 325–336.

91. When the *aerarium* ceased to belong to the senate, this distinction between the *aerarium* and *fiscus* naturally ceased as well as both of them were now part of the treasury of the Caesar and, accordingly, later jurists used the words *aerarium* and *fiscus* indiscriminately, though properly speaking there was no treasury but that of the Caesar. The senate, however, continued to possess the management of the municipal chest (*arca publica*) of the city (Vopiscus, *Aurelian*, 20). This distinction between *fiscus baeticae* and *tarraconensis* has added the mention of *arca* to indicate the office that deals with the management of this collection, clearly understanding that the Baetica province was senatorial while the *tarraconensis* was imperial.

92. See above, nt. 34.

93. It is necessary to bear in mind that the office *a rationibus* became the *collegium rationalis* under Septimius Severus: see Mommsen (1996), p. 331; Kłodziński (2018), pp. 294–295.

94. *Hist. Aug. Alex. Sev.* 32.5; 22.1.

95. Broekaert (2008), p. 219.

96. Laffi (1965), p. 197. See also C. 11.6.

97. It appears in other inscriptions in a general sense see e.g. *CIL* III 12044 = *CIL* III 13569 = *InscCret-01*, Lyttos 00189 = *AE* 2007, 00043; *EpThess-01*, 00053 = *EKatoMak* 00014 = *AE* 1998, 01214 = *AE* 1999, 01405 = *AE* 1999, 01411 = *AE* 2001, 01757.

98. Laffi (1965), p. 197.

APPENDIX

Table 6.3 Inscriptions in marbles from Dokimeion (Phrygia).

Place	Date	Inscription	Notes	Sources
Phrygia	Prior to AD 136	*loco IV b(racchio) III / Sur(a) III co(n) s(ule) II (ad 107) j CCXXXVIII/ RMA Pal(ma) II co(n) s(ule) (ad 109) / VFR Vop(isco) co(n) s(ule) (ad 114) / b(racchio) tert(io)*	*Bracchia* might reflect the movement of quarried stones from one *brachium* to the next, to clear the access to the quarry sections, or the rearrangement or stockpiling areas. The term *locus* starts to appear in the first decades of the 2nd cent. AD and is a fixed element in the inscribed formula. *Locus* is a designation of the site where a block was freed, and later, of the block itself acting as an annual serial number.	Fant (1989), no. 40; Hirt (2010), pp. 292; 302
Phrygia	After AD 136	*Te[rt]ullo et Sacerdote co(n)s(ulibus) / ex of(ficina) Andaev(i) caesura j Alex(andri) / loco XCIX b(racchio) R*	The term *caesura* probably delimited an area of extraction or a quarry within a quarrying district. It may have been introduced around AD 136 and appears as a fixed element in the labels after AD 147. *Officina* is a term that describes a workshop and, combined with a name in the genitive case, was also introduced in AD 136, although not regularly used until after AD 157. It is important because it designates where the marble was cut and produced.	Fant (1989) no. 127; Hirt (2010), p. 293

Place	Date	Inscription	Notes	Sources
Ostia	AD 96	*L [ ] CR/ / ex r(atione) Olyp(i?) Caes(aris); c) Ve(tere) e(t) [Val(ente)] co(n) s(ulibus*	The mark *ex ratione* is not found on blocks found in Dokimeion, but on the ones from that origin and found at Rome, Leptis Magna and Ostia. The exact meaning of *ratio* is still unknown, but broadly speaking, it refers to the management of the distribution of goods destined for state supply.	Baccini Leotardi (1979) no. 40; Pensabene (1994), p. 325; Hirt (2010), p. 301
Chemtou	Prior to AD 137	*Sura III et Senici(one) II co(n)s(ulibus) ex rat(ione) Felicis Aug(usti) ser(vi) j d(e) n(umero) DCXII XXX j (officina) Tiluris*	The inscription indicates the name of the workshop (*officina*) where the stone was cut, and indicates by the mention of *ex ratione* that the stones were cut on behalf of an imperial official in charge of a *ratio*.	CIL VIII 14560
Chemtou	After AD 137	*Imp (eratoris) Antonini Aug(usti) pii d(omini) j n(umero) vac. of(ficina) Cerii j Stloga et Severo co(n) s(ulibus) j su(b) cura Agathae[—]*	The mention of the emperor in the genitive case indicates that he owned the stone.	CIL VIII 14573

Table 6.4 Recently found decision of Hadrian: Balat (Milet), Archaeological Museum, inv. HU 11.28.3 (N. Ehrhardt, W. Günther (2013) (2016), n.1578 = SEG 63, 2013).

Αὐτοκράτωρ Καῖσαρ θεοῦ
Τραιανοῦ Παρτικοῦ υἱὸς
θεοῦ Νέρουα υἱωνὸς Τραιαν[ὸς]
Ἁδριανὸς Σεβαστός, ἀρχιερ[εὺς]
μέγιστος, δημαρχικῆς ἐξοθσία[ς]
τὸ ιε᾽, ὕπατος τὸ γ᾽, πατὴρ
πατρίδος Μιλησίων τοῖς ἄρχουσιν
καὶ τῶι δήμωι
    χαίρειν.
Ναθκλήρων οἰκον ἔχειν
δίδωμι ὑμῖν καὶ τὸν νόμον
καθ᾽ ὃν ἠξίωσαν συντετάχθαι
βεβαιῶ.   Ἐπρέσβεθεν
Κοσσούτιος Φρόντων
καὶ Αἰλιανὸς Πολίτης.
    Εὐτυχεῖτε.
Ἐπὶ ὑπάτων Σεργίου Λεαίνα
Π[ον]τιανοῦ καὶ Μ.᾽Αντων[ίου
Ῥουφίνου---]
	The Emperor Caesar Traianus Hadrianus Augustus, son of the divine Trajan *Parthicus* and grandson of the divine Nerva, *pontifex maximus*, with tribunician power for the 15th time, consul three times, *Pater patriae* (says) Greetings to the magistrates, council, and to the people of the Milesians. "I concede to you the possibility to form an association of shippers and I confirm the regulations according to which they have asked to be organised. Cossutius Fronto and aelianus Polites carried out the embassy. Farewell!" Under the consuls Sergius Laenas Pontianus and M. Antonius Rufinus (Translation by Salway (2019), p. 42.)

Chapter 7

Roman Documentation Concerning Shipping in Bulk

Gianfranco Purpura

According to a 'primitivist' conception, Rome conquered, explored and administered an empire in the last two centuries of the Republic with an oral mentality and very little use of written documents. Now, if not considered false, this view is at least understood to be far from the truth.[1] In fact, everyday documents are increasingly demonstrating the use of complex and sophisticated practices to achieve quite remarkable administrative results.

The use of writing and the systematic use of documents were essential to the development of an immense territory and the subsequent increase in trade. The spread of writing can be connected, more than has previously been assumed, to contact with Hellenistic civilisation.[2] Romans used many different kinds of lists, such as those concerning various social and privileged orders, 'registers' of tribes and centurions, creditors and debtors of the *aerarium*, subjects exempted from tax or those entitled to benefit from the sale of public grain. In addition, other lists ranked the beneficiaries of lots associated with the *coloniae*, public domains and water disbursements. Moreover, even during the ancient period, territorial and geographical maps and 'passports'[3] were essential.[4] Documentation was especially important in the world of business, especially in maritime dealings and in ports.[5] In these environments, documentation lent support to an oral tradition and made the use of writing indispensable. Scripts were sometimes personally traced on merchandise or by an intermediary on the same containers, since many rich private financiers were illiterate,[6] as was sometimes also true of the seamen involved in maritime transport.

Although an oral mentality remained deep-rooted in public practice (for example, by the persistence of a secondary evaluation of documents and the consolidated habit of reading them aloud and quoting them by heart and, therefore, in an approximate manner),[7] in the context of commercial and maritime activities this was obviously not possible.[8]

P. Bingen 77 comprises a fragment of a register from a large port (perhaps Alexandria) in the second century AD that contains detailed information concerning the docking of eleven ships over two days, some carrying the goods of several merchants. The document contains precise and technical information regarding the place of departure (for example, of a grain ship with capacity for as much as 22,500 *artabae* coming from Ostia), the cargo transported, the type of ship, its capacity, the duration of the voyage, the name of the vessel, the owner, the captain, the crew, the individual on whose behalf the cargo was transported and, perhaps, even the berths at which the vessels were to be docked.[9] The document demonstrates, beyond any doubt, the widespread use of writing, not only in the bureaucratic practices of port officials, but also in the economic transactions between merchants and seamen. In this latter connection, rich documentation has survived in the papyri and wax tablets (especially in private archives, such as the Puteolan archive of the Sulpicii) and also in the individual records of daily life – the objects of economic traffic – on which inscriptions were frequently traced, and which have sometimes been poorly understood or neglected, and to which this contribution will draw special attention.

More specifically, the chapter aims at directing attention towards bulk transport, which both gave rise to legal issues concerning the discharge of cargo to numerous merchants (*vectores*)[10] and facilitated the itinerant trade of commodities (in reality the most common kinds of goods transported around the empire), particularly to avoid the 'breaking of the cargo' by the repeated loading and unloading of numerous goods at a variety of destinations.[11] It is also clear that bulk transport, in addition to avoiding this nuisance and permitting loading and unloading to be carried out more quickly, could have made possible a significant reduction in the size of the vessel and the use of a few large suitable containers, such as *pithoi* or *dolia*.[12] These were more advantageous than numerous individual amphorae or other separate containers. For the purposes of identification, pozzolan stoppers were used for wine amphorae and clay or lead seals in connection with baskets and sacks containing various goods[13]; and when it came to the transport of fungible goods belonging to various merchants (such as *garum* or other products transported in large containers) who entrusted their merchandise to a ship with multiple destinations connected by a single route, wooden and lead labels were used.[14]

Although this practice was closely related to business models adopted at different times, it is only in Roman imperial navigation, or rather at the end of the Republican age and at the beginning of the Empire, that trading ships with large quantities of heterogeneous merchandise belonging to different merchants embarked not only on direct routes, but also on itineraries with numerous stops and frequent 'cargo breaks'. Although large cargoes, such as the more than 4,200 amphorae and other wares recently traced to Alonnessos (c. 420–400 BC),[15] were already being transported during the classical Greek age, it seems that only from the second century BC onwards did large cargo ships, like those at the Albenga, with an estimated load of between 500–600 tons consisting of 11,500–13,000 Dressel 1B wine amphorae together with sacks of hazelnuts and wheat, the Spargi (c. 110 BC), which was about 35m long and eight or ten metres wide, or the Madrague de Giens (c. 75–60 BC), with a load of about 375–400 tons and 6,000–7,000 amphorae, become common as carriers of heterogeneous loads, both for direct and segmented routes.[16]

That fact, in truth, has been somewhat controversial, since according to some maritime historians of the ancient world, such as J Rougé[17] or L Casson,[18] Roman imperial navigation mainly took place along fast, direct routes.[19] Others, however, have argued that, just as in the Middle Ages, slow itinerant transport and trade, characterised by cabotage (tramping), was prevalent or at least just as common as navigation along direct routes.[20] On the basis of the wreck of the *Cala Culip IV*, it has been possible to differentiate between the Mediterranean's principal ports, which large ships on direct routes tended to travel between, and secondary ports, which smaller vessels engaged in redistribution by *cabotage* travelled to from the main ports.[21] According to X Nieto:

> 'Quand il s'agit de bateaux de grande taille, avec une capacité de plus de 7,000 amphores, comme dans le cas de Spargi ou de la Madrague de Giens, il nous parait fort improbable qu'une telle opération de réorganization ait pu être envisagée pour seulement livrer quelques douzaines ou même centaines d'amphores. En outre, il est douteux qu'elle eût pu être rentable, tant à cause de l'allongement considérable de la durée du voyage qu'elle aurait occasionnée que par le coût de la main-d'oeuvre qu'elle aurait réclamée.'[22]

He concludes:

> 'Aussi pensons-nous plutôt que ces embarcations de transport en gros avaient à acheminer des cargaisons homogénes depuis la région productrice jusqu'au port principal par une route directe.'

At first sight, the transfer of particularly bulky goods that were not easy to remove from the ship, such as whole *dolia* and marble blocks, seems rather unlikely and would appear to indicate the use of direct routes. Equally, the arrangement of the stowed goods on board could certainly impose a loading-unloading sequence that in some cases necessitated the following of a strict order (that is, because certain goods could not be removed before others), which is also incompatible with a redistributive model.[23] However, as the *Cabrera III* or the *Sud Perduto 2* wrecks show,[24] transport in bulk, even in amphorae carrying undifferentiated consignments, all of the same type and quality, reopens the possibility of itinerant routes even for large ships. This would have made it possible to perform different deliveries at multiple stops on planned voyages, so as to provide the additional flexibility to temporarily reroute the vessel to take advantage of news about the opening of a favourable market.

It has recently been shown that, for nautical reasons, there could not have been a clear contrast between deep-water and coastal navigation during the Roman period and that even in the case of the former, these routes were necessarily subject to interruption in certain areas and at certain times of the year.[25] It seems to me that only without 'cargo breaks', and therefore with deliveries in bulk, would it have been possible to benefit from any intermediate commercial stopovers. Indeed, even small boats frequently engaged in operations that could be described as 'cabotage' (that is, sailing from cape-to-cape, from gulf-to-gulf),[26] could have been involved in long-distance trade. If this were the case, they would not have been engaged exclusively in local commerce and their role would not have been limited to mere redistribution. It therefore seems possible to conclude: 'c'est sans doute la combinaison des deux pratiques au sein des mêmes routes qui a constitué la norme'.[27]

The slow pace of most of the trips documented in P. Bingen 77, compared to the expected sailing times of small *akatoi* (*actuaria*) – that is, vessels engaged in short- and medium-distance commercial transport with mixed forms of propulsion – has been explained with reference to temporary stopovers for weather reasons.[28] However, it could also be explained with reference to the execution of occasional short-distance intermediate journeys, carried out in connection with an improvised itinerant trade (which could also involve large ships), which was not necessarily constrained by a pre-arranged route.[29]

Based on the recent discovery in the port of Marseille of crate fragments bearing the customs seals of one of the stations of the *Quadragesima Galliarum*,[30] and from the infrequency of epigraphic mentions by the staff in charge of collecting *portorium* (*portitores*), it has been inferred that interprovincial traffic must necessarily have passed through a limited number of ports equipped with the infrastructure capable of ensuring the collection of customs duties. The infrastructure was designed to certify the clearance of transported goods through customs at exclusive sites within the relevant fiscal area at which authorisation for marketing and redistribution was sought.[31] These processes created an incentive to trade along direct binary routes along which merchandise was only disembarked at specific customs stations, thus avoiding the extension of sailing times and related bureaucratic requirements.

Looking to the *Monumentum Ephesenum* (9 July, AD 62), however, §9, ll. 22–26 provides a long list of ports, together with the location of the coastal settlements in the Roman province of Asia, where customs offices were located (with such a great degree of detail that we know the size of the different *stationes*).[32] In addition, §16, ll. 40–42 indicate that in the absence of contractors *in loco*, the receipt of the *professio* was entrusted to the highest magistrate in the nearest city; and that numerous local communities were entitled to maintain for their own benefit, with the permission and under the control of Rome, the privilege of gathering taxes that they had collected before the Roman conquest, further expanding the already detailed list of places where it would have been possible to dock and pay duties, even for large ships. From a practical perspective, it does not seem that there was any real issue arising from the payment of taxes, not least because of an alleged shortage of customs stations in the coastal areas of Asia, or in other areas of the empire for that matter, since it would have been possible to pay tax at the nearest city. This was the consequence of a political framework that spanned a unified Mediterranean that was increasingly inclined not to suffer any kind of hindrance in merchant exchanges, even over long distances.

According to A Bresson,[33] however, upon landing in Greek cities during the Roman period, any merchandise that was to be put up for sale was unloaded and, the relevant import duties having been paid, export duties were levied on the unsold goods that had to be re-embarked. In places where sale by samples was practiced (δεἴγμα), this inconvenience could be avoided by exhibiting a sample for a limited period, which saved the need to load and unload the cargo. Not only could this hindrance therefore be avoided by increasing the frequency of sale by sample, but also (and above all) by concentrating these sales in those ports open to foreigners and at which local redistribution took place.

If, however, boats of a certain size could dock without hindrance, due to the presence of custom stations, in places where trading in commodities in bulk out of holds that had become increasingly capacious was considered practicable, it is necessary to explain how this had become possible without the need to 'break the cargo' and therefore to waste time and manpower – all plausible economic objections that have been put forward. In short, it is due to the use of sample jars (δεἴγματα), little amphorae, little sacks, and small sealed flasks – that made this approach more and more feasible – both for dry goods and for liquids.

The practice of late-Republican bulk transportation is attested to in the following well-known text:

'D. 19.2.31 (Alf. 5 *dig. a Paulo epit.*):
Several people shot their grain together into Saufeius' ship, after which the latter returned his share of the grain to one of them out of the common pile and the vessel was lost. The question was asked whether the others could proceed against the *nauta* with respect to their share of the grain by raising an action for *onus aversum?* He responded that there were two kinds of things placed out [in virtue of a contract of letting and hiring], either on terms that the very same thing is given back (such as when clothes are placed out to a fuller for cleaning) or property of the same kind (as when refined silver is given to a smith to make vases or gold to make rings): in the former case the thing remains the property of the owner, whereas in the latter he becomes *in creditum*. The same principle exists in relation to *depositum*: for if someone made a deposit of a certain amount of money and neither enclosed it nor handed it over under seal, but rather by counting it out, the person with whom the deposit was made was bound to do nothing more than to deliver back an equivalent sum. Accordingly, it would appear that the grain was made Saufeius' and had been handed over in the appropriate way. Now if each person's grain had been separately enclosed by means of partitions or wicker baskets or some other kind of container, so that the consignment of each could be told apart, we are not able to make an interchange, but rather the person to whom the grain belongs can bring a *vindicatio* to recover what the *nauta* had delivered. And so he rejected actions for *onus aversum*, because if, on the one hand, the goods were of such a kind that, on being handed over to the *nauta*, they immediately became his and the merchant *in creditum*, it did not appear to be a case of *onus aversum*, inasmuch as they belonged to the *nauta*; but if, on the other hand, the same thing that was handed over was owed in return, the *actio furti* would lie for the *locator*, so that an *iudicium* for *onus aversum* was superfluous. If then the goods were handed over in such a way that they could be delivered back in kind, the conductor is liable only to the extent of his fault (this much being owed in matters contracted for the benefit of both parties); and it is hardly blameworthy that he [i.e., the *nauta*] restored the grain to one of them out

of the common pile, seeing that it was necessary for him to make a return to one or other person first, even though he made the position of the one better than that of the others by doing so.[34']

Though the text is among the most controversial of the Digest's fragments, modern scholarship is inclined to acknowledge its substantial genuineness.[35] Following the transport of a quantity of wheat in bulk that had been embarked by several merchants on Saufeius' ship, Saufeius had returned a portion of the common grain at a port of call to one of the merchants.[36] Later, the ship perished with all the cargo, provoking the other merchants (*ceteri*) to ask Alfenus whether they could bring an action for 'diminution of the load'. The action, however, was excluded in the jurist's response, which referred to a fundamental distinction used by Roman lawyers to frame agreements for the transport of goods within the contract of letting and hiring: namely, between *duo genera rerum locatarum*, which is to say, on the one hand, those things for which the *nauta* was obliged to return identical goods that had been handed over (*idem*) and, on the other, those for which they committed to return only a quantity of the same kind (*eiusdem generis*).

In the first case, the goods were affixed with a mark upon loading, so that they could be identified exactly upon delivery (χειρέμβολον).[37] This identification was made both in the interest of the merchant, who desired that the same goods should be returned, while remaining their owner and bearing the consequent risk in the case of loss (*casum sensit dominus*)[38]; and, above all, in that of the *nauta*, who loaded the cargo and was therefore exempted from bearing the risk of transportation, since they did not become owner of the merchandise.

In the second case, however, which concerned transport in bulk, a *mutatio dominii* occurred, so that the *nauta* held the object of the contract *in creditum*, which bound them only to deliver a different object consisting of the same material (*eiusdem generis*), owing to the indestructibility of the *genus* even in the case of *vis maior*.[39] So far as bulk transport was concerned, then, the merchant ended up having to bear the risk. Consequently, a merchant on Saufeius' ship who had received back their share of wheat should, according to the text, have considered themselves fortunate; and equally Saufeius, by returning the first consignment of grain, free from fault or liability. The question remains, though, why the other merchants, who remained creditors following the change of ownership that resulted from the transport in bulk, asked Alfenus for an opinion about raising an action for 'diminution of the load'?

It is clear that, at the time the *quaestio* was put to Alfenus, for merchants loading goods in bulk the distinction between the *duo genera rerum locatarum*, which could have grounded the argument that the *mutatio dominii* had transferred the risk to Saufeius, was already precluded.[40] From this point of view, the explanation proposed by L Ménager that the entire ship had been leased as a whole by several merchants for a joint transport in bulk cannot be accepted.[41] Indeed, it would have made no sense to invoke the *mutatio dominii* and the consequent shouldering of the risk by the *nauta*, who would have been responsible only for the good condition of the boat. In these circumstances, the wheat would have remained the property of the merchants, which cannot be reconciled with Alfenus' declaration that, 'secundum quae videri, triticum factum Saufeii et recte datum'. Could Saufeius have been accused of *aversio* if the merchants had leased the ship for themselves? The only option is to assume a *locatio ad onus vehendum*, which necessarily involved a planned route under Saufeius' command and the acquisition of the property by the *conductor* in bulk[42]; and therefore not merely the availability of abstract shares owned by each of the merchants, as would have been normal,[43] for the purposes of carrying out the *opus*.

It seems that following the increase in trade, of risks and the consequent recognition of the edictal clause relating to *receptum* – which is believed to have been in operation by the end of the second century BC[44] – the mercantile owners of goods identified by a χειρέμβολον could pay the *navicularius* a slightly higher freight to assume responsibility under a *receptum*. As it was, the risk under the *receptum* was equivalent in scope to the risk that carriers already assumed on account of the change of ownership under a contract *ad onus vehendum* for the transport of the goods of multiple merchants that were identified by *genus*. If this inevitably raised the cost of transporting goods identified and guaranteed by *receptum*, which merchants used frequently to their advantage in response to the increasing danger of piracy in the second and first centuries BC, the introduction of the *receptum* basically ended up equating, in terms of the risk transferred to the *navicularius*, the regime that governed goods *signatae* that were subject to a *receptum* with those transported in bulk (which remained less costly to ship). This advantage may have resulted in a more frequent recourse to this sort of transport, which is known to have become more popular during the first century BC.[45] However, the fact that the carrier, both under the *receptum* and when conducting transport in bulk, was now burdened by the considerable risks associated with *vis maior*, compelled the praetor to mitigate this responsibility by accepting, only a few decades after the time of Alfenus Varus, an *exceptio* that could be pleaded in connection with contracts guaranteed by *receptum* and which the jurist Labeo considered to be 'not inequitable'.[46]

This explanation also permits us to assume that the unlimited liability that should have resulted from the automatic application of the principles governing the handling of things identified by *genus* was excluded – even in the case of transport in bulk. In fact, if the *nauta* who had undertaken the *receptum* and therefore bound themselves *salvas merces in portum perducere* (in return for a higher freight) could have been exempted from the risks of shipwreck and piracy, but not from other perils falling under so-called *casus minores* (that is, for example, *incendium, iactus mercium, ictus fulminis, mortes servorum, latronum hostiumve incursus, fugae servorum, ruina, rapinae, tumultus, animalium casus mortesque* and so forth) – which would still have justified the *receptum*[47] – it follows that, even before the *exceptio labeoniana*, a subjective responsibility limited only to *culpa* had been recognised in all ordinary cases of *locatio conductio* concerning transport for *navicularii* who did not demand a higher freight. This recognition would have fitted well with a competitive and consolidated maritime practice that was adapted to conditions in which a ship could disappear along with its entire cargo and crew. Certainly, in the case of a bulk transport interrupted by *vis piratarum* or *naufragium*, nothing could be attributed to Saufeius that constituted a violation of the regular responsibility to furnish *diligentia*.

For this reason, the *ceteri* had no other choice than to try to advance – in the words of the request to Alfenus as it has been (rather unhappily) reported in the text of the Digest[48] – a desperate attempt to make out a breach of contract for 'diversion from the planned route'.[49] The merchants, claiming therefore to have been disadvantaged, were aiming not just to obtain a share of the quantity of grain that had actually been returned, but at the full recovery of their respective consignments on account of unequal treatment. The alternative proposed by Alfenus was either an *actio furti* in case of transport of identifiable goods or its exclusion in the event of bulk transport, due to the *mutatio domini*. On the facts, this excluded Saufeius from liability for *furtum*, *culpa*, or from any allegation of unequal treatment, 'since he had to return it to somebody first'.

Altogether, it is apparent that the Roman jurists, when confronted by the customs that were widely diffused in Mediterranean Hellenistic practice among merchants of various nationalities, who would come to be known at least from the Augustan age as ναυλωτικαί or ναυλῶσεις, tried to frame them – as in the case of maritime loans or general average – using the Roman legal instruments that were known and available to them.[50] In the case of the lease of an entire ship (*locatio/conductio per aversionem*), either for a certain time period or for a journey (which was the simplest and easiest way to solve the problem of transporting goods when a suitable means of transport was lacking); or in which space was hired for the stowage of goods on board a vessel with a predetermined destination (*locatio rei*); the merchant was designed as the *locator*, who assumed the risk of loss or damage to the goods, and the *nauta* as the *conductor*, having been employed by the merchant. The same was true if several merchants had joined together to hire a single ship or distinct spaces, occupied by marked goods, with the intention that it should follow a predetermined route either with a single stopover or multiple landings. However, if the merchandise had not been marked upon loading and was to be transported in bulk *ad onus vehendum* – thus providing the *nauta* with greater autonomy, at least at that early stage of Roman transport – it would have travelled at the risk of the *nauta*, who quite naturally would have been rather reluctant to accept it.

With the recognition of the *receptum*, Roman carriers would have been placed on a par with foreigners, bearing the risk for goods for which a higher freight had been paid and which would necessarily have to be marked to identify them. However, the increase in the responsibility of Roman *nautae*, both for marked goods on account of the *receptum* and for unmarked goods on account of the *mutatio domi- nii*, would have led at first to the recognition of the exclusion of liability for *force majeure* in relation to bulk goods. This accorded with Mediterranean practice, which had for some time conceived of the contract of transport as a 'μίσθωσις' and, in particular, as an 'ἐργολαβία'.[51] In that sort of contract, the *nauta* presented themselves as the *conductor*, who took up the performance of a task (*opus*) that obliged them to answer only if there had been a specific incident while the goods were in their custody or if a lack of diligence could be specifically attributed to them (though not in the case of *force majeure*, where responsibility could only be assumed by the inclusion of an explicit clause, as in the case of the *receptum*).[52]

Finally, the *exceptio labeoniana* also recognised that *navicularii* who entered into a *receptum* could be exempted from shipwreck and attacks by pirates, though the clause *receptum salvam fore* continued to provide protection to merchants for losses caused by minor perils (*casus minores*): a point of no small significance.

Without a *receptum*, therefore, and whether the goods were marked or unmarked, all merchandise now travelled at the merchant's risk, as was already the case in the Hellenistic practice of *annona* transport, where the responsibility of the carrier for river transport had its contractual, non-legal basis in Graeco-Egyptian law. As A Cenderelli persuasively argued in contrast to AJM Meyer-Termeer,[53] the repeated inclusion of express clauses of guarantee in nautical contracts (ναυλωτικαὶ συγγραφαί) by consignors, cannot be explained, as Meyer-Termeer believed, by an attempt to make the carrier more attentive towards the custody of the cargo and to establish proof of the obligation to this effect; but rather by the fact that the regime of river transport in Egypt did not automatically include absolute or unlimited responsibility in relation to the ship or goods respectively and was therefore subject to agreement in return for a higher freight, as was true of the Roman regime at the end of the Republican age.

The progressive and natural juxtaposition of Roman with Hellenistic maritime practices might have been cultivated by specific contacts made for this purpose. It has been suggested, for example, that the visit to Egypt by several Romans, such as Lucius Mummius in 112 BC, was carried out precisely to learn about methods of advanced agricultural administration, the transport of grain along the Nile to Alexandria, Ptolemaic trade and so forth, aspects of which later spread westward.[54]

In the Roman world, these practices informed, for example, the method by which merchandise was embarked, supported by the *locatio mercis vehendae*, attested to by witnesses, but recorded *ad probationem tantum* by a probationary act, which could have taken the form of a *testatio* (that is, a kind of ceremony before witnesses). The creation by the *nauta* and their subordinates of various kinds of χειρέμβολα (on pozzolana, lead, clay, wood and so forth) in connection with the receipt, stowage and custody of goods was aimed first at avoiding the risks implicit in bulk transport and then toward identification of merchandise; but it no longer gave effect to the transfer of the risk, which the *nauta* could now voluntarily assume by entering into a *receptum*. Hence the preparation of three lists to accompany the goods: one for the merchant, another for the *nauta* and the last for the recipient.[55]

In fact, the control of the goods to be handed over to the recipient, identified by the marks and verified on arrival, by issuing a receipt, would have been greatly facilitated by the use of written documents.[56] This mercantile practice had already carried on for some time in Egypt and elsewhere across the Mediterranean, where transport documents were used to ensure the correct identification of merchandise, its quality and quantity and to set out the various standard measures (such as the σηκώματα, or *mensae ponderariae*) that were employed to check volume and weight.[57] These controls were performed both at the time of boarding (παράδοσις), with the delivery of a perforated *tessera* hung on a special instrument, and at the time of unloading, when the return of the *tessera* enabled the continuous monitoring of the handling of the goods during weighing (ζυγοστασία) and storage.[58] In addition, the δείγματα[59] was indispensable not only for sales by sample, but also in the documentation concerning bulk transport for the verification of the quality of the property that was returned. Certainly, the use of δείγματα,[60] archaeological examples of which have been found increasingly in the commercial environment of ancient ports, lent itself well to the practice of conducting sales by sample, as it enabled the costs associated with the unloading of goods and customs procedures to be postponed until the sale of the merchandise was assured (which was symbolised by the delivery of the sealed sample in advance).

A sample could also travel under seal in the hands of a supervisor (ἐπίπλοος).[61] This was done to ensure the quality of the goods following loading, navigation and unloading, and to reduce the chance of disputes arising upon arrival (that is, when the goods were unsealed) by checking for damage to the merchandise or for evidence of fraud. In the end, a sample, in the case of the bulk transport of low-quality goods (excluding, therefore, products that, on account of their own particular specificity, could only be returned *in specie*) was perfectly adequate for the purpose of verifying the return of quantities of goods of the same kind belonging to different carriers. These goods were carried in bulk, avoiding the waste of time and effort associated with the emptying of the hold for the return of merchandise that, perhaps, had been placed under many other goods in the bottom of the hull of a large ship. For quality control in the case of liquids, it was necessary to take the liquid from the transport containers, barrels, amphorae or *dolia* and then compare it to the unsealed sample. For this purpose, terracotta or bronze 'pipettes', which have been frequently found at shipwreck sites, were used. These were perforated at the bottom and worked by submerging the lower end of the vessel to enable the syphoning of the liquid from the amphorae, *dolia* or barrels through a hole at the other end of the pipe for comparison with the contents of the δείγμα.[62]

There are now many small containers known with traces of writing, which come from commercial and port environments, and which may have been δείγματα. Of course, not all of them were used for the same purpose. One of the first to be identified[63] was connected with a public grain transport dated 1 November, 2 BC,[64] which consisted of two different vessels sailing in convoy with one or two δεῖγματα, though the consignment itself was considered homogeneous and unitary. The samples were sealed by the two pilots and accompanied by two legionary ἐπίπλοοι, who were entrusted with the supervision of an identical quantity of wheat (that is, 433 ¼ *artabae* each, in addition to a supplement of half an *artaba* for each supervisor, perhaps as scrap). But why, given that there were two different vessels with two pilots and two supervisors entrusted with identical quantities, would the fiscal grain be transported in common with one or two samples for both?

One possible explanation is that the two hulls were not of equal size. One was smaller, loaded at most up to the parapet (. . . εἰς παράφραγμα), that is, up to the ridge of the side, while the other was of greater capacity and was therefore capable of containing the rest of the grain, including the supplement.[65] In this case, by sailing in convoy in the calm waters of a great river, it was possible to create a δεῖγμα, and perhaps even a duplicate for safety, which mentioned the total burden of both cargoes totaling 866 ½ *artabae*. This mention would have been completely unjustified if there had been two separate transports that were not considered as a unit. In practice, it seems that, having loaded the smaller of the two vessels with half the grain and assigned it to a supervisor, the prudent approach was to load the surplus onto another boat of greater capacity. This vessel carried an identical quantity (besides the supplement), which explains the existence of one or two δεῖγματα, each sealed by the two pilots, entrusted to the custody of the two ἐπίπλooι, and loaded into two different ships.

It is likely that such practices, which were certainly also used in the private Hellenistic trade of goods transported in bulk, both in connection with ships carrying the loads of several merchants with δεῖγματα, or even, as we have seen, several ships with one or more δεῖγματα, gave rise to the Roman practice of using sample jars. These are attested to by archaeological finds such as those discovered at Pompeii, which usually reveal the nature and content of the *exemplar*, the recipient, the carrier and sometimes even the means of transport.[66] It is impossible, however, to infer from these finds whether the transport to which they were connected was in bulk (particularly of wheat), though neither can this be excluded. Since samples of wheat were intended for the use of a specific shipper, there was no reason to mention other merchants who might possibly have been loading the same products in bulk onto the same ship. It was only the shared responsibility of the pilots and overseers of a state cargo embarked on two ships that, since they were considered as a unit, led to the double-mention in SB VI 9223. The use of samples was motivated not by legal formality, but practical necessity, which leads us to add another text to the two short Pompeian inscriptions reported above that have been the object of intense scholarly examination: *CIL* IV 9591.[67] However, even this *exemplar*, although it presents a text rich in details not reported in other samples, does not clarify whether it was accompanying a bulk transport of merchandise belonging to different *vectores*. Indeed, it has been noted that 'from these specimens it can be deduced that many small anepigraphic containers (*amphorae* or jars) may have been *deigmata*', without it being possible to work out the precise use for which the container was intended.[68]

For this reason, samples have tended to be divided into two basic categories: the first of which pertains to 'accompanying samples',[69] which ensured that a load was not adulterated during transport and that the product was identical to the one handed over on departure. These control samples are best known from, for example, the leather bag of the pilot Chaeremone (which briefly stated the nature of the product, the carrier, the place of departure and the destination, but which lacked any other information), and especially for the transport of fiscal wheat or barley on the Nile.[70] Certainly, these samples were also employed in the trade between private individuals of dry products and liquids and, above all, for the transport of fungible goods belonging to multiple merchants carried in bulk within the same ship (that is, goods *eiusdem generis* to be returned on arrival).

The second category of *exemplaria* or δεῖγματα consists of 'tasting samples' – sent for publicity purposes – which were intended to advertise to potential buyers products that were stored at a distance or on a ship moored at the quay. The availability of these samples avoided the need to unload the merchandise and pay import duties before the transaction was complete. These numerous samples, like the one found in Arles that 'advertised' the Alban wine of a certain Valerius Proculus, available in 140 *dolia* from 60 containers (*sexsagenaria*) and to be placed on the market following the receipt of any orders, did not bear the name of the recipient in the dative.[71] According to D Djaoui, it is also possible that the multiple Baetican oil jars found in the ports of Arles, as well as in Fos (in 14 specimens), in Rome, or in Ostia, were *exemplaria*[72]; many for tasting, but others accompanying a cargo. Since these jars are often devoid of *tituli picti* or graffiti, it is difficult to identify their use with any degree of certainty.

It must also be kept in mind that the use of writing (for example, in tracing the recipient's signature, sometimes in the form of initials) does not always lend an insight into the use of the container, since the sample bearing the transporter's seal, now destroyed, could have been entrusted to a supervisor – a δειγμακαταγωγός in the context of fiscal transport – or to a private carrier. This remitted the sample to the personal custody of an ἐπίπλοος, who on arrival could have handed it over directly to the recipient for inspection, without any need for specific writing relating to other *vectores* or to the quantity, which in any case had to be determined in the accompanying documents, which, as has already been said, were drawn up in triplicate (so called 'delivery notes').[73]

A rudimentary 'delivery note', graffitied with spelling errors and other infelicities, has been identified on a Lamboglia 2 amphora from the first century BC. The interior of the amphora, which was found in 2006 in the service canal of the island of St Francis of the Desert in Venice's northern lagoon, contained significant resinous traces.[74] In fact, at least five names (given in the genitive of possession),[75] which were evidently those of the recipients, are mentioned, each followed by the number of amphorae to be delivered and the respective weight of each batch.

The text stands as evidence for the transport on a single vessel of a consignment of goods shipped by several merchants, most likely '38, 35 tonnellate di carico, alle quali corrisponderebbero più di 30.000 litri di vino' acquired 'direttamente dal/dai produttori vinicoli, stabilendo il prezzo in base alla sua qualità e quantità, concordando inoltre che il prodotto venisse consegnato in anfore (e cioè vinificato)'.[76]

However, in the absence of any indication that goods of different types were to be returned to different merchants, it must be assumed that the cargo was homogeneous (that is, all of the same quality) and differed only with respect to the number of amphorae and their collective weight.[77] The persistence of the quality of a cargo *eiusdem generis*, which may be treated as if it had been transported in bulk, even if the consignments were not actually mixed together, as in the case of ships with *dolia*[78] or amphorae containing wine that was of the same kind and, therefore, to be returned indiscriminately, could have been guaranteed by one or more accompanying samples.

Finally, once again, as in the case of the anepigraphic *exemplaria*, we can observe the unsystematic, occasional use to writing, insofar as poorly traced notes were graffitied on ordinary objects, by people whose profession compelled them to adapt to the indispensable requirements of written documentation.

BIBLIOGRAPHY

Albanese, B. (1971), 'Per la storia del *creditum*', AUPA 32, pp. 5–180.

Amelotti, M. and Migliardi Zingale, L. (1984), 'Una dichiarazione di *naukleros* del 237 a. Cr. in un papiro inedito della collezione genovese', in *Sodalitas. Scritti in onore di Antonio Guarino*, Vol. 6 (Naples: Jovene), pp. 3009–3019.

Amirante, L. (1958), *Ricerche in tema di locazione* (Milan: Giuffré).

Andreau, J., Rossi, L. and Tchernia, A. (2017), 'CIL IV, 9591: un transport de blé entre Ostie et Pompéi, I parte', MEFRA 129(1), pp. 329–337.

Andreau, J., Rossi, L. and Tchernia, A. (2019), 'CIL IV, 9591: un transport de blé entre Ostie et Pompéi, II', MEFRA 131(1), pp. 201–216.

Ankum, H. (1981), '*Tabula Pompeiana* 13: Ein Seefrachtvertrag oder ein Seedarlehen?', IVRA 29, pp. 156–173.

Arnaud, P. (2005), *Les routes de la navigation antique. Itinéraires en Méditerranée* (Paris: Errance).

Arnaud, P. (2012), 'Ancient sailing-routes and trade patterns: the impact of human factors', in D. Robinson and A.I. Wilson (eds), *Maritime Archaeology and Ancient Trade in the Mediterranean* (Oxford: Oxford Centre for Maritime Archaeology), pp. 61–80.

Arnaud, P. (2019), 'Aux marges du formalisme juridique romain: le contrat de naulisme', *Annuaire de Droit Maritime et Océanique* 37, pp. 365–388.

Aubert, J.J. (1999), 'Les *institores* et le commerce maritime dans l'Empire romain', *Topoi* 9, pp. 145–164.

Beltrame, C. (2012), *Archeologia marittima del Mediterraneo. Navi, merci e porti dall'antichità all'età moderna* (Rome: Carocci).

Benke, N. (1987), 'Zum Eigentumserwerb des Unternehmers bei der *locatio conductio irregularis*', ZRG RA 104, pp. 155–273.

Bernard, H. (2007), 'Nouvelles épaves hispaniques de Corse: Sud Perduto 2 (Bonifacio) et Marina di Fiori (Porto Vecchio)', in J. Pérez Ballester and G. Pascual Berlanga (eds), *Comercio, redistribution y fondeaderos. La navigacion a vela en el Mediterraneo. Actas V Jornadas de Arqueología Subacuática, Gandia 2006* (Valencia: Universitat de València), pp. 461–471.

Berni Millet, P. and Gorostidi Pi, D. (2013), '*Iulius Valerianus et C. Iulius Iulianus: mercatores* del aceite bético en un *signaculum* de plomo para ánforas Dressel 20', *JRA* 26, pp. 167–190.

Beseler, G. (1925), '*Aequitas*', *ZRG RA* 45, pp. 453–467.

Bessenyö, A. (2001), 'Das Rätsel der actio oneris aversi. Eine Exegese von D. 19.2.31', in G. Hamza (ed), *Iura antiqua–iura moderna. Festschrift für Ferenc Benedek zum 75. Geburtstag* (Pécs: Kiadó), pp. 23–55.

Biscardi, A. (1975), (1975), '*Actio oneris aversi*', *Novissimo Digesto Italiano (NNDI)* 1, pp. 267–268.

Bove, L. (2006), 'TPSulp. 80 (= Tab. Pomp. 47): un *mandatum per epistulam* (con χειρέμβολον: Ulp. D. 4.9.1.3)?', in M. Silvestrini, T. Spagnuolo Vigorita, and G. Volpe (eds), *Studi in onore di Francesco Grelle* (Bari: Edipuglia), pp. 21–25.

Bramante, M.V. (2014), 'TH 4 e la prassi romano-campana «*de re rustica*»', *Index* 42, pp. 141–163.

Bresson, A. (2008), *L'économie de la Grèce des cités, II, Les espaces de l'échange* (Paris: Armande Colin).

Candy, P. (2021), '"Judging beyond the sandal": Law and rhetoric in D. 19,2,31 (Alf. 5 dig. a Paulo epit.)', *ZRG RA* 138, pp. 310–337.

Cardilli, R. (1995), *L'obbligazione di praestare e la responsabilità contrattuale in diritto romano (II sec. a.C. - II sec. d.C.)* (Milan: Giuffrè).

Carvajal, P.I. (2008), '*Receptum nautarum* and the Grenf. II, 108 Papyrus', *Index* 36, pp. 583–602.

Casson, L. (1971), *Ships and Seamanship in the Ancient World* (Princeton, NJ: Princeton University Press).

Cavallo, G. (1991), 'Gli usi della scrittura nel mondo romano', in B. Andreae (ed), *Princeps urbium. Cultura e vita sociale dell'Italia romana* (Milan: Garzanti-Scheiwiller per Credito Italiano), pp. 171–251.

Cenderelli, A. (1981), 'Review of A.J.M. Meyer-Termeer, *Die Haftung der Schiffer im griechischen und römischen Recht*', *RHD* 49, pp. 180–185.

Colls, D., et al. (1977), 'L'épave Port-Vendres II et le commerce de la Bétique a l'époque de Claude', *Archaeonautica* 1, pp. 3–145.

Cresci Marrone, G. (2009), 'Insediamenti indigeni della Venetia verso la romanità', *Antichità Altoadriatiche* 68, pp. 207–220.

Cresci Marrone, G. (2011), 'Novità epigrafiche da *Iulia Concordia*', *Quaderni di Archeologia del Veneto* 27, pp. 212–214.

Cresci Marrone, G. (2015), 'Anfora iscritta da San Francesco del Deserto', in L. Malnati and V. Manzelli (eds), *Brixia. Roma e le genti del Po. III-I secolo a.C. Un incontro di culture* (Florence: Giunti), pp. 56–58.

De Dominicis, M.A.F. (1950), 'La clausola edittale *salvum fore recipere* esclude in età classica la responsabilità per custodia dei *nautae* nel caso di forza maggiore?', *St. vari di St. del Dir. Rom.* (Padua: Penada, 1933–1937), pp. 1–53.

De Marco, N. (2003), 'L'*Actio oneris aversi*. Appunti su di un equivoco ricostruttivo', *Labeo* 49, pp. 140–159.

De Robertis, F.M. (1952), *Receptum nautarum: studio sulla responsabilità dell' armatore in diritto romano, con riferimento alla disciplina particolare concernente il caupo e lo stabularius* (Bari: Cressati).

De Robertis, F.M. (1958), 'Ancora sul *receptum nautarum*', *RDN* 24, pp. 241–266.

De Robertis, F.M. (1965), 'D. 19.2.31 e il regime dei trasporti marittimi nell'ultima età repubblicana', *SDHI* 31, pp. 92–107.

De Santis, E. (1945), 'Interpretazione del fr. 31 D. 19.2 (*Alfenus libro V digestorum a Paulo epitomatorum*)', *SDHI* 11, pp. 86–114.

De Sarlo, L. (1939), *I Digesta di Alfeno Varo* (Milan: Giuffré).

Della Corte, M. (1946), 'Pompei, Scoperte epigrafiche (Reg. I, ins. VII-VIII e varie)', *Notizie degli Scavi di Antichità* 7, pp. 110–112.

Djaoui, D. and Tran, N. (2014), 'Une cruche du port d'Arles et l'usage d'échantillons dans le commerce de vin romain', *MEFRA* 126(2), pp. 1–16.

Djaoui, D. (2014), 'Découverte d'un pot mentionnant la société des DD Caecilii dans un contexte portuaire situé entre 50–140 apr. J.C. (découverte subaquatique à Arles, Bouches-du-Rhône, France)', in R. Morais, A. Fernández, and M. José Sousa (eds), *As produções cerâmicas de imitação na Hispania (II Congresso Internacional da SECAH - Ex Officina Hispana)*, Vol. 2 (Porto: Universidade do Porto), pp. 161–178.

Djaoui, D. (2015), 'Les pipettes en terre cuite: preuve indirecte de l'utilisation des tonneaux sur Arles et Fréjus à la période flavienne, Abécédaire pour un archéologue Lyonnais', in S. Lemaître and C. Batigne Vallet (eds), *Abécédaire pour un archéologue lyonnais – Mélanges offerts à Armand Desbat* (Autun: Mergoil), pp. 207–214.

Djaoui, D. (2015), 'Prélever le vin au tonneau!', in L. Sieurac and A. Genot, *Arelate*, Vol. 4 (100Bulles), pp. 54–55.

Drexhage, H.J., and Ruffing, K. (2008), 'P.Bingen 77 und der Handel zwischen Asia Minor und Aegypten', in E. Winter and F. Biller (eds), *Festschrift für Elmar Schwertheim zum 65. Geburtstag*, Vol. 1 (Bonn: Rudolf Habelt), pp. 153–165.

Duncan-Jones, R. (1990), *Structure and Scale in the Roman Economy*, (Cambridge: Cambridge University Press).

Fiori, R. (1999), *La definizione della locatio conductio. Giurisprudenza romana e tradizione romanistica* (Naples: Jovene).

Firmati, M. (2014), 'Sigilli di *mercatores* per doli dal porto di Pisa', in A. Buonopane, S. Braito, and C. Girardi (eds), *Instrumenta Inscripta V, Signacula ex aere. Aspetti epigrafici, archeologici, giuridici, prosopografici, collezionistici, Atti del Convegno Internazionale (Verona, 20–21 sett. 2012)* (Rome: Scienze e Lettere), pp. 383–391.

Forschner, B. (2011), 'Das Schiff des Saufeius', *Forum Historiae Iuris* 11, pp. 1–23.

France, J. and Hesnard, A. (1993), 'Une *statio* inédite du Quarantième des Gaules et les opérations commerciales dans le port romain de Marseille (place Jules-Verne)', *JRA* 8, pp. 78–93.

France, J. (2001), *Quadragesima Galliarum: l'organisation douanière des provinces alpestres, gauloises et germaniques de l'Empire romain: 1er siècle avant J.-C.-3er siècle après J.-C.* (Rome: École française de Rome).

Frösen, J. (1980), 'Chi è il responsabile? Il trasporto del grano nell'Egitto greco e romano', *Annali della Facoltà di Lettere e Filosofia. Università di Perugia. 1. Studi classici* 4, pp. 161–176.

Geraci, G. (2004), 'Mensura, pondus e probatio nel rifornimento granario di Roma imperiale (e di Costantinopoli)', in F. Elia (ed), *Politica retorica e simbolismo del primato: Roma e Costantinopoli (secoli IV-VII): Atti del Convegno Internazionale (Catania, 4–7 ottobre 2001): omaggio a Rosario Soraci* II (Catania: CULC), pp. 155–181.

Geraci, G. (2012), 'Sekomata e *deigmata* nei papiri come strumenti di controllo delle derrate fiscali e commerciali', in V. Chankowski and P. Karvonis (eds), *Tout vendre, tout acheter. Structures et équipements des marchés antiques (Actes du Colloque d'Athènes, 16–19 juin 2009)* (Bordeaux: Ausonius), pp. 347–363.

Geraci, G. (2018), 'Feeding Rome: The Grain Supply', in C. Holleran and A. Claridge, *A Companion to the City of Rome* (Malden: Wiley-Blackwell), pp: 219–246.

Gofas, D.C. (1975), 'ΛΟΓΩΙ ΠΡΟΒΑΣ ΣΙΤΟΥ. A contribution to the interpretation of an early byzantine fiscal inscription', *RIDA* 22, pp. 233–242.

Gofas, D.C. (1977), 'La vente sur échantillon a Athenes d'après un texte d'Hypéride', in J. Modrzejewski, D. Liebs, and H.J. Wolff (eds), *Symposion 1977. Vorträge zur griechischen und hellenistischen Rechtsgeschichte. (Akten der Gesellschaft für griechische und hellenistische Rechtsgeschiente, Bd. 3)*, pp. 121–129.

Gofas, D.C. (1993), Études d'histoire du droit grec des affaires. Antique, Byzantin et Post-Byzantin (Athens: La société archéologique à Athènes).

Gofas, D.C. (1994), 'Encore une fois sur la *Tabula Pompeiana* 13', in G. Thür (ed), *Symposion 1993. Vorträge zur griechischen und hellenistischen Rechtsgeschichte (Graz-Andritz, 12–16 September 1993)* (Cologne and Vienna: Böhlau), pp. 251–266.

Gonzalez Romanillos, J.A. (2004), 'Observaciones sobre la responsabilidad en el *receptum nautarum*', *Seminarios complutenses de derecho romano* 16, pp. 277–286.

Guéraud, O. (1933), 'Deux documents relatifs au transport des céréales dans l'Égypte romaine', *Annales du Service des Antiquités de l'Égypte* 33, pp. 59–64.

Guéraud, O. (1950), 'Un vase ayant contenu un échantillon de blé (δεῖγμα)', *JJP* 4, pp. 106–115.

Hadjidaki, E. (1996), 'Underwater Excavations of a Late Fifth Century Merchant Ship at Alonnesos, Greece: the 1991–1993 Seasons', *Bulletin de Correspondance Hellénique* 2, pp. 561–593.

Hauben, H. (1997), 'Les propriétaires de navires privés engagés dans le transport de blé d'état à l'époque ptolémaïque', in B. Kramer, W. Luppe, H. Maehler, and G. Poethke (eds), *Akten des 21. Internationalen Papyrologenkongresses* (Berlin: Teubner), pp. 430–448.

Heilporn, P. (2000), 'Registre de navires marchands', in H. Melaerts (ed), *Papyri in honorem Johannis Bingen octogenarii (P. Bingen)* (Leuven: Peeters), pp. 339–359.

Horden, P. and Purcell, N. (2000), *The Corrupting Sea: A Study of Mediterranean History* (Oxford: Wiley-Blackwell).

Huvelin, P. (1929), Études d'histoire du droit commercial romain (histoire externe-droit maritime) (Paris: Recueil Sirey).

Jakab, É. (2000), 'Vectura pro mutua: Überlegungen zu TP 13 und Ulp. D. 19, 2, 15, 61', *ZRG RA* 117, pp. 244–273.

Jakab, É. (2006), 'Vertragsformulare im *Imperium Romanum*', *ZRG RA* 123, pp. 71–101.

Lafaye, G. (1919), '*Tessera*', in *DAGR*, Vol. 5 (Paris: Hachette Livre), p. 132.

Lequément, R. (1975), 'Étiquettes de plomb sur des amphores d'Afrique', *MEFRA* 87(2), pp. 667–680.

Ligios, M.A. (2020), '*CIL* IV, 9591: riflessioni in materia di impresa di navigazione e di prassi commerciale marittima', *AUPA* 63, (forthcoming).

Liou, B. and Morel, M. (1977), 'L'orge des Cavares: une amphorette à inscription peinte trouvée dans le port antique de Marseille', *RAN* 10, pp. 189–197.

Longo, S. (2019), *Emptio venditio et locatio conductio familiaritatem aliquam inter se habere videntur. Le fattispecie gaiane oggetto di dibattito giurisprudenziale* (Turin: Giappichelli).

Manganaro, G. (1988), 'La Sicilia da Sesto Pompeo a Diocleziano', *ANRW* II.11.1, pp. 3–89.

Marichal, R. (1974–1975), 'Rapports sur les conférences. Paléographie latine et française', *Annuaire 1974–1975. École Pratique des Hautes Études*, IVe section 107, pp. 524–527.

Marlière, E. and Torres Costa, J. (2007), 'Transport et stockage des denrées dans l'Afrique romaine: le rôle de l'outre et du tonneau', in A. Mrabet and J. Remesal Rodríguez (eds), *Africa et in Hispania, Études sur huile africaine* (Barcelona: Instrumenta), pp. 85–106.

Marty, F. (2002), 'Aperçus sur les ceramiques à pâte claire du golfe de Fos', in L. Rivet and M. Sciallano (eds), *Vivre, produire et échanger: reflets méditerranéens (Mélanges offerts à Bernard Liou)* (Montagnac: Monique Mergoil), pp. 201–220.

Mataix Ferrándiz, E. (2020), '*CIL* IV 9591: Propuesta reconstructiva de una *locatio conductio* para el transporte de mercancías por mar', in V. Revilla Calvo, A. Aguilera Martín, Ll. Pons Pujol, and M. García Sánchez (eds), *Ex Baetica Romam. Homenaje a José Remesal Rodríguez* (Barcelona: Universidad de Barcelona), pp. 787–820.

Mayer i Olivé, M. (2008), '*Opercula*, los tapones de ánfora: un indicador económico controvertido', in M. Hainzmann and R. Wedenig (eds), *Instrumenta inscripta latina II. Akten des 2. Internationalen Kolloquiums, Klagenfurt, 5–8 maggio* (Klagenfurt: Verlag des geschichtsvereines), pp. 223–239.

McCormick, R. (2001), *Origin of the European Economy: Communications and Commerce. A.D. 300–900* (Cambridge: Cambridge University Press).

Ménager, L.R. (1960), '*Naulum et receptum rem salvam fore.* Contribution à l'étude de la responsabilité contractuelle dans les transports maritimes, en droit romain', *RHD* 38, pp. 177–213.

Merola G.D. (2001), *Autonomia locale governo imperiale. Fiscalità e amministrazione nelle province asiane* (Bari: Edipuglia).

Metro, A. (1995), 'Locazione e acquisto della proprietà: la *c.d. locatio-conductio "irregularis"*', *Seminarios Complutenses de Derecho Romano* 7, pp. 191–216.

Minaud, G. (2004), 'Regard sur la comptabilité antique romaine: la mosaïque de l'aula des mensores à Ostie, des doigts et des comptes', *MEFRA* 116, pp. 437–468.

Nicolet, C. (1994), 'À la recherche des archives oubliées: une contribution à l'histoire de la bureaucratie romaine', in S. Demougin (ed), *La mémoire perdue* (Paris: Éditions de la Sorbonne), pp. v–xvii.

Nieto, X. (1997), *Le commerce de cabotage et de redistribution, La navigation dans l'Antiquité* (Aix-en-Provence: Édisud).

Oliveri, F., et al. (2015) *Sicily and the Sea* (Amsterdam: Allard Pierson Museum).

Pace, B. (1958), *Arte e civiltà della Sicilia antica: Cultura e vita religiosa* (Sicily: Editrice Dante Alighieri).

Pavis D'Escurac, H. (1976), *La Prefecture de l'Annone Service Administratif Imperial d'Auguste à Constantin* (Rome: École française de Rome).

Pavolini, C. (2000), *La ceramica comune. Le forme in argilla depurata dell'antiquarium* (Rome: Instituto Poligrafico e Zecca dello Stato).

Pelloso, C. (2016), '*Custodia, receptum* e responsabilità contrattuale', *Seminarios Complutenses de Derecho Romano* 29, pp. 263–302.

Pryor, J.H. (1987), *Geography, Technology, and War: Studies in the Maritime History of the Mediterranean, 649–1571* (Cambridge: Cambridge University Press).

Pryor, J.H. (1989), 'The voyage of Rutilius Namatianus: From Rome to Gaul in 417 C.E.', *Mediterranean Historical Review* 4, pp. 271–280.

Purpura, G. (1975), 'Alcuni rinvenimenti sottomarini lungo le coste della Sicilia Nord-Occidentale', *Sicilia Archeologica* 28–29, pp. 57–84.

Purpura, G. (1981–1982), '*Tabulae Pompeianae* 13 e 34: due documenti relativi al prestito marittimo', *Atti della Accademia di Scienze Lettere e Arti di Palermo* 5(2), pp. 449–474 = (1984), in *Atti del XVII Congresso Internazionale di Papirologia* (Naples: Centro internazionale per lo studio dei papiri ercolanesi), pp. 1245–1266.

Purpura, G. (1996), 'Scritture sull'acqua. Testimonianze storiche ed archeologiche di traffici marittimi di libri e documenti, X Rassegna di Archeologia subacquea di Giardini Naxos, 28 ottobre 1995', *AUPA* 44, pp. 361–382.

Purpura, G. (1997), 'Attività marittime e rinvenimenti archeologici nella Sicilia romana', in *Atti del Convegno 'La marittimità in Sicilia'* (Naples), pp. 67–74 = (1996), in *Studi romanistici in tema di diritto commerciale marittimo* (Soveria Mannelli: Rubbettino), pp. 328–336.

Purpura, G. (1999), *Diritto, papiri e scrittura*, 2nd edn (Turin: Giappichelli).

Purpura, G. (2005), '"Passaporti" romani', *Rivista Italiana di Egittologia e Papirologia* 82(1–2), pp. 131–155 = (2004), *AUPA* 49, pp. 207–239.

Purpura, G. (2005), 'La provincia romana d'Asia, i publicani e l'epigrafe di Efeso (*Monumentum Ephesinum*)', *IVRA* 53, pp. 177–198.

Purpura, G. (2013), 'Alle origini delle consuetudini marittime mediterranee. *Symbola, sylai e lex Rhodia*', in A. Lovato (ed), *Convegno 'Ordinamenta Maris' Trani, 30/31 maggio 2013*, pp. 1–20.

Purpura, G. (2014), 'Il χειρέμβολον e il caso di Saufeio: responsabilità e documentazione nel trasporto marittimo romano', *AUPA* 57, pp. 127–152.

Rocco, B. (1971), 'Nuovi piombi mercantili dalla Sicilia greca', *Sicilia Archeologica* 4, pp. 27–36.

Rostovtzeff, M. (1900), *Catalogue des plombs de l'antiquite, du Moyen Age et des temps modernes conserves au Department des medailles et antiques de la Bibliotheque nationale* (Paris: Rolin et Feuardent).

Rougé, J. (1964), 'Tempête et littérature dans quelques textes chrétiens', in *Oikouménè. Studi paleocristiani in onore del Concilio Ecumenico Vaticano II* (Catania: Università di Catania), pp. 61–75.

Rougé, J. (1966), *Recherches sur l'organisation du commerce maritime en Méditerranée sous l'Empire romain* (Paris: S.E.V.P.E.N).

Russo, L.V. (1996), *La rivoluzione dimenticata. Il pensiero scientifico greco e la scienza moderna* (Milan: Feltrinelli).

Salido Domínguez, J. (2013), 'El transporte marítimo de grano en época romana. Problemática arqueológica', in R. Morais, H. Granja, and A. Morillo (eds), *O Irado Mar Atlantico. O naufrágio bético augustano de Esposende (Norte de Portugal)* (Braga: Sersilito), pp. 139–178.

Salinas, A. (1871), 'Piombi antichi siciliani. Primo articolo', *Annali dell'Istituto di Corrispondenza Archeologica* 38.

Solazzi, S. (1936), 'Appunti di diritto romano marittimo: L'*actio oneris aversi*', *RDN* 2, pp. 268–280.

Thür, G. (1994), 'Die Aestimationsabrede im Seefrachtvertrag: Diskussionsbeitrag zum Referat Dimitri C. Gofas', in G. Thür (ed), *Symposion 1993. Vorträge zur griechischen und hellenistischen Rechtsgeschichte (Graz-Andritz, 12–16 September 1993)* (Cologne and Vienna: Böhlau), pp. 267–271.

Toniolo, A. (2007), 'Una bolla di consegna per un trasporto di anfore di I sec. a.C.', *Quaderni di Archeologia del Veneto* 23, pp. 183–187.

Varone, A. (2005), 'Schede di pitture e anforette (deigmata)', in G. Stefani (ed), *Cibi e sapori a Pompei e dintorni* (Pompei: Flavius), pp. 15–17 and 104–106.

Varone, A. (2015), 'L'Anforetta del grano', in C. Parisi Presicce and O. Rossini (eds), *Nutrire L'Impero: Storie di alimentazione da Roma e Pompei. Roma, Ara Pacis Augusta, giugno-novembre* (Rome: L'Erma di Bretschneider), pp. 20–21.

Varvaro, M. (2008), *Per la storia del certum. Alle radici della categoria delle cose fungibili* (Turin: Giappichelli).

Vélissaropoulos, J. (1980), *Les nauclères grecs: recherches sur les institutions maritimes en Grèce et dans l'Orient hellénisé* (Geneva and Paris: Droz).

Vera, D. (2006), 'Un'iscrizione sulle distribuzioni pubbliche di vino a Roma (*CIL* VI, 1785 = 31931)', in M. Silvestrini, T. Spagnuolo Vigorita, and G. Volpe (eds), *Studi in onore di Francesco Grelle* (Bari: Edipuglia), pp. 303–317.

Wilinski, A. (1960), 'D. 19.2.31 und die Haftung des Schiffers im altrömischen Seetransport', *Annales universitatis Mariae Curie-Sklodowska* 7, pp. 353–359.

Wolf, J.G. (1979), 'Aus dem neuen pompeianischen Urkundenfund: Der See-frachtvetrag des Menelaos', *Freiburger Universitätsblätter* 65, pp. 23–36.

Zilliacus, H. (1939), Neue Ptolemäertexte zum Korntrasport und Staatdarlehen, *Aegyptus* 19, pp. 59–76.

Zucca, R., et al. (2016), 'Nota sull'amministrazione e l'economia delle città del Promunturium Mercurii (Africa Proconsularis)', *Antichità Altoadriatiche* 85, pp. 295–309.

NOTES

1. Nicolet (1994), pp. X–XI. The original text (*http://www1.unipa.it/dipstdir/docenti.htm* (last accessed 30 September 2021)) was translated from Italian into English by Emilia Mataix Ferrándiz and Peter Candy, who offered me the opportunity to publish in this collection of studies. I am very grateful to them both for the opportunity offered to me and the effort made.

2. On the gap between Romans and Greeks, cf Russo (1996).

3. Purpura (2005), pp. 131–155.

4. Nicolet (1994), pp. XI–XII. On the absence of nautical maps, cf Arnaud (2005), pp. 46–60.

5. Purpura (1996), pp. 361–382.

6. Cf, for example, Tab. Pomp. 13 (= *TPSulp.* 78 r), in which it is declared that the surety, who was present, was illiterate (' . . . *coram ipso, quod is litteras nesciret . . .* '). Purpura (1981–82), pp. 449–474. For a different interpretation, see Wolf (1979), pp. 33–36; Ankum (1981), pp. 156–173; Gofas (1994), pp. 260–266; with the contribution of Thür (1993), pp. 267–271; Jakab (2000), pp. 244–273 (with bibliography); and the chapter by P Candy later in this volume.

7. Purpura (1999), pp. 90–91.

8. Cavallo (1991), pp. 239 and 244.

9. Heilporn (2000), pp. 339–359, esp. p. 344; Drexhage and Ruffing (2008), pp. 153–165.

10. Cf D. 19.2.31 (Alf. 5 *dig. a Paulo epit.*) and the literature cited in Purpura (2014), pp. 138–143, on the well-known text about bulk transport from the end of the Roman Republic.

11. For the practice of transporting the goods of different merchants on a single ship, see, for example, D. 14.2.2 (Paul. 34 *ad ed.*): '*Cum in eadem nave varia mercium genera complures mercatores coegissent praetereaque multi vectores servi liberique in ea navigarent . . .* ' and D. 14.1.1.3 (Ulp. 28 *ad ed.*): '*Magistri autem imponuntur locandis navibus vel ad merces vel vectoribus conducendis . . .* '.

12. At the Galata Museum of the Sea in Genoa, the date of the birth of the modern container is given as 1956.

13. These are the little-studied commercial lead labels: Rostovtzeff (1900), pp. 7–416; Lafaye (1919), p. 132; Salinas (1971) (brief notes in *Id.* (1871), extracted from the Rivista Sicula); *Id.* (1864); Pace (1958), pp. 418–420; Rocco (1971), pp. 27 and 36. It has been argued that a commercial lead label with the image of a boar in the recto and a *kantharos* on the verso was used to mark the exported merchandise of Verres, just

as in the case of another governor, Q. Iunius Blesus, proconsul of Africa in AD 22–23: Manganaro (1988), p. 40 nt. 194; Purpura (1997), pp. 71–72. On the use of other containers, such as barrels, cf Marlière and Torres Costa (2007), pp. 85–106.

14. The *Annaba* wreck (Algeria) contained 'African' amphorae with lead strips wrapped around the handles, indicating that the contents came from various *officinae*. Lequément (1975), pp. 667–680, assumed that these workshops were African industries for the processing of fish. For a lead label from a facility dedicated to the preparation of *garum* at S. Vito Lo Capo (Trapani), see Oliveri (2015), p. 24.

15. Hadjidaki (1996), pp. 561–593.

16. According to Heilporn (2000) pp. 352–359, the ship from Ostia in P. Bingen 77, l. 10, was similar in size.

17. Rougé (1964), pp. 61–75.

18. Casson (1971), pp. 270–291.

19. McCormick (2001), pp. 103–114; Beltrame (2012), p. 174.

20. Pryor (1987), pp. 25–39; *Id.* (1989), pp. 271–280; Duncan-Jones (1990), pp. 7–29; Reynolds (1995), pp. 131–135; Horden and Purcell (2000); Arnaud (2005), p. 6.

21. Nieto (1997), pp. 152–154.

22. Nieto (1997), p. 154.

23. Beltrame (2012), p. 176.

24. Nieto (1997), p. 154; Arnaud (2005), p. 112. The cargo of the Augustan Sud Perduto 2 wreck has been attributed based on inscriptions to three different *vectores*: those of Port-Vendres II, a small boat sunk between AD 41/2 and 50 and to at least nine different shippers; Bernard (2007), pp. 461–471; Colls et al. (1977), p. 139; Arnaud (2012), p. 72.

25. Arnaud (2005), pp. 5–46; 97–148; 231–232.

26. Arnaud, (2005), p. 60.

27. Arnaud, (2005), pp. 118–125.

28. Heilporn, (2000), p. 342.

29. Arnaud, (2005), pp. 107–125.

30. France and Hesnard (1995), pp. 78–93; France (2001).

31. Arnaud (2005), p. 115; *Id.* (2012), p. 64.

32. *Mon. Eph.* § 30, ll. 71–72; Merola (2001), pp. 209–219; Purpura (2005), pp. 188–200.

33. Bresson (2008), pp. 101–105; Arnaud. (2012), p. 65.

34. For the translation, Candy (2021), p. 313:

'In navem Saufeii cum complures frumentum confuderant, Saufeius uni ex his frumentum reddiderat de communi et navis perierat: quaesitum est, an ceteri pro sua parte frumenti cum nauta agere possunt oneris aversi actione. respondit rerum locatarum duo genera esse, ut aut idem redderetur (sicuti cum vestimenta fulloni curanda locarentur) aut eiusdem generis redderetur (veluti cum argentum pusulatum fabro daretur, ut vasa fierent, aut aurum, ut anuli): ex superiore causa rem domini manere, ex posteriore in creditum iri. idem iuris esse in deposito: nam si quis pecuniam numeratam ita deposuisset, ut neque clusam neque obsignatam traderet, sed adnumeraret, nihil alius eum debere apud quem deposita esset, nisi tantundem pecuniae solveret. secundum quae videri triticum factum Saufeii et recte datum. quod si separatim tabulis aut heronibus aut in alia cupa clusum uniuscuiusque triticum fuisset, ita ut internosci posset quid cuiusque esset, non potuisse nos permutationem facere, sed tum posse eum cuius fuisset triticum quod nauta solvisset vindicare. et ideo se improbare actiones oneris aversi: quia sive eius generis essent merces, quae nautae traderentur, ut continuo eius fierent* *et mercator in creditum iret, non videretur onus esse aversum, quippe quod nautae fuisset: sive eadem res, quae tradita esset, reddi deberet, furti esse actionem locatori et ideo supervacuum esse iudicium oneris aversi. sed si ita datum esset, ut in simili re solvi possit, conductorem cul-pam dumtaxat debere (nam in re, quae utriusque causa contraheretur, culpam deberi) neque omnimodo culpam esse, quod uni reddidisset ex frumento, quoniam alicui primum reddere eum necesse fuisset, tametsi meliorem eius condicionem faceret quam ceterorum.'*

35. Albanese (1971), pp. 88–100; De Marco (2003), pp. 143–149; Fiori (1999), 68–79; Cardilli (1995), pp. 261–276. For a recent treatment, see Longo (2019), pp. 226–229, esp. p. 229; Varvaro (2008), pp. 37–47 and 118–121 accepts the authenticity of the text and considers it in the context of the history of the category of *res quae pondere numero mensura constant.*

36. De Marco (2003), p. 141 nt. 4 believes that the close temporal relationship between the start of the unloading operations and the loss of the ship, as postulated by De Santis (1945), p. 94, on the basis of the tightness of the syntax in the expression '*red-diderat de communi et navis perierat*', indicates that upon arrival at the destination the unloading started with the return of the grain to one of the merchants, which was then immediately followed by the loss of the ship. Cf also, Benke (1987), p. 194 nt. 118. For the port itself, or rather the continuation of the journey to other ports, see Cardilli (1995), p. 271 nt. 104. On the other hand, the inquiry concerning the 'diversion of the cargo' suggests that not all the shippers had contracted with Saufeius to go to the same destination (cf De Marco (2003), p. 141 nt. 2). Albanese (1971), p. 89 doubts that the restitution could have taken place before departure.

37. On the χειρέμβολον and for the diverse theories that have been advanced, cf Purpura (2014), pp. 127–152, esp. pp. 133–143. On some seals from Pisa, cf Firmati (2014), pp. 383–391; and for a *signaculum* on Dressel 20 amphorae, cf Berni Millet and Pi (2013), pp. 167–190; and, generally, Mayer i Olivé (2005), pp. 223–239.

38. The assumption of the risk by the merchants, both at the time of Alfenus and Justin-ian, is also attested to in Sen. Ben. 7.10.2: '*nullam excusationem (maiores) receperunt . . .* ' and in Inst. 3.14.2: '*Et is quidem qui mutuum accepit, si quolibet fortuito casu quod acce-pit amiserit, veluti incendio ruina naufragio aut latronum hostiumve incursu, nihilo minus obligatus permanet*'. '*Is quidem qui mutuum accepit*' does not refer to the borrower of the *pecunia traiecticia*, nor to a *nauta-*carrier in bulk, *sine recepto*, after the time of Alfenus.

39. 'Dalla *locatio* di cose generiche derivava una responsabilità illimitata in caso di man-cata consegna, come fin troppo chiaramente si evince dal testo in questione': De Robertis (1965), p. 101 nt. 35; p. 107 nt. 78; Cardilli (1995), pp. 263–276; Purpura, (2014), p. 141.

40. On the freedom from liability of the *nauta*, cf De Robertis (1965), p. 104 nt. 53: 'è certo che per il *naufragium*, anche nell'ipotesi più radicale di contratto garantito mediante receptum, soccorreva, fin dall'età di Labeone, apposita eccezione liberatoria: e siamo solo a qualche lustro di distanza da Alfeno Varo'. Fiori (1999), p. 76, hypothesises that the *complures* had proposed a legal reconstruction of the case that was not accepted in the response, by requesting a criminal action similar to the *actio furti* in the belief that they were the owners of the wheat: 'Se così fosse, potremmo immaginare che al contrario Alfeno, ritenendo che non vi fosse alcuna comunione tra i mercanti e che la proprietà del grano fosse passata a Saufeio, abbia risposto che non c'è stata alcuna *aversio*'.

41. Ménager (1960), p. 182.

42. D. 19.2.31 (Alf. 5 *dig. a Paulo epit.*): '*quoniam alicui primum reddere eum necesse fuisset* . . .'.
43. In this regard, there has been talk of a *locatio irregularis*. Fiori (1999), p. 80: 'la giuris-prudenza tardo-repubblicana non escludeva il ricorrere di una *locatio conductio* anche in quei negozi in cui si realizzava un trasferimento di proprietà'. Amirante, L. (1958), pp. 59–65, indicates 'che il responso non distingue due tipi di locazione, ma soltanto duo genera di *res locatae*. Sicché, l'eventuale passaggio del dominio è soltanto "una conseguenza della qualità della cosa consegnata" e non implica in alcun modo una distinzione nell'ambito del *locatum-conductum*'.
44. Cf the lucid summary of the issue by De Robertis (1952), pp. 5–13 and the recon-struction by Ménager (1960), pp. 177–182, esp. pp. 197–198. According to traditional opinion the *receptum* was introduced by the Praetor to increase the responsibility of the *nauta* for the goods of merchant *vectores*. Cf De Robertis, (1952), pp. 32–51, on the other hand, for whom the *receptum* reduced the *nauta*'s responsibility, since it would have made him responsible only for the goods for which the *receptum* had been paid (also, Rougé (1966), p. 384). Note, however, that according to the pre-existing rules governing contracts of letting and hiring the *res signatae*, for which a *receptum* had not been paid, could still have continued to be transported at the risk of the merchant *vec-tor*, even if this were less convenient for the *nauta*, who neither received the revenue generated by a *receptum* nor enabled transport to take place without 'breaking the cargo'. According to Gonzalez Romanillos (2004), pp. 277–286, the *receptum* was only designed to cover the theft of, and damage to, goods that were on board.
45. Purpura (2014), pp. 143–145.
46. D. 4.9.3.1 (Ulp. 14 *ad ed.*): '*Labeo scribit, si quid shipwreck aut per vim piratarum perierit, non esse iniquum exceptionem ei dari*': on which, De Robertis (1952), p. 85, 102; Id. (1958), pp. 256–66; Id. (1965), p. 106; Cardilli (1995), p. 264.
47. De Robertis (1952), p. 86 and nt. 4.
48. Purpura (2014), pp. 139–140. Consequently, neither the untechnical expression '*actio oneris aversi*', nor the references to a *confusio* (*frumentum confunderunt*) or *communio* (*reddere de communi*) among the *complures*, are interpolations or in any way indicate the use of language that ought not to be attributed to Alfenus: De Santis, (1945), pp. 98–114; De Sarlo (1939), p. 57; Metro (1995), pp. 210–216. For the inaccuracy of the *complures*: Wilinski (1960), pp. 353–359; De Robertis, (1965), p. 271 nt. 102; Fiori, (1991), p. 76.
49. The term '*aversio*', therefore, ought not to be translated in its technical sense (that is, as 'misappropriation of the cargo', but in its main and non-technical sense, indicating that the carrier had followed an unsuitable route that favoured only one of the mer-chants (cf the chapter by É Jakab later in this volume). According to Biscardi (1975), pp. 267–268, the theories concerning the character of the mysterious *actio oneris aversi* can be substantially reduced to three (since the thesis that it was an special *actio furti*, recognised by the *ius civile*, is now abandoned): (a) the *actio oneris aversi* was a con-tractual action similar to the *actio locati*, which early fell into desuetude following the generalisation and development of its counterpart (Huvelin (1929), pp. 115–119); (b) the *actio oneris aversi* was the *actio locati* as applied to the case of *oneris aversio* (Beseler (1925), p. 467); (c) the *actio oneris aversi* was the praetorian *actio furti adversus nau-tas* by another name (Solazzi (1936), pp. 268–280). More recently, Bessenyö (2001), pp. 23–55, has suggested that it was a *condictio triticaria*, on the basis that Saufeius' relationship with the *complures* was configured as a *mutuum* (p. 54) and the view of Forschner (2011), pp. 1–23, who considers it an obsolete penal action. As De Marco

(2003) has convincingly argued, however, the expression has not been properly understood, since the *complures* did not use it in a technical sense. The marked generality of the *quaestio* put to the jurist as a last resort by the dissatisfied merchants, who were accustomed to agree upon the routes to be followed for each navigation, as in the *syngraphe* of Lacritus and those recorded in the orations of pseudo-Demosthenes more generally (see, also, the famous Callimachus loan reported in D. 45.1.122.1 (Scaev. 28 *dig.*)), could suggest that they proposed a diversion, which ended up making the condition of one better than that of the others, who therefore aimed at the recovery of their respective shares. But Alfenus, right at the end of the *responsum* ('*quoniam alicui primum rede eum necesse fuisset*'), excludes the admissibility of the proposed action – we remember – in relation to clearly identified goods, the misdirection of which could have led to *culpa* (*actio locati*) or even liability for *furtum* (*actio furti adversus nautas*).

50. Vélissaropoulos (1980), pp. 268–311; Arnaud (2019), pp. 378–380. According to Arnaud, P. Koel. 3 147 (30/27 BC) is the oldest extant document, before P. Oxy XLV 3250 (AD 62) (on which, see the chapter by P Candy later in this volume), which Vélissaropoulos considered the most ancient. It should be noted that, according to Arnaud, in the period before the empire, small batches of goods could frequently be exempted from the use of written forms. In fact, it appears that no more than seven documents are known for the first three centuries of the empire.

51. Vélissaropoulos (1980), pp. 282–300.

52. Already, De Dominicis (1950), pp. 72–73; Purpura, (2014), p. 147; on *custodia*, *receptum*, and contractual liability, see Pelloso (2016), pp. 263–302.

53. Cenderelli (1981), pp. 180–185. Cf also Jakab (2006), pp. 91–101; Purpura (2014), p. 147.

54. Frösen (1980), p. 175.

55. This person introduces themselves in an epistolary form in *TPSulp.* 80 (= Tab. Pomp. 47), which Bove interpreted as a *mandatum per epistulam* with χειρέμβολον (Bove (2006), pp. 21–25). On this question, however, see Purpura (2014), pp. 134–136 and 148–149. In the *annona* transport from Egypt they released 'una lettera di carico con le ricevute richieste in tre copie. Una spetta allo stratego, una al sitologo del magazzino centrale e la terza per accompagnare il carico. Il sitologo invia il suo rapporto sul carico direttamente ad Alessandria': Frösen (1980), pp. 171–176.

56. P. Grenf. II 108 (AD 167), for example, has been interpreted as a receipt released by the recipient of the goods that also confirmed the regularity of the delivery ('*quas has res intra scriptas meas sanas salvas recepisse scripsi*'); others, however, have considered it a copy of the agreement by which the *nauta* assumed the *periculum*, following entry into a *receptum*. De Robertis (1952), p. 157 nt. 1; Carvajal (2008), pp. 599–602.

57. Geraci (2012), pp. 347–352.

58. Minaud (2004), pp. 460–468; Purpura (2013), pp. 1–20; Id. (2014), p. 132.

59. For Roman archaeological discoveries at the port of Marseille and Pompeii, see Liou and Morel (1977), pp. 189–197. The text on the little amphora found at Marseille reads as follows: '*Massil(iam) ou Massil(iensi) Rubrio / [..]sino / hord(ei) Cavar(um) / sicci mundi / i m(odii) mille (et quingenti)*' (To Marseille, for Rubrius . . . sinus, 1,500 *modii* of barley (from the land of) the Cavares, dry, clean . . .). For the Alexandrian evidence, Guéraud (1933), pp. 62–64; Id. (1950), pp. 107–112, which, in addition to the previous find, has a leather bag with the inscription: '*Exemplar / hordei missi per Chae/remonam Anubionis / gubernatorem - ex no/mo memphite a<d> metropolin*' (Barley sample sent with the pilot Chaeremone, son of Anubius, from the Memphite nome to the metropolis); on

which, see Geraci (2004), pp. 163–178. Concerning the different uses of δείγματα, in both Greek and Roman commerce, cf Rougé (1966), 419–421; D'Escurac (1976), pp. 231–239; Amelotti (1984), pp. 3009, 3010 nt. 4 and 3019; Gofas (1970); *Id.* (1993), pp. 233–245; Geraci (2012), pp. 155–181; *Id.* (2018), pp. 231–246. For papyri and other literature relating to trade between private individuals from the third century BC to the fifth/sixth century AD: P. Cairo Zen. III 59522; P. Cairo Zen. IV 59696; P. Col. I 51; P. Oxy. I 113; CTh. 14.4.9. A tablet from Herculaneum (TH 4) dated 2 September, AD 60, which contains the words '*signa salvo praestari*' (relating to the integrity of the seals on wine containers in a *stabulum*) guaranteed – in a manner similar to the δείγματα *frumentari* – both the quantity and quality of wine made available for tasting (the *degustatio*), especially since this took place through sealed *ampullae* accompanying the *dolia* so as to avoid opening the container: Bramante (2014), p. 150; Vera (2006), pp. 309–315. The hole found in the lower part of the body of numerous amphorae, closed by a stopper, probably served to facilitate the *degustatio*, without breaking the seal of the amphora (cf Purpura (1975), p. 63, figure 8).

60. Gofas, (1993), pp. 139–145; *Id.* (1977), pp. 121–129.

61. P. Stras. 31, 6 (third century AD).

62. Djaoui (2015), pp. 207–214; Djaoui, Sieurac, and Genot (2015). A ritual sprinkler, operating on the same principle and dating to the eighth century BC, was found, together with other vases, under the Mugonia Gate in Rome (cf *Archeologia Viva*, 83, Sept/Oct. 2000, p. 47). For intentionally pierced amphorae, cf above, nt. 59.

63. SB VI 9223: Νομοῦ ὀξ(υρυγχίτου) / Ἀμμώνιος Ἀμμωνίου κυβερνήτης πλοίου δημοσίου οὗ ἐπίσημον α..ς, δι' ἐπιπλόου Λουκίου Οὐκλατίου στρατιώτου / λεγεῶνος κβ σπείρης β κεντερωνέας Μαξίμου Στολτίου, καὶ Ἑρμίας Πετάλου κυβερνή(της) ἑτέρου πλοίου / οὗ ἐπίσημον Αἴγυπτος, δι' ἐπιπλόου Λουκίου Καστρικίου στρατιώτου λεγεῶνος κβ σπείρης δ' κεντερωνέας / Τίτου Πομπηίου. Ἔστιν δ<ε>ῖγμα οὗ ἐμβεβλήμεθα ἀπὸ γενη(μάτων) κη (ἔτους) Καίσαρος, ὁ μὲν Ἀμμώνιος εἰς παράφραγμα / (πυροῦ) (ἀρταβῶν) υλγδ ὁ δὲ Ἑρμίας ὁμοίως (πυροῦ) (ἀρταβῶν) υλγδ (γίγονται) αἱ ἐμβεβλημέναι διὰ Λεωνίδου καὶ Ἀπολλωνίου σιτολ(όγων) ἀπηλιώ(του) / μερίδος κάτω<<ι>> τοπαρχ(ίας) (πυροῦ) (ἀρτάβαι) ωξςL καὶ προσμεμετρήμεθα ταῖς ἑκατὸν ἀρτάβ(αις) (πυροῦ ἀρτάβης) (ἥμισυ), τὴν δὲ ἐμβολὴν πεποι-/ήμεθα ἀπὸ β τοῦ Ἀθὺρ ἕως δ τοῦ αὐ(τοῦ) μηνός καὶ συνεσφραγίσμεθα τῇ ἀμφο(τέρον) σφραγῖδι, τοῦ μὲν Ἀμμω(νίου) / ἧς <ε>ἰκὼν Ἄμμωνος, τοῦ δὲ Ἑρμίου ἧς <ε>ἰκὼν Ἁρποκράτης. (Ἔτους) κθ Καίσαρος Ἀθὺρ δ. (2ª mano) Ἑρμίας καὶ Ἀ<μ>μώνι<ο>ς ἐσφραγίσμ<εθ>α τὰ δ<ε>ίγματα. (Ἔτους) <κθ> Καίσαρος Ἀθὺρ ιθ' ('Del nomo Ossirinchite. Ammonios figlio di Ammonios, pilota di un'imbarcazione pubblica il cui emblema è A . . . sotto la scorta del sovrintendente (ἐπίπλοος, 'sopraccarico') Lucius Oclatius, soldato della XXII legione, 2a coorte, centuria di Maximus Stoltius, ed Hermias, figlio di Petalos, pilota di un'altra imbarcazione il cui emblema è l'Egitto, sotto la scorta del sovrintendente (ἐπίπλοος, 'sopraccarico') Lucius Castricius, soldato della XXII legione, 4a coorte, centuria di Titus Pompeius. Questo è il campione (δείγμα) del carico che abbiamo ricevuto in consegna dai raccolti dell'anno 28 di Cesare (Augusto): Ammonios fino al parapetto artabe di grano 433 e ¼, ed Hermias egualmente artabe di grano 433 e ¼, fanno in totale, caricate sotto la responsabilità di Leonidas e di Apollonios, sitologi della meris occidentale della toparchia inferiore, artabe di grano 866 e ½, e abbiamo aggiunto un supplemento di 1/2 artaba di grano ogni cento artabe. Abbiamo effettuato il carico dal 2 di Hathyr fino al 4 dello stesso mese e abbiamo apposto i nostri due rispettivi sigilli (. . . συνεσφραγίσμεθα τῇ ἀμφο(τέρων) σφραγῖδι . . .), quello di Ammonios il cui

marchio è un'immagine d'Ammone e quello di Hermias la cui impronta è una figura di Arpocrate. L'anno 29 di Cesare (Augusto), 4 di Hathyr (1 novembre 2 a.C.). [2a mano]: Io Hermias e io Ammonios abbiamo sigillato i campioni. L'anno 29 di Cesare (Augusto), 19 di Hathyr (16 novembre 2 a.C.)') (translated into Italian by Geraci (2012), p. 355). Guéraud (1950), p. 111, correctly notes that 'le transport est effectué par deux barques jumelles: il faut concevoir les deux quantités de blé, non pas comme deux cargaisons qui se trouvent être égales, mais comme les deux moitiés d'une cargaison unique et homogène: c'est pour cela que leur égalité est poussée jusqu'au 1/4 d'artabe, que le deigma se réfère indifféremment aux deux bateaux, et que l'ipographe est au nom des deux kybernatai. Tout ceci n'exclut d'ailleurs pas qu'il ait pu exister un second vase sem-blable au nôtre, de sorte que chaque bateau ait eu le sien. La chose est même vraisem-blable si j'ai correctement rétabli le texte fautif de la ligne 10. Mais les choses sont faites de telle manière qu'un seul vase puisse, au besoin, faire foi pour toute la cargaison des deux bateux'. Unfortunately, the uncertainty of the reading of l. 10 (see Guéraud, p. 114) cannot be resolved with reference to the image presented in Guéraud's publica-tion, which is compounded by the difficulty of checking the document that belongs to the Cairo Museum (no. 88756). It seems, however, that the considerations at p. 114 are well-founded and therefore that two separate sample jars were prepared for reasons of safety for each boat, while the loads in the two hulls were considered a homogeneous unit. Moreover, the papyri show that even for a single boat, several sample jars could be prepared: H. Zilliacus (1939), pp. 62, ll. 13–14 and 32–34; with the observations of Guéraud, (1950), pp. 108 and 114.

64. For an accurate list of shipwrecks with archaeologically verifiable cargoes of cereals, see Salido Dominguez (2013), pp. 139–177.

65. In the Hellenistic age, these were typically small river boats (250, 300, 700 *artabae*). Large boats could have exceeded 10,000 *artabae* and even as much as 18,000 *artabae*: Hauben (1997), pp. 437. For maritime vessels of the second century AD, P. Bingen 77 indicates an increase in tonnage, though the average remains less than 2,500 *artabae*, apart from a hull of 22,500 and another of 7,000 *artabae*. See above, nt. 9.

66. *Notizie degli Scavi di Antichità* (1946), p. 110; CIL IV 5894 with *Add.*, p. 725: '*Ante (mis-sum) [e]xenplar tritici / in nave C. Senti Omeri; / Ti Claudi Orpei / vect(oris)*' (Wheat sam-ple (sent) in the ship of Gaius Sentius Homer, of the carrier Titus Claudius Orpheus) and Inv. 12316: '*Exsemplar tritici / Plutioni Calventi C(ai) ser(vo)*' (Wheat sample (sent) to Plutio, slave of Calventius Caius); on which, Varone (2005), pp. 105–106.

67. CIL IV 9591: '*Ante exemplar / tr(itici) m(odiorum) X̅VCC (quindecim milium ducento-rum) / in n(ave) cumba amp(horarum) MDC (mille sescentarum) tutela Iouis et / Iuno(nis) parasemi Victoria P. Pompili / Saturi mag(ister) M. Lartidius Vitalis domo Clupeis. (vacat) Vect(ura) Ostis a(. . .) IIC- (duobus centesimis) sōl(ven)do / [in margine] Gratis m(odii) CC (ducenti) / S(ine) F(raude) pr(idie) Idus octobr(es)*' (Sample preceding 15,200 *modii* of wheat transported on the cargo ship (*cumba*) under the protection of Jupiter and Juno with the insignia of Victory owned by Publius Pompilius Saturus. Captain of the ship Marcus Lartidius Vitalus, originally from Clupea. (*vacat*) a 2 per cent transport fee to be paid at Ostia. (In the margin) 200 free *modii*. Without fraud, 14 October). So according to the recent revisions by Andreau, Rossi and Tchernia (2017), pp. 329–337; and *Id.* (2019), pp. 201–216. The *exemplar*, however, also has an inscription on its reverse (that is, 'b') side, which, like the inscription on side (a) is written in black (and not red) ink: Varone (2005), p. 104 nt. 133; *Id.* (2015), p. 20. Thus, in a third hand, '*Rustico ab . . .* '. This was not taken into consideration, as it was thought to be

connected to the domestic re-use of the container in Pompeii. However, there is no indication in the dative of the recipient, for whom the sample was made. Aubert (1999), p. 156, based on a version of the text that has now been revised by Andreau, Rossi, and Tchernia, read 'Rustico', though this interpretation does not take into account the inscription on side (b). 'Rustico' is indicated with the same black ink as the writing on side (a). I am therefore more inclined to accept a proposal by De Romanis to dissolve at l. 6 the *a*(. . .) in *a*(*ccipienda*) and the *S*(*ine*) *F*(*raude*) of Della Corte (1946), pp. 110–112 = AE 1951, 165, in favour of *S*(*olutio*) *F*(*acta*), a choice followed by Varone, Mataix Ferrándiz, and Ligios. Suddenly the interpretation of the discovery could be rather different. Cf Marichal (1974–1975), pp. 524–527; Geraci (2012), p. 356; Zucca et al. (2016), pp. 304–307; Varone (2005), pp. 104–105; Id. (2015), pp. 20–21; Mataix Ferrándiz (2020), pp. 787–820; Ligios (2020).

68. Geraci (2012), p. 356 nt. 48; Andreau, Rossi, and Tchernia (2017), p. 11 nt. 40.
69. So Andreau, Rossi and Tchernia (2017), p. 7.
70. Guéraud (1933), pp. 62–64. For the text, see above at nt. 59. Guéraud observes that it is not a question of barley sent directly to Alexandria via the Memphite nome, but rather to the nome's metropolis. The vagueness of the expression *ex nomo memphite* could indicate that it was not possible to indicate exactly which of the various collections of villages was the origin, which in any case could have been useful when it came to re-using the same container for other consignments coming from other locations within the same nome.
71. Djaoui and Tran (2014), pp. 1–16.
72. Djaoui (2014), pp. 161–178. For Fos, see Marty (2002), p. 211; for Rome and Ostia, see Pavolini (2000), figures 34, 58, and 75.
73. See above, nt. 55.
74. Toniolo (2007), pp. 183–187; Cresci Marrone (2009), pp. 213–215; Id. (2011), pp. 212–214; Id. (2015), p. 302. I would like to thank PA Gianfrotta for reporting the discovery to me.
75. Based on a recent rereading of the report by Cresci (2015), p. 56: 'Le particolarità paleografiche nella resa delle lettere appaiono cronologicamente compatibili all'uso primario del contenitore come veicolo di derrate e non a un suo successivo riutilizzo'. See, also, Toniolo (2007), p. 184.
76. Toniolo (2007), p. 186.
77. On the need to check the size and weight, see Geraci (2012), pp. 159–160; Id. (2018), p. 347.
78. Purpura (2014), pp. 149–151.

Chapter 8

Loans and Securities: Tracing Maritime Trade in the Archive of the *Sulpicii*

Éva Jakab

PUTEOLI AND THE SEA

The archive of the Sulpicii is a valuable collection of documentary texts witness-ing the economy and society of an ancient city in the first century AD. Today's visitors, seeing the modest archaeological finds in modern Pozzuoli, can hardly imagine the pulsating life in the forum and port two thousand years ago. The bay of Puteoli provided a convenient natural harbour where ships could safely anchor, protected from storms.[1] When the writing tablets of the archive were drawn up, Puteoli was the most important port of Rome. Even larger seagoing ships could dock there in order to unload their merchandise and to transport them on river or land routes to Rome.[2] Ostia and Portus, the artificially developed harbours of Rome that were extended following the invention of hydraulic concrete, were only established later.[3]

The sea routes from Puteoli, for example to Carthage or Alexandria, belonged to the fastest connections between Italy and Egypt/Africa. Sailing along the west bank of Sicily, the journey took twelve to fifteen days.[4] Taking the rather risky Strait of Messina, it could even be done in nine days.[5] In any case, the return journey took more time: along the African coast or via Greece, one had to sail on average as long as forty days.[6] The convenient location of Puteoli and its natu-ral harbour made the city an important trading centre; its enormous importance has been confirmed by ancient literary sources as well as modern archaeological research (scrutinising sailing routes and shipwrecks).[7]

Regarding the great economic importance of the city it seems rather strange that maritime trade has hardly left any traces in the archive of the Sulpicii.[8] One single document, *TPSulp.* 78, testifies a direct connection with transma-rine activities. It is a *cheirographon* of a certain Menelaos, a *nauta* or merchant of Greek origin from the city of Keramos, Asia Minor. In AD 38, Menelaos con-cluded a freight contract, a *naulotike* in Puteoli (l. 9).[9] Unfortunately, the text of this *naulotike* is not preserved; the document that came down only contains a receipt that was linked to it: Menelaos acknowledged – in his Greek mother tongue – that he had received from a certain Primus 1,000 denarii (= HS 4,000). The Sulpicius bank seems to have been involved in the business as a paying agent: obviously Primus, the slave of Publius Attius Severus, disbursed the freight through the bank.[10] Considering the location and the economic importance of Puteoli, ought we to be surprised at the preservation of only one legal transaction concerning maritime trade? Did the Sulpicii really stay away from contracts with shipmen and merchants? Were they not interested in the lucrative maritime business?

Such disinterestedness would be rather strange because there were high-ranking businessmen in Puteoli and Herculaneum who invested large amounts in maritime trade. It suffices to mention Vestorius, who was involved in business with Atticus and Cicero and also in financing overseas trading activities.[11] It is well known that the Sulpicii also acted as financial brokers and middlemen: they supported the operations of businessmen and lent them money directly or took out loans from investors and found reliable borrowers for them.[12] In the following I try to shape some models concerning the Sulpicii's possible participation in transmarine trade activities. The focus is on loan agreements and real securities. The writing tablets in the Sulpician archive show sixty-one payments or acknowledgements of debt for a total value of c. 1,022,000 sesterces.[13] Before going into details, some (fragmentary) documents should be recalled which report on considerable amounts changing hands through the Sulpician bank; they might also have supplied start-up capital for trading enterprises.

One document dated 22 December, AD 57,[14] reports the sale of a ship and its cargo (*sub praecone*) at auction[15]; the cargo consists of the considerable quantity of 18,000 *modii* of grain. In line four, *Sidone* might indicate the origin of the cargo or of the ship. The skipper, son of a certain *Theodorus S* (his name is not preserved) seems to be a peregrine of Greek origin.[16] Camodeca reconstructed in the first line *C(aius) S[--]*[17] which suggests that one of the Caii Sulpicii was a party at the auction: considering the dating it must have been Caius Sulpicius Cinnamus.[18] The 18,000 *modii*, counting in weight, amounts to about 120 tons.[19] In lines eight to nine only a few words can be read: '*nave . . . avertisset . . . obligata esset . . . protopraxia*'[20] – the words seem to refer to an illegal activity, perhaps embezzlement or customs fraud. In legal vocabulary, '*avertere*' denotes acts that are against the law or against contractual terms.[21] Commonly, '*protopraxia*' specifies a privilege of the fiscus in asserting claims, also against third parties.[22] The word is mostly met in legal relationships involving tax authorities – although, according to Pliny, the proconsuls of Bithynia also granted such a privilege to urban communities.[23] It should be left open here whether *protopraxia* referred to a port tax imposed by the municipium of Puteoli[24] or to a sale tax imposed by the state.[25] For the present topic it suffices to state that the Sulpicii took part in a transaction that was in some way connected with maritime trade.

TPSulp. 80 is a business letter announcing the arrival of some goods; a ship called Octa[26] is expected to arrive with a considerable amount of wine and wine products (*acetum, defrutum*, perhaps also *mulsum*).[27] *Urnalia sicula* are mentioned in the document (line three); the Sicilian *urna* corresponds to half a Roman amphora.[28] Using Sicilian wine vessels can be a link to the origin of the merchandise; likely the ship was loaded in a Sicilian port.[29] The letter seems to have been sent earlier, before the arrival of the ship, to a certain Aphrodisius – maybe to give him time for preparations to receive the cargo properly.

All three documents quoted (*TPSulp.* 78, 80, and 106) seem to indicate the Sulpicii's engagement in sea trade. In *TPSulp.* 78 the payment of the freight for a sea voyage goes through the bank; and in *TPSulp.* 106 the bank may have been involved in the bankruptcy of a trading company. The simple business letter in *TPSulp.* 80 might have been intended as evidence of a pledged cargo, maybe given as security for maritime loan (to give just one possible connection to the bank). The protagonists of all three documents had predominantly Greek names: they represent shipmen and merchants coming from the eastern Mediterranean to try their luck in Puteoli. It is fair to assume that they were deeply rooted in Greek culture, including Greek legal culture. The monetary transactions documented in the writing tablets could have provided sufficient starting capital for their trading activities.

G Camodeca arranged two *tabulae* under the title *Rationum Fragmenta*, whose common external feature is their unusually large format: 5.2 x 20.2 cm and 4.5 x 20.8 cm. Both are entries in account books (*rationes*, *codex rationum* or *codex accepti et expensi*).[30] *TPSulp.* 94 was drawn up by Gaius Sulpicius Faustus on 3 June, AD 42: 'What is written below by Gaius Sulpicius Faustus'. Afterwards follow the date and the actual entry: 'To Eunus, vicarius of Amarantus Hyacinthianus, slave of Tiberius Claudius Caesar Augustus Germanicus, 50,000 sesterces'. A month later, on 3 July, AD 42, 50,000 sesterces were paid again to Eunus. On 9 July, another 25,000 sesterces were paid to a certain Thallus, vicary slave of Phorus. Neither of the tablets gives any information about the *causa* of the transactions; it may be that some maritime business was being conducted in the background.

The loan agreements (*mutua*) of the archive also attest to the transfer of significant sums of money: in one of them, Gaius Sulpicius Cinnamus paid out HS 20,000 to a certain Marcus Lollius Philippus (*TPSulp.* 54); in another Euenus Primianus credited HS 10,000 to C. Novius Eunus (*TPSulp.* 51); following which a further HS 10,000 are loaned (in *TPSulp.* 52); in the next, Gaius Sulpicius Faustus gave a loan of HS 20,000 to a certain Lucius Marius Iucundus (in *TPSulp.* 53).

There are also high amounts booked in the so-called *nomina arcaria*: C. Sulpicius Cinnamus disbursed HS 30,000 to a certain Magia Pulchra (in *TPSulp.* 63) – repayment was promised by her in a *stipulatio*, with a strict deadline. In *TPSulp.* 72, the repayment of HS 30,000 is confirmed by Gaius Sulpicius Cinnamus; and *TPSulp.* 75 records on the payment of HS 20,000. At that time, a medium-sized ship with a capacity of sixty to eighty tons would have cost around HS 57,000 to 68,000 in Italy. Such a ship could transport 10,000 *modii* of grain; and a full cargo unloaded in Puteoli could have been sold for HS 40,000. On the other hand, a merchant paid a much lower price when they acquired their cargo of 10,000 *modii* in Alexandria: a papyrus from the village of Tebtynis records HS 1 to 2 per *modius*, that is HS 10,000 to 20,000 for a full cargo.[31] With this in mind, a merchant or shipman given around HS 10,000 or 20,000 would have had sufficient capital to start a maritime enterprise.

MARITIME LOANS AS REFLECTED BY LAWYERS

This contribution looks for traces of the Sulpicii's participation in maritime business activities. As mentioned above, the archive does not contain any documents that explicitly refer to a maritime loan. However, significant money transactions, entries in *rationes*, loans and securities are attested to which could have been connected with maritime trade.

Mutuum, loan, was an old *stricti iuris* unilateral 'real' contract under Roman law; the borrower became owner of the money handed over (*pecunia numerata, pecunia mutua*) with the task to return the same equivalent.[32] The lending was (theoretically) gratuitous: that is, no interest could be charged. Notwithstanding this limitation, in everyday practice interest was agreed separately, mostly by promising in a *stipulatio*. In a money loan, all material risks were on the borrower.[33]

The legal construction of maritime loans differed from that of *mutuum* in essential points.[34] It was a conditional loan with special interest and risk agreements:

'D. 22.2.1 (Mod. 10 *pand.*):
Transmarine (*traiecticia*) is the (loaned) money which is sent across the sea: if it is spent where it was lent it is not "transmarine".[35]

Modestin emphasised that money lent for the purpose of a voyage (*pecunia traiecticia*) had special rules: the legal effects of which occur when the voyage with the money (or the merchandise purchased from it) began, which is to say when the ship took leave of the port of departure.[36] Both parties were protected by this condition: the higher rate of interest became due only when the increased risk (*periculum maris*) started; and the lender's risk was also limited to a trip that was already underway.[37] If the voyage was cancelled the high interest could not be claimed – rather the rules of a regular loan ('land loan') applied.[38]

The terminology of maritime loans was far from homogenous: the commonly used phrases '*faenus nauticum*', '*pecunia traiecticia*' specified the contract by its special terms (maritime interest or money on a voyage).[39] The Roman jurists, treating cases involving maritime loan transactions, refer to the agreement with rather different phrases: '*periculum creditoris*', '*maius legitima usura faenus*', '*usurae et sortem*', '*usurae maritimae*', '*salva navis sortem cum certis usuris recipiam*'.[40] In one text, Scaevola called the high interest '*pretium periculi*'[41] and felt it necessary to distinguish such types of contracts from *aleae*, or gambling. Maritime agreements had aleatory features but remained within the scope of legally recognised contractual practice. Scaevola argued that the high interest agreed between the parties actually remunerated the high risk on the lender.[42] The lawyer gave two striking examples: lending money to a fisherman to buy fishing equipment and lending money to an athlete to finance their training.[43] In both cases, an entrepreneur was pre-financed for a foreseeably profitable activity. The lender made a considerable advance payment for a contractually defined purpose[44]; they deliberately took the high risk that the condition (the hoped-for profit) would never be satisfied so that repayment could not be demanded. Though Scaevola did not mention it, the contracts treated by him fit exactly that of a maritime loan.[45]

Pecunia traiecticia was money lent for a voyage for the purpose of trading (and with the agreement that the money would be returned when the ship arrived safely with the hoped-for profit). Maritime loans were lent within a strict time limit[46]: the lender's risk was restricted to a precisely set period. Several disputes arose about the highly relevant deadline – in particular, whether the appointment was kept, especially for the return journey. The lawyers decided commonly upon the agreement between the parties (*id quod actum est*).[47]

In this sense, Modestin stated that the lender took the risk from the day on which *navigare* began:

'D. 22.2.3 (Mod. 4 *reg.*):
In the case of a transmarine loan the risk falls on the creditor from the day on which it is agreed that the ship should leave (the port).'[48]

Actually, '*navem navigare conveniat*' sums up here two relevant points: the day agreed and the day on which the voyage actually started. If sailing was prevented by storm on the appointed day the lender did not take the risk.[49] On the other hand, the lender's risk ended when the ship safely arrived at the port of destination ('*salva nave*', '*si salva navis pervenerit*').[50] The repayment of the loan was immediately due upon arrival, including the high interest.[51]

The common term of every maritime loan, *salva nave*, often needed legal interpretation: it had to be cleared by lawyers when it did occur. It was important to classify the exact date because the assumption of the risk terminated upon arrival – that is, when the loan became due. The borrower (the merchant or shipman who just set foot on land) had to pay back the entire amount of the maritime loan including interest – and upon mooring the ship, their 'insurance' terminated. If the cargo was subsequently lost, be it on a docked ship, on the quay or in a warehouse, *omne periculum* met the borrower alone.

This is the conclusion that was confirmed by Paul as he settled a dispute on a maritime loan with an unusual security arrangement:

'D. 22.2.6 (Paul. 25 *quaest.*):
A *faenerator* (money lender) lent money at a maritime rate and took some goods on the ship as pledge; when the entire debt could not be paid from these goods, he took other goods that were loaded on other ships and pledged to other money lenders, if there was a surplus . . .'[52]

A *faenerator* (moneylender) lent a certain amount of money *usuris maritimis*, on 'maritime interest' (that is, the high interest commonly accepted only in maritime loans). The moneylender insisted on a special mortgage agreement: he demanded a hypothec not only over the goods acquired using the money borrowed but also over all the merchandise belonging to the same merchant carried in any other ship.[53] After the ship with the mortgaged goods went down due to *periculum maris*, the lender wanted to take possession of his debtor's other goods in the other ships (in other words, he wanted to assert his extended lien). The question that arose was whether the moneylender has to bear the entire damage because the ship had been lost within the agreed time. On this, Paul responded that a diminution of the pledge is usually at the expense of the borrower, not the lender. However, the lawyers emphasised that maritime loans were given on terms that the creditor can claim for repayment only if the ship arrives safely within the agreed time. Therefore, the borrower is not liable if the condition does not occur. It means that the creditor's risk terminates alternatively: when the ship safely arrives or when the agreed deadline expires. If the first ship was lost within the time limit the loss of the mortgage therefore fell on the moneylender because the condition failed. Indeed, the creditor could only claim for repayment or for the surplus from the auction of the other goods (mortgaged in other ships) if the condition was fulfilled (that is, the ship arrived safely, *salva navis intra statuta tempora*) but later the mortgaged goods lost value for some other reason. The 'other reasons' could indicate cases such as the loss of the ship after its arrival, while lying at anchor in a port.[54] In this case all damages, including those caused by *vis maior*, fell on the borrower alone. Obviously, the creditor's claim for repayment (and their access to the mortgaged goods) did not automatically expire when the ship was lost.[55]

EXCURSUS: SAUFEIUS' CONTRACT OF CARRIAGE

A similar situation could be assumed in the famous Saufeius case:

> 'D. 19.2.31 (Alf. 5 *dig. a Paulo epit.*):
> Several people shot their grain together into Saufeius' ship, after which the latter returned his share of the grain to one of them out of the common pile and the vessel was lost. The question was asked whether the others could proceed against the *nauta* with respect to their share of the grain by raising an action for *onus aversum*? . . .'[56]

Several merchants poured together their grain into Saufeius' ship[57]; after a sea voyage the ship arrived safely at the port of destination[58] and Saufeius began to hand over the transported grain to each merchant. As it happened, he only managed to return his share to one of them; presumably by measuring the grain out of the ship.[59] Thereupon the ship suddenly foundered.[60] The merchants who lost their grain tried to pass their damage on to the *naukleros*; Alfenus was asked for advice.[61]

The lawyer took a broad approach and evaluated the usual contractual practice with its terms on liability and risk allocation. He emphasised that objects are commonly hired for transport in two ways: either the same object is to be returned (*idem redderetur*) or an object of the same kind (*eiusdem generis*). If the grain was poured together into the ship, the skipper had to deliver to each carrier his share by weighing it out after the ship had arrived safely; he owed not the same thing, only a certain amount out of the grain on board: *eiusdem generis*, although the *naukleros'* obligation to deliver was limited to the goods on his ship.

In commercial practice, it was not customary to stipulate a ranking among carriers; even in Saufeius's case, there is no trace of this. Alfenus dealt with the problem of whether the carriers who lost their grain could raise an *actio oneris aversi* against Saufeius because of misappropriation – and he denied it.[62] Even the freight contract (*locatio conductio*) was excluded as a basis for a lawsuit against the *naukleros*, because this only made him responsible for *culpa*, not for *casus*.[63]

What risks and liabilities were Saufeius's transporters exposed to? Assuming that they were grain merchants it is likely that they financed their cargo by raising maritime loans – and all the grain was lost with the ship. Thinking of the case from this point of view, their great despair is easy to understand. After the safe arrival of the ship the condition was fulfilled, the *faenerator* stopped taking any risk and the maritime loan became due (including its high interest). However, the goods acquired using the money went down with the ship. From this point on, all the risks were on the merchant alone. He had to bear the consequences of his misfortune – very likely the disaster ended in bankruptcy for him.

Summing up: all the cases discussed above demonstrate that carriage by sea and maritime loans were intertwined in many ways and formed a peculiar network for risk sharing and risk allocation. The decisions of the Roman lawyers draw attention to the fact that contract formulas used in everyday life frequently fall back on Hellenistic ideas. For example, Scaevola seems to reflect on non-Roman practice by emphasising that mere informal agreements (*pacta sine stipulatione*) are sufficient for 'expanding the obligation' (*ad augendam obligationem*).[64] In another case, Papinian deals with the remuneration of a slave who accompanied the cargo – the same practice can be observed in Greek maritime loans.[65] Elsewhere, Pomponius and Labeo remark upon the situation in which 'there is no one on the side of the *promissor* who can be sued for a maritime loan'.[66] Obviously, moneylenders used to demand a guarantor, likely a citizen of the community where the contract was signed. However, it was only possible if the borrower was sufficiently known and networked in the city or port in question.[67] If the borrower was a stranger with no local connections, they could hardly have met this expectation. For this case Labeo suggests that a *testatio*, an objectively stylised and witnessed document should be drawn up – as was usual in the Greek law of transmarine loans.[68]

MARITIME LOANS IN ACTION

No wax tablets about *pecunia traiectitia* have survived from ancient Italia. Nevertheless, the writings of the Roman lawyers inform us how such agreements looked like in action. For instance, a transmarine loan is paraphrased in the well-known contract of Callimachus:

> 'D. 45.1.122.1 (Scaev. 28 *dig.*):
> Callimachus took from Stichus, a slave of Seius a maritime loan in the province of Syria for a sea voyage from Berytus to Brentesium. It was lent for the full two hundred days of navigation under pledge and hypothec over the goods purchased at Berytus and to be brought to Brentesium and over those that would be bought at Brentesium and taken on board to Berytus. It was agreed between them, that after Callimachus reached Brentesium he should sail off to Syria before the next *ides* of September with other goods bought and the goods on the ship . . .'[69]

The text was incorporated under the title *De verborum obligationibus* in the Digest, because the most important terms of the contract were confirmed in a *stipulatio* (*obligatio stricti iuris*). It is unclear in which language the legal document was originally drawn up. Undoubtedly, the borrower's stipulation is quoted in Latin, but the basis contract, the *daneion nautikon*, might have been set up in Greek as well.[70] Indeed, even the very first phrases indicate a Hellenistic context: *mutua pecunia nautica* reminds of the Greek terminology of transmarine loans (*nautika, nautikon daneion*).[71] Stichus, a slave of a certain Seius (both typical stock names)[72] was obviously engaged in maritime business. He made a loan to Callimachus who was probably a *nauta* or *emporos* of Greek origin; the money was paid out on the usual terms of transmarine loans (*pecunia nautica*). The contracting parties fixed the entire sea route: from Berytus in Syria to Brentesium in Italy. The loan was granted for the outward and return journey, but for a maximum of 200 days[73]; the latest possible date to set off back was settled for the Ides of September (based on the usual sailing season). If Callimachus failed to sell his goods or to buy new merchandise by then, he is no longer allowed to set sail.[74] Instead of bringing the trip to an end, he should pay the entire amount owed in cash to the lender's representative on board, who was instructed to bring the coins to Rome by land.

It is of particular interest for our topic that the lender had a mortgage over the entire cargo (referred to as *pignus vel hypotheca* in the text).[75] The borrower promised in a stipulation (*cautio*) that he will faithfully adhere to the terms of the agreement (*eaque sic rata fieri fide rogavit . . . promisit*). The stipulation was properly formulated using '*promittere*' instead of the solemn verb *spondere*, which was kept just for Romans.[76] This is a strong indication that at least one of the parties must have been a non-Roman. Scaevola deals with complications due to the delayed return journey (I will not go into that here).[77]

The agreement, merely summarised in D. 45.1.122.1, actually includes more than one legal transaction: a transmarine loan (*pecunia traiectitia*), an extensive mortgage agreement and a verbal obligation (*stipulatio*). The narrative is limited to the relevant facts; dogmatically insignificant details are consequently left out. There is no information about the amount borrowed or the interest agreed. However, the exact sailing route and the latest possible date for the return trip are highlighted. Obviously, these terms were essential for Scaevola's decision, because they marked the limits of the risk allocation fixed in the agreement between the parties. The security by way of *pignus* and *hypotheca* was agreed over the full cargo bought at Berytus and replaced in Brentesium; it actually reflects Greek custom and fits the principle of surrogation.[78] Callimachus' contract confirms that the 'sea law' of the Romans was strongly influenced by trading practices from the Eastern part of the Mediterranean world.[79] The few legal documents reporting on commercial loans from the heyday of the Roman Empire are also mostly preserved on papyrus and in Greek. It seems appropriate, therefore, to look at some of the transmarine loans preserved from fourth century BC Athens.

EXCURSUS: MARITIME LOANS IN FOURTH-CENTURY BC ATHENS

In Demosthenes' speech against Lakritos (oratio 35) the complete text of a *syngraphe* (loan contract) is preserved. A few terms are of high importance for the present topic:

> 'Androkles . . . and Nausicrates lent to Artemon and Apollodorus of Phaselis 3,000 drachmas of silver for a voyage from Athens to Mende or Scione, and from there to Bosporus, and, if they wish, on the left-hand side as far as the Borysthenes, and back to Athens . . . on security of 3,000 Mendaean jars of wine . . . They pledge these, not owing any money to anyone else on this security, nor will they obtain any further loan on it. They will convey back to Athens in the same boat all the goods from the Pontus purchased with proceeds from the outward cargo. If the goods reach Athens safely, the borrowers will pay the accruing money to the lenders in accordance with the agreement within twenty days of their arrival at Athens in full . . . They will place the security intact under the control of the lenders until they pay the accruing money in accordance with the agreement. If they do not pay within the agreed time, the lenders shall be permitted to pledge the pledged goods and to sell them at the prevailing price . . . '[80]

Demosthenes' arguments are focused on the common terms of transmarine loans, as usually agreed between the parties. To summarise the facts: Androkles and his friend Nausicrates gave two brothers, Artemon and Apollodor (both from Phaselos) 3,000 drachmas on the usual terms of transmarine loans. Right from the start, the young borrowers were helped by their brother Lakritos in handling the business: even the deed was designed by him. The money was lent for a round trip Athens–Mendé–Skione–Bosporus–Northern Pontos–Athens and the entire cargo was mortgaged to the moneylenders. In the *syngraphe*, the borrowers undertook to use the 3,000 drachmas to buy 3,000 *keramia* of wine in Mendé and load it into their ship. They also assured the lenders that the cargo would not be mortgaged to any other creditor and that no further loan would be taken out for the same cargo and that Androkles and Nausicrates would remain the sole pledgees for the whole round trip. If the ship returned safely to Athens, capital and interest would be due within twenty days. According to the *syngraphe*, only the value of goods that were lost at sea could be deducted from the amount owed.[81]

Based on the *syngraphe*, a non-possessory pledge arose over all goods brought onto the ship.[82] It was a replacement and a forfeit pledge: all rights of the lender ended with the loss of the goods and the pledge became the property of the lender if the borrower did not repay the money (including interest) within the agreed time after the ship safely arrived.[83] Based on Dem. 32.14, it can be assumed that the lender was allowed to seize the pledged merchandise if the borrower behaved fraudulently – even before the agreed deadline expired.[84]

Artemon and Apollodor promised to secure physical control over the cargo for the lenders as soon as the ship laid anchor and to maintain their control during the twenty days open for repayment. If the borrowers failed to perform, the pledge forfeited to the lenders' property from the date on which the loan became due. The deed does not reveal how physical control might have been taken. However, Demosthenes' arguments assume that the entire cargo had to be immediately unloaded after docking the ship at the port of destination; and this seems to correspond to the usual practice.

Androkles (the plaintiff) repeatedly mentions that the *emporoi* of Athens, who invested their money in maritime trade, gathered impatiently at the port and waited for the arrival of the ships. In the ports all over the Mediterranean world a network of agents operated who observed the movements of the ships and regularly reported on it. By these agents the lenders were warned in good time about every ship approaching. As soon as the ship anchored in Piraeus, the creditors laid hands on the goods pledged to them for their transmarine loans.[85]

If the Phaselites had acted honestly, they would have anchored in Piraeus and immediately unloaded the cargo. The goods would then have been secured in a warehouse in the port district. The borrowers, however, tried instead to perpetrate fraud: they stayed away from the harbour, anchored off in a small bay and hung around (for twenty-five days) the marketplaces with 'samples', likely of the grain they carried on the ship.

Similarly, Demosthenes' speech against Zenothemis (oratio 32) refers to the loading, unloading and storage of grain, as well as to the access of the lenders to the pledged goods. The speech was written for a close relative of the orator, a certain Demon, who lent a larger amount in terms of a transmarine loan to the *emporos* Protos. Protos sailed away in the ship of the *naukleros* Hegestratos to Syracuse on a grain-trading expedition. The wording of the *syngraphe* between Demon and Protos is not preserved, nor did the trial itself take place between the contracting parties.

Demosthenes' speech is rather confusing; it is not easy to understand the complicated story. Summarising the main facts, it can be stated that several *emporoi* (not only Protos) sailed in the same ship, including a certain Zenothemis. They safely reached Syracuse, acquired their merchandise (mostly grain), loaded it into the ship and were about to return to Athens. However, on their way back they were hit by a powerful storm on the open sea;[86] the ship was badly damaged and almost went down (Demon's tale that the ship was holed by the captain himself seems to be fictitious).[87] Due to the storm they had to change course and set in at Cephallenia because the ship had to be repaired (the mast and sails were especially badly damaged). It can be assumed that Zenothemis gave an 'emergency loan' and later, once in Athens, tried to get back his money from his fellow travellers, including Protos.

His claim could be based on Rhodian sea law that stated that a *naukleros* could pass on the costs of repair (especially of the mast and sails) to his carriers because shipmen and merchants travelling in the same ship formed a kind of risk sharing community. For this reason, Zenothemis is likely to have seized the cargo in Piraeus, in the port of destination. How did he end up as the defendant in the trial? His switching from plaintiff to defendant resulted from the special rules of litigation concerning possession/ownership under Greek law. As already mentioned above, Protos initially agreed a mortgage over the entire cargo with Demon, his creditor on terms of a transmarine loan, and Demon's lien extended until capital and interest were returned. This conflict, the competition between different hypothecs, is the real point in the ongoing procedure.

For the present paper, only the events after the arrival of the ship are relevant. The ship was repaired, sailed off from Cephallenia and arrived safely at Piraeus.[88] Demosthenes indicates that all the lenders who provided any funding for the Syracuse voyage immediately rushed to the docking ship.[89] Those who took out maritime loans with security over the merchandise immediately tried to take control of the ship and its cargo. The fellow travellers, on the other hand, whose business was financed by other creditors, tried to get the cargo to a safe place as quickly as possible. Here and elsewhere in the speech it is stressed that the goods were immediately unloaded and brought ashore. It is obvious that the cargo was mainly housed in the surrounding storage facilities, to which the moneylenders were provided with fair access.[90]

The grain purchased using the money lent by Demon was also unloaded and was likely stored in a warehouse. Storage rental offered a reasonable way to borrowers and lenders to ensure that they retained shared access and shared rights over the goods.[91] Protos also followed common practice: after their safe arrival he looked for unloading and storage facilities. It seems that this all happened shortly before Zenothemis tried to get possession of his grain. It is likely that Protos had not yet paid back Demon's transmarine loan and therefore that the twenty days available to him had not yet expired. In any case, Protos acted correctly, by dutifully taking the interests of his creditor, Demon, into consideration.

Zenothemis's intervention, however, messed everything up. His speech has not come down to us, but it can be assumed that he argued in his defence that he lent money for fixing up the ship after the storm in order to facilitate the continuation of the voyage.[92] According to Rhodian sea law, each carrier was obliged to bear their share of repair costs due to *force majeure*. It seems that Protos had yet to pay his share, which explains why Zenothemis broke into the warehouse with legal force and took the grain under his control.[93] In Greek law, a legal dispute about ownership (both for immovables and movables) was conducted by means of a so-called *dike exoules*.[94] If Zenothemis wanted to file an action against Protos as the grain's possessor, he had to enter into possession with (ritual) force: '[i]f the owner denied the intruder's right, he touched him and led him out again' (*exagein, exeillein*).[95] After these formal acts of violence, the intruder could bring a *dike exoules* on account of their 'expulsion'.

Zenothemis, however, when he was claiming the grain, consistently refused to be 'led out' by Protos. The reason was that he did not want to recognise Protos as his opponent in the litigation. He must have known that Protos traded with borrowed money: according to Rhodian sea law the repair costs of a ship could be deducted from the sum payable on a maritime loan. Protos seems to have refused to compensate Zenothemis: that is why Zenothemis wanted to be 'led out' by Demon instead. This, he saw, was his only chance to get at his money: namely, by demanding it from Demon, the lender of the maritime loan.

FINANCING LONG-DISTANCE TRADE IN PTOLEMAIC AND ROMAN EGYPT

The essential terms of maritime loans can also be observed in some papyri from Ptolemaic and Roman Egypt. A fragmentary document, SB III 7169 (second century BC), confirms that risk-bearing by moneylenders was even a common financing model for transmarine or long-distance trade.[96] In this deed, a transmarine loan was lent to five *synploi*, merchants, who planned their voyage in the same ship to the Aromatophoros in the Punt where they wanted to trade in perfume and other luxury items.[97] The money was borrowed for an unusually long period, a whole year. Repayment was due after the ship arrived in an Egyptian port along the Red Sea coast and the moneylenders assumed the risk until this moment. The parties, however, agreed a rather long 'tolerance time' of fifty, seventy, eighty or ninety days[98]: that is, the usual time for crossing the desert and shipping the goods down the Nile to the *emporion* in Alexandria. There are no security agreements in the document: the parties might have fixed a general mortgage in a separate document.[99] However, in line thirteen a phrase can be reconstructed which sounds rather similar to the risk allocation in the Lakritos speech.[100]

A later document, SB XIV 11 850 (= VI 9571), dated 9 Meicher (13 February), AD 149, preserves a bank notice connected with a maritime loan[101] that was issued in Theadelphia in Roman Egypt.[102] A certain Marcus Claudius Sabinus, a representative of a public bank,[103] informs two merchants, Zoilos and Kallimedes, both from Askalon,[104] that their loan is about to be disbursed. Two Roman citizens, Gaius Longinus Celer and Tiberius Claudius Chares, are named as creditors.[105] There are also two further people, Sostratus and Sosus (also from Askalon, co-owners of the ship) who were added to the list of borrowers in line five. So there are a total of four borrowers who, as *synnaukleroi* in the same ship (line six), receive and are jointly liable for a transmarine loan (*daneion nautikon*, line seven).[106] Likely, their trade was carried out with the small ship between Askalon and Alexandria.[107] In line seven, reference is expressly made to a *syngraphe nautike* that served as that basis for the transaction.[108] The bank participated as a paying agent in the business. Lines seven and eight also tell us that a copy of the deed was kept in the bank.[109] As security, the entire cargo and the ship were pledged (lines eight to nine).

A similar arrangement can be assumed as the background to a second papyrus from Roman Egypt (SB XVIII 13167, second century AD).[110] The fragmentary piece records a trading trip financed with transmarine loans: line thirteen mentions a *daneion-syngraphai* that specified the deadline for repayment and was considered the *causa* of the present security deed.

The journey was intended for Muziris on the Indian coast.[111] The borrower promised (after his return) to transport the goods (purchased using the loan proceeds) through the desert to Koptos and store them in the bonded warehouse (lines nine to eleven); which is to say, he was responsible for the land transport after the safe arrival of the ship in a port on the Red Sea.[112] The overland route followed the caravan route to Koptos where the goods were required to be loaded onto a ship and transported down the Nile to Alexandria.

The lender's representative accompanied the transport at every stage and all the warehouse storages were checked by him. He was charged with sealing every storage unit to ensure the safety of the merchandise and the creditor's control: the goods should not be taken away by the borrower nor by third parties (at least until the maritime loan was repaid). Upon arrival in Alexandria, the goods were to be placed again into a storehouse under the seal of the creditor (or his representative), to which he should have ready access. There is a list of merchandise on the verso of the security deed, likely made for the Roman customs authorities.[113]

Unfortunately, the loan contract itself is not preserved. Rather, the document merely relates the detailed security agreement between the parties.[114] For the present topic, the pledge of the merchandise is of high importance, together with the ceaseless control and access of the creditors over the mortgaged goods that were purchased from their money (lines five to nine). The creditors asked that the pledged goods should be placed under their control for the duration of the voyage and the *emporos* promised it solemnly. If the borrower did not perform, the creditor had the right to take possession of the merchandise (line fifteen) and then to sell or re-pledge them at his discretion.[115]

The document also demonstrates that although the goods were under a customs seal between the port of arrival and the *tetarte* in Alexandria,[116] the creditor was still able to affix his private seal to mark his right of disposal (which he could only make use of once the goods had arrived in Alexandria). The transport was organised and paid for by the *emporos*, since the merchandise actually belonged to him (*kyrieia*), though on the strength of his mortgage a primary right of access and disposal belonged to the lender (*chratesis*).

The security deed even regulated the paying of customs and duties: the *tetarte* (25 per cent of the total value) had to be laid out in cash or in kind to the customs authorities in Alexandria. If the *emporos* became insolvent, the lender could stand in for them: they could lay out the *tetarte* to free the goods from the bonded warehouse. There was no opportunity for converting the merchandise into money before all these additional costs had been paid.

It is obvious that financing long-distance trading activities was a complicated affair. An *emporos* needed considerable start-up capital to purchase goods; to pay for oversea and caravan transport; and to lay out (before selling their merchandise) the high import taxes for the Roman authorities. If they were rich enough to pay all of these, they also had to return the transmarine loan and its high interest: until repayment, the goods were controlled by the lender, subject to the mortgage.

A maritime loan could not meet the whole capital demands of such a trading trip by itself. The main purpose of maritime loans was to secure the cargo on the high seas, in order to shift the sea risk (*vis maior*) onto the lender. The *emporos* therefore still needed considerable sums to pay freight costs, customs duties, agents and so forth. These additional costs were financed either from their own assets or from further loans, so-called 'land loans', which were lent at a much lower rate of interest. Maritime trade thus operated through a sophisticated system of internal and external financing. Although the text of SB XVIII 13167 is rather damaged and its interpretation is controversial, it is a valuable document that helps us to understand the economic context in which ancient maritime trade took place. Having these commonly applied business models, which are well documented from the fourth century BC to the second century AD, also throws new light upon the legal documents of the Vesuvian region.

TABULAE POMPEIANAE

The wax tablets from Puteoli are quite distant in terms of time and space from the agreements in Demosthenes' speeches and from the maritime loans on the Red Sea. Nevertheless, a certain continuity can be assumed in the contractual practices that were so closely connected with Mediterranean trade. Suffice it to say that the borrower had twenty days open to repay the maritime loan after the safe arrival of the ship: a custom that finds expression in the Codex Theodosianus, the Novellae of Justinian,[117] and in the *syngraphe* of Lakritos in the fourth century BC. Similarly, the mortgage over the entire cargo and the lender's access to the goods acquired using their money were typical examples of 'general terms' that applied everywhere in the ancient world. In SB XVIII 13167, the precisely regulated transport route from the Red Sea to Alexandria, which was strictly controlled by the creditor or their agent, drew attention to another important characteristic of long-distance trade: along the main routes and in the frequented ports, well-built and well-guarded warehouses were available for *naukleroi* and merchants to use. The remains of a similar infrastructure, foundations and wells of big *horrea*, privately or publicly owned, have been discovered in Puteoli, Ostia and Portus as well.[118]

TPSULP. 45: HESYCHUS RENTS SOME STORAGE PLACE IN PUTEOLI

Under *TPSulp.* 45, G Camodeca re-edited three *tabulae* that provide a well-preserved text referring to a rental agreement. The triptych, sealed by witnesses,[119] was drawn up in Puteoli on 2 July, AD 37.[120] The *scriptura interior*, the inner writing with its protected text, is on the second page of the first panel and on the third page of the second panel. The *scriptura exterior* repeats and makes the whole agreement freely accessible. Comparing the two versions, significant differences can be observed: the outer script was written in more or less correct Latin, while the inner script shows conspicuous vulgarisms. The difference can be explained through certain peculiarities of Mediterranean notarial practice: commonly, the outer script was prepared by an educated, well-skilled scribe while the inner script was written by the party themselves: they just copied or wrote down after dictation. In the following I will cite from the *scriptura exterior*.[121] The document is a *chirographum*, a subjectively styled deed written in the first person singular.[122]

The *tabulae* present a contract of letting and hiring concerning some kind of storing facility in Puteoli: '*Diognetus . . . scripsi iussu Cypaeri domini mei coram ipso me locasse Hesycho*'. Diognetus, the slave of a certain C. Novius Cypaerus, recorded that he had let to Hesychus (on the orders of his master) some storage rooms in the *horrea Bassiana*.[123] The reference *iussu domini* indicates that the slave contracted in the name of his master.[124] The document concerns the business of Cypaerus: all the rents flow to him. Diognetus acted directly on behalf of his master, not out of his *peculium*. The other party was also unfree: Hesychus, the slave of a freedman called Euenus Primianus (lines five and six) hired on behalf of his master two storerooms for some grain on the upper and lower floor of the warehouse called *Bassiana*.[125]

There were different technologies used for storing grain: either the grain was poured together, mixed with that of other customers on terms that the same amount must be returned (*eiusdem generis*); or the grain was poured into separate compartments when the same amount from the same compartment must be returned (that is, 'beschränkte Gattungsschuld'); or (as a further possibility) the grain was stored in sacks and the same thing, the same sacks with the same grain, had to be returned (*eandem rem*).[126]

In *TPSulp.* 45, one learns that a large quantity of Alexandrian wheat was brought into the upper storeroom (no. 12) of the *horrea Bassiana* (the deed does not specify an exact quantity). Storage room no. 12 must have been a lockable cell into which the grain was probably poured in.[127] When due, the *horrearius* had to return the same wheat (*eandem rem*). However, his liability could be rather different depending on the method of delivery: whether the grain had to be measured out or just picked up by the tenant.[128] Lines nine and ten describe the second storage room: a vaguely shaped place on the lower floor, between the pillars, where 200 sacks were brought in filled with legumes; again, the *horrearius* had to return the same sacks (*eandem rem*).[129]

'*Quod pignori accepit hac die a Caio Novio Euno*': now we read that both wheat and legumes were pledged, which indicates that they must have served as real security for an unspecified debt (lines nine to ten and thirteen to fourteen). The parties agreed on a *merces* of one *sestertius* per month: probably it was a symbolic sum necessary for the effectiveness of the bilateral contract of letting and hiring (that is, a peppercorn rent).[130]

To summarise: C. Novius Cypaerus was in the storage business, making a profit by renting out storage space. His slave, Diognetus, stood by his side to do the daily routine work. *TPSulp.* 45 was issued by Diognetus. Storage spaces were rented to Hesychus, the slave of the (freed) Euenus Primianus. The grain stored there actually belonged to C. Novius Eunus, from whom Hesychus received it as a pledge ('*quod pignori accepit . . . quos pignori accepit ab aeodem Eunum*').

There are further documents in the archive that inform us about some credit transactions that took place in the background. Two of the triptychs were drawn up about loans: one on 18 June and another on 2 July. These documents confirm that Hesychus lent money twice to C. Novius Eunus and in both deeds Alexandrian wheat and legumes were given as security and stored in the *horrea Bassiana*. The first loan came down in *TPSulp.* 51, which was documented on 18 June, AD 37. According to this document C. Novius Eunus received 10,000 sesterces from Hesychus. The second loan was drawn up two weeks later, on 2 July (edited in *TPSulp.* 52), in which he borrowed a further 3,000 sesterces from the same lender. In the first loan document, no deadline for repayment was set; the borrower even promised that he would immediately return the sum borrowed at any time if requested. The parties agreed also a real security over 7,000 *modii* of Alexandrian wheat and 4,000 *modii* of sacked legumes ('*pignoris arrabonisve nomine*').[131]

The link to the storage rental in *TPSulp.* 45 is apparent. However, the suggestion that the grain was only stored in the warehouse for the first time on 2 July, with the second loan agreement, is not convincing. It is likely that C. Novius Eunus, a grain merchant, brought his grain much earlier, immediately after the arrival of the ship and its unloading near to the *horrea Bassiana*.[132] In my view, it must have happened before he borrowed the first loan, which is to say the 10,000 sesterces from Hesychus. Unfortunately, no documents concerning this legal transaction have been preserved.

There is, however, a remarkable phrase – '*penes me*' – in *TPSulp.* 51 (line five of *tabula* three) which is mostly understood to mean at that time C. Novius Eunus still had the pledged grain 'with him'.[133] In a strict sense, '*penes me*' is not a technical legal term; it cannot be unequivocally linked to possession or ownership under Roman law. It seems that it just meant 'with me' as opposed to 'with you, under your control'. It might have simply specified that the moneylender, Euenus Primianus, did not have yet a physical control over the pledged goods (we will soon return to this point).

In the second loan, written on 2 July, C. Novius Eunus borrowed a further 3,000 sesterces from the same lender, Euenus Primianus (*TPSulp.* 52). The loan was also cashed in this case by his slave Hesychus. The parties agreed a real security over the same grain and legumes, again stored in the *horrea Bassiana*. It is explicitly stated that the 3,000 should be due in addition to the 10,000 sesterces already borrowed.[134]

The wording of the two loans seems almost identical. However, there is a striking difference in the terms that fix the pledge: where *TPSulp*. 51 has '*dedi ei pignoris arrabnisve nomine . . . quae omnia reposita habeo penes me*', *TPSulp*. 52 has only '*dedi ei pignoris . . . quot est positum*'. The different wording is a strong argument that the physical control over the pledged grain must have been changed with the second loan.[135] On 18 June, the borrower, C. Novius Eunus still referred to the grain as *penes me* (*TPSulp*. 51), but this phrase is missing in the second loan that was drawn up two weeks later (*TPSulp*. 52). This does not appear to have been a coincidence: on 2 July, a rental agreement was written in which Hesychus, the lender's slave, was already named as a tenant (*TPSulp*. 45). Apparently, the second loan was paid out on the condition that the lender was entitled to direct access to the pledged grain.[136] It must be considered that the grain was in the *horrea Bassiana* the entire time – only the tenant's name was exchanged.[137]

Obviously, warehouse rentals were common and useful tools to secure free access for moneylenders to the goods pledged to them.[138] Under Roman law, a tenant was never given any possessory right – that is, no *civilis possessio*; no legal protection. This lack of protection notwithstanding, being a tenant secured for the lender an unhindered and exclusive access to the storerooms where the pledged goods were kept.[139] The lender's factual position was considerably strengthened, since they were able to keep others away from the pledged property, including the merchant themselves.[140] Transactions like this were commonly documented by a set of deeds. It can be assumed that, in addition to the loan and rental agreement, a security deed with a *conventio/datio pignoris* was also drawn up for Hesychus (or more precisely for Euenus Primianus, in our case).

SULPICIUS FAUSTUS RENTS STORAGE ROOMS IN PUTEOLI

TPSulp. 46 also records an agreement on rental of storerooms in a *horreum*, the *tabulae ceratae* having been dated 13 March, AD 40.[141] The triptych is rather damaged. In the following, we will consider the better-preserved *scriptura exterior* (Tab. III, pag. 5).[142] A certain Nardus, slave of Publius Annius Seleucus, wrote on behalf of his *dominus*, who was not able to write (lines three to five), that he let some storage rooms in the *horrea Barbatiana*.[143] The phrase '*scripsi me locasse coram et iussu Seleuci domini mei*' states that the slave acted as an intermediary in his owner's business. C. Sulpicius Faustus was the other party in the contract, a representative of the older generation of the Sulpicii. The banker hired some storage space in the *horrea Barbatiana* where 13,000 *modii* of Alexandrian wheat was to be kept. The average cargo of a grain ship at that time was between 10,000 and 50,000 *modii* (about 68 to 340 tons).[144] It means that the grain stored by C. Sulpicius Faustus could have made up the entire cargo of a smaller ship.

Nardus promised that the grain would be measured out by his owner and his slaves when it became due: '*quae admetietur dominus meus cum servis suis*' (lines nine to ten). It can be assumed that that the grain was just poured together in a locked space for the purpose of storage.[145] The method of returning it by weighing out is reminiscent of similar clauses that were widespread and commonly used in freight contracts all over the Mediterranean world.[146] In freight contracts, weighing out the cargo at the port of destination referred to an implied risk allocation: the risk of quantity (loss from the grain during transport) was passed on to the *naukleros*.

In *TPSulp*. 46, the term indicated the liability of the *horrearius*[147]: he had to bear any loss of quantity, due, for example, to any damage that occurred during storage.[148] A distinction has to be made between this special risk distribution (regarding damage affecting quality during storage) and the general risk-bearing clause agreed among the parties (as it has come down in *TPSulp*. 79); we shall come back to this soon.

There is no time limit in the rental concluded between Publius Annius Seleucus (represented through Nardus) and C. Sulpicius Faustus. On the other hand, a monthly rent of 100 sesterces was fixed, which appears to have been a usual market price, compared with the one sesterce agreed upon in *TPSulp*. 45.

Some documents of the archive provide further information on the economic and financial background of this business. On the same day on which the storage place was hired, L. Marius Iucundus (a freedman of Dida) borrowed 20,000 sesterces from C. Sulpicius Faustus. However, there is neither a deadline nor a pledge mentioned in the loan contract: these terms were fixed in separate documents.

Soon, just two days after the first two deeds (rental and loan), a security agreement was concluded and drawn up between the same parties (*TPSulp*. 79).[149] In the phrase '*Scripsi me dedisse Caio Sulpicio Fausto pignoris nomine . . .* ', L. Marius Iucundus declared that he had given C. Sulpicius Faustus a pledge of over 13,000 *modii* of Alexandrian wheat stored in the storage place no. 26 of the *horrea Barbatiana*. There is also a reference to the *causa*: that is, the debt of 20,000 sesterces documented in a *chirographum* – '*quae per chirographum scripsi me ei debere*' (lines seven to eight) – contained in a loan deed (*TPSulp*. 53).

TPSulp. 79 also specified an exact deadline for repayment: '*si idibus Mais primis ea HS . . . quae supra scripta sunt, non dedero, solvero, satisve fecero*' (line nine).[150] It is striking that the loan document (*TPSulp*. 53) did not mention any deadline: only the security deed (written two days later) set the day of performance (15 May). L. Marius Iucundus therefore only took a short-term loan. Probably the two months were intended to serve as bridging finance that was necessary for some trading business of his.

Still more can be said about the money transactions between L. Marius Iucundus and C. Sulpicius Faustus. As we saw above, the portfolio consisted of several documents, each of which only recorded those details that were relevant to the transaction at hand (in other words, the details that had to be proved in a possible trial). The *chirographum* about the loan kept only the declaration that 20,000 sesterces were received and must be returned: '*scripsi me accepisse et debere*' (lines three to four). Certainly, the parties were aware that a pledge would also be agreed in due course and a separate document would be drawn up on that account. This explains why they did not care about fixing a deadline in the loan contract. The day of repayment was important above all for the security deed because the creditor's right to alienate was linked to it: when performance failed, the creditor was entitled to sell the pledged objects, for example by putting them up for auction: '*sub praecone de condicione pignoris . . . vendere*' (line eleven).[151]

There is a remarkable clause in lines fourteen to fifteen: '*Utique id triticum, quo de agitur, omni periculo esset meo heredisve mei*'. L. Marius Iucundus explicitly declares that all the risk regarding the stored grain is on him alone (or on his legal successors). On the other hand, as we have seen above, *periculum quantitates* means that any reduction of the quantity without fault was passed on to the *horrearius* by the rental agreement (*TPSulp.* 46). Comparing the two deeds it can be assumed that the borrower's risk in *TPSulp.* 79 (in the *pignoris datio*) related to the full loss of the pledged property while *TPSulp.* 46 conforms with the common rules of liability and risk-bearing in letting and hiring, which fixed the liability of the *horrearius* for *custodia*. Regarding the '*omni periculo esset meo*' clause the possibility could be considered that the parties wanted to exclude the impact of Greek legal concepts. Under Greek law, with the loss of the pledged goods the entire debt also expires. Not so in *TPSulp.* 79, where the loss of the pledged goods had to be borne by the debtor.[152]

Let us shortly reconstruct again the sequence of events: L. Marius Iucundus stored 13,000 *modii* of Alexandrian wheat in Puteoli, in the *horrea Barbatiana*. The quantity suggests that it may have been a shipload that had just arrived from Alexandria. Presumably, the cargo was brought ashore immediately following on the safe arrival of the ship: the *saccarii* unloaded and the *mensores* measured it immediately.[153] Likely, the merchant L. Marius Iucundus stored the grain in a warehouse in the port district, in the *horrea Barbatiana*. It can be assumed that he concluded a *locatio conductio* with the *horrearius* or with his agent: unfortunately, this document has not survived. The ship should have arrived in Puteoli shortly before the events recorded in *TPSulp.* 53 and 79 (*chirographum* of a loan and pledge over the wheat) took place. In any case, it is certain that L. Marius Iucundus received 20,000 sesterces as a *mutuum* on 13 March, which were paid out by C. Sulpicius Faustus. At the same time, the storage space in which the grain was kept was hired by the moneylender. Two days later, a security deed (*pignoris datio*) was also drawn up in which the pledge, the due date and the lender's right to alienate were recorded.

TO SUMMARISE

Most scholars who have dealt with the credit transactions of C. Novius Eunus and L. Marius Iucundus have not considered the possibility that the pledged grain could happen to be merchandise from overseas trade. As we have seen above, overseas trade was mainly financed by transmarine loans. It is likely that the grain stored in the *horrea Bassiana* and *Barbatiana* that was used as security for the purpose of raising loans was originally bought in Alexandria with *pecunia traiecticia* and shipped to Puteoli. Certainly, maritime loans have left no direct traces in the legal transactions preserved in the archive of the Sulpicii. However, the documentary sources which came down from Egypt, especially the Muziris papyrus, imply that financing by transmarine loans was a common practice in long-distance trade. Why should it not also be assumed that C. Novius Eunus and L. Marius Iucundus used outside money received as transmarine loans in their grain businesses in Alexandria? The cases introduced above have shown that storage facilities that were available for hire may have played an important role in the storage and preservation of real security. There is only one further step needed to connect the grain cargo from Alexandria with bridging loans and storage rentals as security.

Recently, E Chevreau has suspected maritime loans in the background of *TPSulp.* 45, 46, 51, 52, 53, and 79.[154] She argued that Euenus Primianus originally lent 10,000 sesterces as a transmarine loan to Caius Novius Eunus and that the 3,000 sesterces documented in *TPSulp.* 52 should be interpreted as the interest owed.[155] However, her argument is not really convincing. Above all, it is unclear why the interest rate of a single *daneion nautikon* at the time of Demosthenes can apply for maritime loans in Puteoli in the first century AD.[156]

However, a network of transmarine and land loans as described above could provide a suitable explanation for hiring storage places in hedging transactions. When C. Novius Eunus and L. Marius Iucundus purchased their cargo of Alexandrian wheat out of *pecunia traiecticia* in Alexandria, the grain must have been pledged to the moneylenders in the manner typical of a *daneion nautikon*. Callimachus' contract confirms that this practice was also familiar to the Romans, and, in particular, to merchants and lawyers as well.[157] Scaevola calls the pledge agreed '*pignus vel hypotheca*'. U Von Lübtow has already underlined that the jurists may have deliberately addressed the Greek law of hypothec, which commonly applied in maritime loans all over the ancient Mediterranean world.[158] When the grain was bought out of the proceeds of maritime loans and shipped from Alexandria to Puteoli, the lender's (non-possessory) lien lasted until capital and interest were returned.

The Muziris papyrus demonstrates that the pledged goods were kept under the control of the lender or his representative during the whole trip. The cargo was even sealed by him to prevent any theft or embezzlement. In addition, the parties even agreed that the lender would pay the tax (*tetarte*) if the *emporos* became insolvent (though he was entitled to auction the goods in return). The contract's contemplation of the possibility that the lender might struggle to maintain his liquidity combined with the considerable additional costs (freight and so forth) associated with long-distance trading indicate that *emporoi* often depended upon interim financing (or bridging loans). After the safe arrival of the ship at the port of destination, the first debts to be satisfied were the maritime loans.

In Demosthenes' speech against Lakritos we learned that the moneylenders waited impatiently in Piraeus for ships returning from long-distance trading expeditions, in order to get the cargo – which was pledged for a *daneion nautikon* – under their control. The *faeneratores* of Puteoli may have acted in a similar way. The warehouses of Piraeus played a practical role in exercising physical control – as described, for example, in the Zenothemis speech. This speech also confirms that the parties sometimes shared access: Protos, the borrower, unloaded his grain and brought it to a warehouse – he must have hired some storage place. The storage grain was 'with him', which means that he had the right to dispose of the property (*kyrieia*). However, because the grain was bought out of a maritime loan lent by Demon to Protos, the business was financed with outside money, which meant that Demon kept *chratesis* (some kind of ownership) over the merchandise and the right of access. Zenothemis wisely refused to recognise Protos as defendant in the ongoing trial. He knew that it was more advantageous for him to arrange the ritual act of 'intruding with force – being led out' with Demon, in order to file a *dike exoules*. *Chratesis* and *kyrieia* were divided between lender and borrower under Greek law. Entering into the hired storerooms would have brought factual control for Zenothemis – but it cannot be equated with *possessio* under Roman law.

Hiring storage facilities for the pledged grain was also closely connected with real security in the archive of the Sulpicii. In this case, the link to overseas trading can be easily implied. In my view, a slightly different story must be assumed in the background of the two portfolios (that of C. Novius Eunus and that of L. Marius Iucundus). *TPSulp.* 45 and 51/52 record two consecutive loans (HS 10,000 and 3,000), each of which was raised on real security. The first loan was drawn up on 18 June, the second on 2 July. The storage room was not hired by the lender until the second loan, dated 2 July, was drawn up. The two weeks between the first loan and the second, when the lender was given access by hiring the storage place, could be reasonably explained by assuming a transmarine loan, lent by a third party, in the background. On 18 June, C. Novius Eunus could even write that the grain was 'with him' (*penes me*). He stated neither his ownership nor his possession in the sense of Roman law but used a rather non-technical term, '*penes me*'. The seemingly untechnical phrase can be explained with reference to the impact of Hellenistic legal ideas: C. Novius Eunus had not yet paid back the maritime loan, therefore his rights *in rem* were still uncertain. In terms of Greek law, the lender still had the better title (*chratesis*) based on the principle of surrogation and also the right of access established by the factual control that he exercised over the pledged goods (as we saw in the Muziris papyrus). C. Novius Eunus, therefore, could only offer a contractually fixed pledge to Euenus Primianus, who lent him a regular ('land') loan. With the HS 10,000 borrowed, C. Novius Eunus was able to return the maritime loan, which must have been due.[159] Then followed a period of two weeks when he must have tried to get rid of his grain at a reasonable price. The events afterwards suggest that he did not succeed: on 2 July, he needed a second loan and had to cede the rent (the storage place with the grain pledged) to Hesychus, the slave of the moneylender Euenus Primianus. In the second loan, the lender apparently insisted upon having factual control over the pledged merchandise, which had since become unencumbered (that is, free from lien).[160]

The credit transaction of L. Marius Iucundus (*TPSulp.* 46, 53, and 79) seems
somewhat different. On 13 March, he received a loan of HS 20,000 and at the
same time ceded his storage room rent to the moneylender, C. Sulpicius Faustus. Neither the loan document nor the warehouse rent mentioned a lien. Two
days later, on 15 March, the parties issued a security deed that fixed all details
of the lien. In these transactions, the grain merchant L. Marius Iucundus faced
the banker C. Sulpicius Faustus. Although the present loan between them was
a regular ('land') loan, the context suggests a previous maritime loan – in my
view with a third party moneylender whose name is not known. It is likely that
the (hastily) withdrawn HS 20,000 were needed to repay a transmarine loan. It
seems that the debt was paid immediately; perhaps the *faenerator* (the lender of
the maritime loan) had an account in the bank of the Sulpicii and the HS 20,000
(just borrowed) were immediately credited to his account. With performance
the hypothec over the grain expired. That is why L. Marius Iucundus was able
to offer the factual control over the grain to C. Sulpicius Faustus at once: the
banker who was one of the parties to the contract of letting and hiring. Actually, the banker's strong position is a good argument that the pre-lien (out of the
transmarine loan) had already expired. It also explains why C. Sulpicius Faustus
was registered as a tenant on the same day as the one on which C. Novius Eunus
received the loan.

In any case, the two portfolios have in common that hiring facilities where
pledged grain was stored were important, practical tools that enabled moneylenders to practise factual control. One is left with the impression that the parties
did not necessarily proceed under the elaborate rules of Roman law.[161] In many
respects, the theory and practice of legal transactions entered into in the context
of maritime trade were borrowed from Greek law, which had a different approach
to ownership and possession. In the Sulpicius archive, the considerable impact of
Greek legal thinking on notarial practice can be readily traced. The moneylenders
of Puteoli do not seem to have particularly cared for *possessio* and the operation of
the *actio Serviana*: rather, they were content with the factual control achieved by
hiring the storerooms with the pledged property, because it gave them exclusive
access to the merchandise. There, the grain was kept safe by the *horrearius* who
would not allow access to anyone except the tenant.

BIBLIOGRAPHY

Abatino, B. (2012), 'Pignoris arrabonisve nomine in TPSulp. 51 (TPN 43): A case
    of diglossia?', *RHD* 80, pp. 311–328.
Adams, C. (2007), *Land Transport in Roman Egypt. A Study of Economics and
    Administration in a Roman Province* (Oxford: Oxford University Press).
Adams, C. (2012), 'Transport', in W. Scheidel (ed), *The Cambridge Companion to
    the Roman Economy* (Cambridge: Cambridge University Press), pp. 218–240.

Alzon, C. (1965), *Problèmes relatifs à la location des entrepôts en droit romain* (Paris: Cujas).

Ankum, H. (1996), 'Observations sur le prêt romain, sujet cher à Henryk Kupiszewski', in W. Wolodkiewicz and M. Zablocka (eds), *Le droit romain et le monde contemporain: mélanges à la mémoire de Henryk Kupiszewski* (Warsaw: University of Warsaw), pp. 59–68.

Arnaud, P. (2005), *Les routes de la navigation antique. Itinéraires en Méditerranée* (Paris: Errance).

Biscardi, A. (1974), *Actio pecuniae traiecticiae: contributo alla dottrina delle clausole penali*, 2nd edn (Turin: Giappichelli).

Broekaert, W. (2017), 'Conflicts, Contract Enforcement and Business Communities in the Archive of the Sulpicii', in M. Flohr and A. Wilson (eds), *The Economy of Pompeii* (Oxford: Oxford University Press), pp. 389–414.

Camodeca, G. (1994), 'Puteoli porto annonario e il commercio di grano in età imperiale', in *Le Ravitaillement en blé de Rome et des centres urbains des débuts de la République jusqu'au Haut-Empire. Actes du colloque international de Naples, 14–16 Février 1991* (Rome: École française de Rome), pp. 103–128.

Camodeca, G. (1999), *Tabulae Pompeianae Sulpiciorum. Edizione critica dell'archivio puteolano dei Sulpicii* (Rome: Quasar).

Camodeca, G. (2001), 'Nuove testimonianze sul commercio marittimo puteolano', in P. Gianfrotta and F. Maniscalco (eds), *Forma maris. Forum internazionale di archeologia subacquea* (Naples: Massa), pp. 85–94.

Candy, P. (2020), 'Parallel developments in Roman law and maritime trade during the Late republic and Early Principate', *JRA* 33, pp. 53–72.

Candy, P. (2021), '"Judging beyond the sandal": Law and rhetoric in D. 19,2,31 (Alf. 5 dig. a Paulo epit.)', *ZRG RA* 138, pp. 310–337.

Casson, L. (1956), 'New Light on Maritime Loans', *Eos* 48(2), pp. 89–93.

Casson, L. (1971), *Ships and Seamanship in the Ancient World* (Princeton, NJ: Princeton University Press).

Casson, L. (1986), 'P. Vindob. G 40822 and the Shipping of Goods from India', *Bulletin of the American Society of Papyrologists* 23, pp. 73–79.

Casson, L. (1990), 'New Light on Maritime Loans: P. Vindob. G 40822', *ZPE* 84, pp. 195–206.

Casson, L. (1991), 'Ancient Naval Technology and the Route to India', in V. Begley and R.D. De Puma (eds), *Roma and India. The Ancient Sea Trade* (Madison, WI: University of Wisconsin Press), pp. 8–11.

Chevreau, E. (2008), 'La *traiecticia pecunia*: un mode de financement du commerce international', *Mémoires de la Société pour l'Histoire du Droit et des institutions des anciens pays bourguignons, comtois et romans* 65, pp. 37–47.

Chevreau, E. (2009), 'La pratique du gage dans les Tabulae Pompeianae Sulpiciorum', in H. Altmeppen et al. (eds), *Festschrift für Rolf Knütel zum 70. Geburtstag* (Heidelberg: CF Müller), pp. 183–196.

Cohen, E. (1992), *Athenian Economy and Society. A Banking Perspective* (Princeton, NJ: Princeton University Press).

Crook, J.A. (1976), *Law and Life of Rome. 90 B.C. – A.D. 212* (New York: Cornell University Press).

De Romanis, F. (2014), 'Time to repay a maritime loan: A note on SB XVII 7169 and SB XVIII 13167 recto', *Sileno* 40, pp. 73–89.

Finkenauer, Th. (2018), 'Drittwirkende pacta im klassischen Recht', *ZRG RA* 135, pp. 178–260.

Fiori, R. (1999), *La definizione della 'locatio conductio'* (Naples: Jovene).

Fiori, R. (2018), 'L'allocazione del rischio nei contratti relativi al trasporto', in E. Lo Cascio and D. Mantovani (eds), *Diritto romano e economia. Due modi di pensare e organizzare il mondo (nei primi tre secoli dell'Impero)* (Pavia: Cedant), pp. 507–567.

Gröschler, P. (2008), 'Die Mittel der Kreditsicherung in den tabulae ceratae', in K. Verboven, K. Vandorpe, and V. Chankowski (eds), *Pistoi dia tén technén. Bankers, Loans and Archives in the Ancient World. Studies in honour of R. Bogaert* (Leuven: Peeters), pp. 301–319.

Harrauer, H. and Sijpesteijn, P.J. (1985), 'Ein neues Dokument zu Roms Indienhandel. P. Vindob. G 40822', *Anzeiger der philosophisch-historischen Klasse / Österreichische Akademie der Wissenschaften* 122, pp. 124–155.

Horden, P. and Purcell, N. (2000), *The Corrupting Sea: A Study of Mediterranean History* (Oxford: Oxford University Press).

Jakab, É. (2000), 'Vectura pro mutua: Überlegungen zu Tab. Pomp. 13 und Ulp. D. 19,2,15,6', *ZRG RA* 117, pp. 244–273.

Jakab, É. (2006), 'Vertragsformulare im Imperium Romanum', *ZRG RA* 123, pp. 71–101.

Jakab, É. (2011), 'Cheirographon in Theorie und Praxis', in K.H. Muscheler (ed), *Römische Jurisprudenz–Dogmatik, Überlieferung, Rezeption. Festschrift für Detlef Liebs zum 75. Geburtstag* (Berlin: Duncker and Humblot), pp. 275–292.

Jakab, É. (2014a), 'Sponsoren und Athleten im römischen Recht: Das Ausbildungsdarlehen der Athleten', in K. Harter-Uibopuu and Th. Kruse (eds), *Sport und Recht in der Antike* (Vienna: Austrian Science Fund), pp. 249–274.

Jakab, É. (2014b), 'Horrea, sûretés et commerce maritime dans les archives des Sulpicii', in J. Hallebeek et al. (eds), *Inter cives necnon peregrinos. Essays in honour of Boudewijn Sirks* (Göttingen: V&R Unipress), pp. 331–365.

Kränzlein, A. (1963), *Eigentum und Besitz im griechischen Recht des fünften und vierten Jahrhunderts v.Chr.* (Berlin: Duncker and Humblot).

Krämer, G. (2007), *Das besitzlose Pfand. Entwicklungen in der römischen Republik und im frühen Prinzipat* (Cologne: Böhlau).

Krampe, Ch. (1995), 'Der Seedarlehensstreit des Callimachus', in R. Feenstra (ed), *Collatio Iuris Romani, études dedieés à Hans Ankum I* (Amsterdam: J.C. Gieben), pp. 207–222.

Lohsse, S. (2016), 'Vom Seedarlehen zur Versicherung in der mittelalterlichen Rechtswissenschaft', *ZRG RA* 133, pp. 372–399.

von Lübtow, U. (1976), 'Das Seedarlehen des Callimachus', in D. Medicus and H.H. Seiler (eds), *Festschrift für M. Kaser zum 70. Geburtstag*, (Munich: Beck), pp. 329–349.

Macqueron, J. (1979), 'Deux contrats d'entrepôts du premier siècle ap. J.-C.: T.Pomp. 7 et 44', in Études offertes à Pierre Kayser (Aix-en-Provence: Presses universitaires d'Aix-Marseille), pp. 199–212.

Martini, R. (2015), 'La custodia di merci dell'horrearius: A proposito di *CIL* VI 33747', *ZRG RA* 132, pp. 154–180.

Meyer, E.A. (2004), *Legitimacy and Law in the Roman World. Tabulae in Roman Belief and Practice* (Cambridge: Cambridge University Press).

Morelli, F. (2011), 'Dal Mar Rosso ad Alessandria. Il verso (ma anche il recto) del «papiro di Muziris» (SB XVIII 13167)', *Tyche* 26, pp. 199–233.

Pellecchi, L. (2018), 'Dimensione economica e azione della giurisprudenza il caso delle garanzie reali', in E. Lo Cascio and D. Mantovani (eds), *Diritto romano e economia. Due modi di pensare e organizzare il mondo (nei primi tre secoli dell'Impero)* (Pavia: Cedant), pp. 445–505.

du Plessis, P.J. (2006), 'Between Theory and Practice: New Perspectives on the Roman Law of Letting and Hiring', *The Cambridge Law Journal* 65(2), pp. 423–437.

Pozsonyi, N. (2018), *Dologi hitelbiztosítékok az ügyleti gyakorlatban. Kauteláris praxis a préklasszikus és a klasszikus korszakban* (Szeged: Iurisperitus K., Pólay E. Alapítvány).

Pringsheim, F. (1916), *Der Kauf mit fremdem Geld. Studien über die Bedeutung der Preiszahlung für den Eigentumserwerb nach griechischem und römischem Recht* (Leipzig: Verlag von Veit).

Pringsheim, F. (1950), *The Greek Law of Sale* (Weimar: Böhlaus Nachfolger).

Pryor, H. (1988), *Geography, Technology and War: Studies in the Maritime History of the Mediterranean, 649–1571* (Cambridge: Cambridge University Press).

Purpura, G. (1987), 'Ricerche in tema di prestito maritimo', *AUPA* 39, pp. 189–337.

Purpura, G. (2014), 'Il cheirembolon e il caso di Saufeio: responsabilità e documentazione nel trasporto maritime romano', *AUPA* 57, pp. 129–151.

Rathbone, D. (1997), 'Prices and price-formation in Roman Egypt', in J. Andreau, P. Briant, and R. Descat (eds), *Economie antique. Prix et formation de prix dans les économies antiques* (Saint-Bertrand-de Comminges: Musée archéologique) pp. 183–244.

Rathbone, D. (2000), 'The Muziris papyrus (SB XVIII 13167): Financing Roman trade with India', *Bulletin Société Archeologie d'Alexandrie* 46, pp. 39–50.

Rathbone, D. (2003), 'The financing of maritime commerce in the Roman Empire, I-II AD', in E. Lo Cascio (ed), *Credito e moneta nel mondo romano* (Bari: Cacucci), pp. 197–229.

Rathbone, D. (2009), 'Merchant networks in the Greek world: The impact of Rome', in I. Malkin, C. Constantakopoulou, and K. Panagopoulou (eds), *Greek and Roman Networks in the Mediterranean* (New York: Routledge), pp. 299–310.

Rathbone, D. and Temin, P. (2008), 'Financial intermediation in first-century AD Rome and eighteenth-century England', in K. Verboven, K. Vandorpe, and V. Chankowski (eds), *Pistoi dia tén technén. Bankers, Loans and Archives in the Ancient World. Studies in honour of R. Bogaert* (Leuven: Peeters), pp. 371–419.

Rickman, G. (1980), *The Corn Supply of Ancient Rome* (Oxford: Oxford University Press).

Rickman, G. (1971), *Roman Granaries and Grain Buildings* (Cambridge: Cambridge University Press).

Rohde, D. (2012), *Zwischen Individuum und Stadtgemeinde. Die Integration von Collegia in Hafenstädten* (Mainz: Verlag Antike).

Rougé, J. (1966), *Recherches sur l'organisation du commerce en Méditerranée sous l'Empire romain* (Paris: S.E.V.P.E.N).

Schanbacher, D. (2006), 'Zu Ursprung und Entwicklung des römischen Pfandrechts', *ZRG RA* 123, pp. 49–70.

Schuster, S. (2005), *Das Seedarlehen in den Gerichtsreden des Demosthenes. Mit einem Ausblick auf die weitere historische Entwicklung des Rechtsinstitutes: dáneion nautikón, fenus nauticum und Bodmerei* (Berlin: Duncker & Humblot).

Sidebotham, S.E. (1991), 'Ports of the Red Sea and the Arabia-India Trade', in V. Begley and R.D. De Puma (eds), *Roma and India. The Ancient Sea Trade* (Oxford: Oxford University Press), pp. 12–38.

Sirks, A.J.B. (1991), *Food for Rome. The Legal Structure of the Transportation and Processing of Supplies for the Imperial Distributions in Rome and Constantinople* (Amsterdam: J.C. Gieben).

Sirks, A.J.B. (2002), 'Sailing in the off-season with reduced financial risk', in J.J. Aubert and A.J.B. Sirks (eds), *Speculum iuris. Roman Law as a Reflection of Social and Economic Life in Antiquity* (Ann Arbor, MI: The University of Michigan Press), pp. 134–150.

Sirks, A.J.B. (2016), 'Chirographs: negotiable instruments?', *ZRG RA* 133, pp. 265–285.

Stroud, R.S. (1998), *The Athenian Grain-Tax Law of 374/3 BC* (Princeton, NJ: The American School of Classical Studies at Athens).

Thomas, J.A.C. (1959), 'Custodia and horrea', *RIDA* 6, pp. 371–383.

Thomas, J.A.C. (1960), 'Carriage by Sea', *RIDA* 7, pp. 489–505.

Thür, G. (1987), 'Hypotheken-Urkunde eines Seedarlehens für eine Reise nach Muziris und Apographe für die Tetarte in Alexandreia (zu P.Vindob.G. 40.822)', *Tyche* 2, pp. 229–245.

Thür, G. (1988), 'Zum Seedarlehen *kata Mouzeirin*. P.Vindob.G. 40.822', *Tyche* 3, pp. 229–233.

Thür, G. (2003), 'Sachverfolgung und Diebstahl in den griechischen Poleis', in G. Thür and F.J. Fernández Nieto (eds), *Symposion 1999 (Akten der Gesellschaft für Griechische und Hellenistische Rechtsgeschichte 17)* (Vienna: Verlag der Österreichischen Akademie der Wissenschaften), pp. 57–96.

Vélissaropoulos, J. (1980), *Les nauclères Grecs: Recherches sur les institutions maritimes en Grèce et dans l'Orient hellénisé* (Geneva: Droz).

Vélissaropoulos-Karakostas, J. (2011), *Droit grec d'Alexandre à Auguste (323 av. J.C. – 14 ap. J.C.) II. Personnes, biens, justice* (Athens: Centre de recherches de l'antiquité grecque et romaine).

Verboven, K. (2017), 'Currency and Credit in the Bay of Naples in the First Century AD', in M. Flohr and A. Wilson (eds), *The Economy of Pompeii* (Oxford: Oxford University Press), pp. 363–386.

Verhagen, H.L.E. (2011), 'Der Verfallspfand im frühklassischen römischen Recht. Dingliche Sicherheit im Archiv der Sulpizier', *RHD* 79, pp. 1–46.

Verhagen, H.L.E. (2013), 'The evolution of pignus in classical Roman law. Ius honorarium and ius novum', *RHD* 81, pp. 51–79.

Virlouvet, C. (2000), 'Les denrées alimentaires dans les archives des Sulpicii de Pouzzoles', *CGG* 11, pp. 131–149.

Wacke, A. (1980), 'Rechtsfragen der römischen Lagervermietung', *Labeo* 26, 299–324.

Wacke, A. (2017), 'Das nach siegreich bestandenem Wettkampf zurückzuzahlende Athleten-Darlehen. Eine Entgegnung auf Eva Jakab', *RIDA* 64, pp. 367–381.

Warnking, P. (2015) *Der römische Seehandel in seiner Blütezeit. Rahmenbedingungen, Seerouten, Wirtschaftlichkeit* (Rahden/Westf: Pharos Studien zur griechisch-römischen Antike).

Wieling, H.J. (1989) 'Privilegium fisci, praediatura und Protopraxie', *ZRG RA* 106, pp. 404–433.

Wilcken, U. (1925), 'Punt-Fahrten in der Ptolemäerzeit', *Zeitschrift für ägyptische Sprache und Altertumskunde* 60, pp. 86–102.

Wilson, A. (2011), 'Development in Mediterranean shipping and maritime trade from the Hellenistic period to AD 1000', in D. Robinson and A. Wilson (eds), *Maritime Archaeology and Ancient Trade in the Mediterranean* (Oxford: Oxford University Press), pp. 35–59.

Wolf, J.G. (2010), *Neue Rechtsurkunden aus Pompeji. Tabulae Pompeianae Novae* (Darmstadt: WBG).

Wolff, H.J. (1978), *Das Recht der griechischen Papyri Ägyptens in der Zeit der Ptolemäer und des Prinzipats II, Organisation und Kontrolle des privaten Rechtsverkehrs* (Munich: Beck).

Wolff, H.J. (2002), *Das Recht der griechischen Papyri Ägyptens in der Zeit der Ptolemäer und des Prinzipats I, Bedingungen und Triebkräfte der Rechtsentwicklung* (Munich: Beck).

Zimmermann, R. (1990), *The Law of Obligations. Roman Foundations of the Civilian Tradition* (Oxford: Oxford University Press).

NOTES

1. Warnking (2015), pp. 142–145; Sirks (1991), p. 252. For the ports see Mataix Ferrándiz (2018), pp. 82–106.
2. Wilson (2011), pp. 49–51 underlined the hierarchy of ports and its influence for the organisation of transport.
3. Claudius started the construction of an artificial port near Ostia in AD 42 which was finished by Nero in AD 64: see Warnking (2015), p. 143; Wilson (2011a), pp. 47–51; Sirks (1991), pp. 252–253.

4. The sailing route from Ostia was actually shorter: Warnking (2015), p. 252.
5. Warnking (2015), pp. 259–265.
6. Warnking (2015), pp. 258–264.
7. See the chapter by P Campbell earlier in this volume; also, Candy (2020), pp. 53–57.
8. Camodeca (1999) re-edited 127 *tabulae*.
9. Geographical indications on personal names may denote the origin of the merchant or the place where he mainly conducted his business: see Rohde (2012), p. 101.
10. Jakab (2000), pp. 244–254; Rathbone (2003), pp. 208–210. Cf the chapter by P Candy later in this volume.
11. Verboven (2017), pp. 364–365.
12. Verboven (2017), p. 371.
13. Verboven (2017), p. 372.
14. For the date see Camodeca (1999), p. 217; though cf Wolf (2010), p. 147.
15. *TPSulp.* 106. The ship is called *Notus*, a popular ship-name in the Greek world: see Casson (1971), pp. 354–355.
16. Camodeca (1999), pp. 217–219; Jaschke (2010), pp. 213–214.
17. Camodeca (1999), p. 217 (although he also considered *Q./C. Fabius*).
18. Gröschler (1997), pp. 57–58.
19. Camodeca (1999), p. 217.
20. *Protopraxia* has been documented in Egypt since the first century AD. The first evidence for it appears in the Edict of Tiberius Alexander, *praefectus Aegypti*, AD 68: see Wieling (1989), p. 407.
21. Heumann and Seckel (1907), p. 46 translates 'wegwenden, abhalten, wegleiten' or 'entwenden, unterschlagen, auf die Seite schaffen'.
22. Wieling (1989), pp. 409 and 432 underlines that it concerns a *versio in rem* (that is, it was not a bankruptcy privilege). The legal classification seems difficult (it was carried out through seizure (*katoche*), after public announcement): Wieling (1989), pp. 408–411. However, the legal sources are from a later period.
23. Plin. *Ep.* 10.108, from the year AD 111. Trajan's answer suggests that *protopraxia* could also be granted to some cities as a privilege: '*quo iure uti debeant . . . ex lege cuiusque animadvertendum est*'. See, also, Plin. *Ep.* 10.109. On *protopraxia*, see Wieling (1989), p. 412.
24. In this sense, Camodeca (2001), p. 91.
25. Jaschke (2010), pp. 216–217 seems to have gone too far with her hypothesis.
26. Jaschke (2010), p. 213 suggests reading *Octavia*; however, the photo published by Camodeca does not really support it.
27. Camodeca (1999), p. 184.
28. Wolf (2010), p. 131.
29. Camodeca (2001), p. 88.
30. Camodeca (1999), pp. 205–206.
31. Rathbone (2003), pp. 198, 202, and 211. For the prices in Egypt cf Rathbone (1997), pp. 186–188.
32. G. 3.90; Crook (1967), pp. 210–211.
33. Buckland (1925), p. 273.
34. Maritime loans are discussed under title D. 22.2 (*De nautico faenore*); the entire *titulus*, however, consists of just nine fragments.
35. D. 22.2.1 (Mod.10 *pand.*): '*Traiecticia ea pecunia est quae trans mare vehitur: ceterum si eodem loci consumatur, non erit traiecticia.*'

36. Zimmermann (1990), p. 183; Chevreau (2008), pp. 40–41. It is widely believed that the maritime loan had to form the seed capital: see Ankum (1996), p. 60; Schuster (2005), p. 192. It seems unlikely that the borrower would have been allowed to travel with the coins and purchase goods on the way: Schuster (2005), pp. 192–193. For maritime loans during the Medieval period, see Lohsse (2016), pp. 377–399.

37. The Roman jurists understood maritime loans as special loans with interest: see Schuster (2005), pp. 186–188; Biscardi (1974), pp. 138–141.

38. Modestin also points out the fragile boundaries between a regular loan and a maritime loan in D. 22.2.3 (Mod. 4 *reg.*).

39. Papinian underlines in D. 22.2.4 pr. (Pap. 3 *resp.*) that the risk allocation is explicitly governed through a term in the contract. If this was missing, the remaining amount was still called *traiecticia pecunia*, though it stood on a regular 'landed' footing, *sine periculo creditoris*.

40. D. 22.2.1 (Mod. 10 *pand.*); D. 22.2.2 (Pomp. 3 *ex Plaut.*); D. 22.2.4 pr., 1 (Pap. 3 *resp.*); D. 22.2.6 (Paul. 25 *quaest.*); D. 22.2.7 (Paul. 3 *ad ed.*).

41. D. 22.2.5 (Scaev. 6 *resp.*). The text was classified by Justinian's lawyers as a *foenus nauticum*, though it originally came from the sixth book of Scaevola's *responsa*. It is strange that maritime loans are not mentioned explicitly in the six books of his *responsa*, nor in the text quoted above. See von Lübtow (1976), p. 334; Chevreau (2008), pp. 40–43.

42. Schuster (2005), pp. 188–195; Krampe (1998), p. 472.

43. Jakab (2014a), pp. 252–255; with a critical view Wacke (2017), pp. 368–371.

44. This is why some authors consider it an innominate contract: Schuster (2005), p. 187.

45. von Lübtow (1976), p. 334.

46. See, e.g. D. 45.1.122.1 (Scaev. 28 *dig.*); Krampe (1995), pp. 209–211; von Lübtow (1976), p. 334; Purpura (1987), pp. 212–215.

47. For the temporal delimitation of the parties' risk spheres, see Krampe (1995), pp. 220–222.

48. D. 22.2.3 (Mod. 4 *reg.*): 'In nautica pecunia ex eo die periculum spectat creditorem, ex quo navem navigare conveniat'.

49. D. 22.2.1 (Mod. 10 *pand.*).

50. D. 22.2.6 (Paul. 25 *quaest.*); D. 22.2.7 (Paul. 3 *ad ed.*).

51. D. 22.2.4 pr. (Pap. 3 *resp.*). See, also, the maritime loan of Callimachus: D. 45.1.122.1 (Scaev. 28 *dig.*). For the problem see also C. 4.33.2, C. 4.33.3, and C. 4.33.5. All three decisions came down from the late third century AD.

52. D. 22.2.6 (Paul. 25 *quaest.*): '*Faenerator pecuniam usuris maritimis mutuam dando quasdam merces in nave pignori accepit, ex quibus si non potuisset totum debitum exsolvi, aliarum mercium aliis navibus impositarum propriisque faeneratoribus obligatarum si quid superfuisset, pignori accepit . . .*'.

53. It may be true that the idea of surrogation remained generally alien to Roman law, as stressed by Schuster (2005), pp. 193–194, but the lawyers never questioned the validity of contractual terms with a similar content.

54. This situation is by no means unthinkable: several sources report of ships sinking at anchor.

55. D. 22.2.6 (Paul. 25 *quaest.*): '*Scilicet tunc cum condicio exstiterit obligationis et alio casu pignus amissum fuerit vel vilius distractum vel si navis postea perierit, quam dies praefinitus periculo exactus fuerit*'.

56. Translated into English by P Candy (for the full translation of the text, see the chapter by Purpura earlier in this volume); Candy (2021), p. 313.

57. 'Sammeltransport': on which, see Fiori (1999), pp. 65–68; Purpura (2014), pp. 138–143. For the transport methods see Sirks (1991), p. 261.
58. The context suggests that it was the port of destination and not just any port 'en route'.
59. For sources about weighing out grain in ports see Sirks (1991), pp. 260–264; Jakab (2006), pp. 92–94.
60. The verb '*perierat*' does not inform about the kind of the accident (maybe fire or storm): see Fiori (1999), p. 66.
61. Whether it was Servius or Alfenus should remain open: see Fiori (1999), pp. 66–67; Candy (2021), Pt IV.
62. Jakab (2006), pp. 87–100; Fiori (1999), pp. 67–72; Purpura (2014), p. 139.
63. Alfenus' decision can be confirmed by contractual practice: in freight contracts from Egypt, the shipper was only liable for damage caused during transport (for instance, theft and water damage) – but never for *force majeure*. It was different in freight contracts with the state: see Jakab (2006), pp. 90–91. See, also, Candy (2021), pp. 324–327.
64. D. 22.2.5.1 (Scaev. 6 *resp*.).
65. D. 22.2.4.1 (Pap. 3 *resp*.). See, also, Dem. 32.8. A similar practice can be found in Roman law texts: e.g. D. 44.7.23 (Afr. 7 *quaest*.); C. 4.32.26.2 (AD 528).
66. D. 22.2.2 (Pomp. 3 *ex Plaut*.).
67. *Collegia* might have had an important social mission: they also acted as a source of references for their members, for instance in credit transactions: see Rohde (2012), pp. 140–144; and the chapter by A Marzano earlier in this volume.
68. Schuster (2005), pp. 130–135.
69. D. 45.1.122.1 (Scaev. 28 *dig*.):

'*Callimachus mutuam pecuniam nauticam accepit a Sticho servo Seii in provincia Syria civitate Beryto usque Brentesium: idque creditum esse in omnes navigii dies ducentos, sub pignoribus et hypothecis mercibus a Beryto comparatis et Brentesium perferendis et quas Brentesio empturus esset et per navem Beryto invecturus: convenitque inter eos, uti, cum Callimachus Brentesium pervenisset, inde intra idus Septembres, quae tunc proximae futurae essent, aliis mercibus emptis et in navem mercis ipse in Syriam per navigium proficiscatur . . .*'.

70. The wording follows the usual formula of objectively styled *testationes*. The mixed language is a strong argument for a Greek *nautolike* in the background.
71. In this sense already von Lübtow (1976), p. 334.
72. Although Scaevola uses blank names, there are indications that the case comes from everyday practice (and not a school case): see Krampe (1995), p. 214; Chevreau (2008), pp. 42–43.
73. von Lübtow (1976), pp. 335–357.
74. To the possibility and risk of off-season trips see Arnaud (2005), pp. 26–28; Horden and Purcell (2000), pp. 139 and 225; Pryor (1988), p. 38.
75. It must have been a contractual pledge without possession based on a Greek model: see Schanbacher (2006), pp. 54–55. Von Lübtow (1976), p. 338 pointed out that *pignus* and *hypotheca* have the same meaning here.
76. G. 3.92–3.
77. See Krampe (1995), pp. 209–215; von Lübtow (1976), pp. 337–345; Biscardi (1974), p. 200; Purpura (1987), pp. 212–224.

78. Pringsheim (1950), p. 205; Pringsheim *Id.* (1916), p. 25; Kränzlein (1968), p. 90; Wolff (1974), p. 94. Although the principle of surrogation was not integrated into the Roman law of *pignus*, the lawyers never questioned its effectiveness in contractual practice.
79. Schuster (2005), pp. 183–186; Chevreau (2008), pp. 38–39.
80. Dem. 35.10–13 (trans. by M. MacDowell). As for the text see Vélissaropoulos (1980), pp. 304–308; Purpura (1987), pp. 203–211; Cohen (1992), pp. 54–55.
81. I do not want to deal here with the problem of interest and profitability: see Cohen (1992), pp. 52–58.
82. Kränzlein (1963), p. 88.
83. Kränzlein (1963).
84. Kränzlein (1963), pp. 88–90.
85. A similar clause is quoted by Dem. 56.38 (for Dionysodoros): on which, see Schuster (2005), p. 122. Dem. 34.8 also records related acts: Chrysippos, to whom Phormion gave a maritime loan for a trade trip to the Crimea, asked one of his slaves and a businessman who lived there to control the cargo. The problems of enforcement have also been treated by Kränzlein (1963), pp. 85–86 and 88–89.
86. Dem. 35.22, 23, 27.
87. For the reconstruction of the case see Thür (2003), pp. 60–77.
88. Dem. 35.5, 9, 14.
89. Dem. 32.14.
90. Kränzlein (1963), pp. 89–90.
91. After the principle of surrogation had taken effect the grain belonged to Demon, the moneylender, because it was bought out of his money (*chratesis*). The borrower, Protos, had just *kyrieia*, the right of disposal.
92. The arguments presented at trial can be reconstructed from the context.
93. Dem. 35.14, 17, 18, 19.
94. Thür (2003), pp. 58–59: 'Bestritt der Besitzer das Recht des Eindringlings, fasste er ihn an und führte ihn wieder hinaus' (*exagein, exeillein*).
95. Thür (2003), p. 59.
96. Thür (2003), p. 64; Wilcken (1925), pp. 86–102; Vélissaropoulos (1980), pp. 308–311; Thür (1987), pp. 241–243.
97. The regions mentioned can be identified along the East coast of Africa: see Wilcken (1925), p. 94; Bogaert (1965), pp. 150–151; Purpura (1987), pp. 227–228. Ointment, perfumes and incense were imported from there, brought to Alexandria and forward to Italy (Puteoli): Jaschke (2010), p. 114 and pp. 130–135.
98. The text is badly damaged.
99. Thür (1987), p. 243.
100. In this sense already Wilcken (1925), p. 94; Thür (1987), p. 243.
101. Wolff (1978), p. 96 emphasised that this kind of deed is called an 'unselbständige' bank-diagraphe in which 'der bankmäßige Vorgang unter ausdrückliche Bezugnahme auf eine anderweit (durch *syngraphe, synchoresis* oder *cheirographon*) erfolgte Beurkundung des der Zahlung zugrunde liegenden Kausalgeschäfts attestiert ist'.
102. See BL VIII 375 and BL XIII 211. An extended interpretation has been given by Thür (2000), pp. 177–186.
103. Thür (2000), p. 183; Purpura (1987), p. 267; Rathbone (2003), pp. 217–220.
104. Biscardi (1974), pp. 212–213.
105. Thür (2000), p. 185; Vélissaropoulos (1980), p. 310; Wolff (1978), p. 97; Rougé (1966), pp. 348–349.

106. Casson (1956), p. 92; Thür (2000), p. 184.
107. Thür (2000), p. 183.
108. Wolff (1978), p. 97, Anm. 75 emphasised that banks also often quoted contracts in their entries that were not directly connected to their own business (that is, 'außerhalb der Bank verbriefte Abmachungen').
109. Thür (2000), pp. 182 and 184. The banks acted as some kind of notarial centre: Wolff (1978), pp. 95–97.
110. The beginning of the text is damaged: see Harrauer and Sijpesteijn (1985), pp. 124–126; Casson (1990), pp. 195–206, Thür (1987), pp. 234–245; Thür (1988), pp. 229–233; De Romanis (1996), pp. 186–192; Rathbone (2000), pp. 39–50; Rathbone (2003), pp. 220–221; Morelli (2011), pp. 199–201.
111. Likely, the voyage went Alexandria–Muziris–Alexandria: see Thür (1987), p. 235; recently, also, De Romanis (2014), p. 80. The town of Muziris can be localised to the north of modern Cochin. Already Pliny wrote about sailing routes to India: Plin. *HN*. 6.104–6.106; see Adams (2007), pp. 228–229; Casson (1991), pp. 8–9.
112. Very likely in Berenike or Myos Hormos; Thür (1988), p. 230. For the ports at the Red Sea see Casson (1991), p. 8; Sidebotham (1991), pp. 12–21.
113. Thür (1987), pp. 244–245; Rathbone (2000), pp. 39–50; and Morelli (2011), pp. 206–216, with a partly new reading.
114. Thür (1987), pp. 240–247 showed that the papyrus preserved just a security deed and not the text of a maritime loan; see also Rathbone (2003), pp. 220–221. It is even controversial where the loan was signed; Thür (1987), pp. 240 and (1988), p. 230 argued for Alexandria; the final destination is an especially strong argument for this view. Morelli (2011), pp. 202–203 saw here a second loan: according to him, the *emporos* repaid the maritime loan after arriving at the Red Sea port and took a second loan for the land transport. Casson (1986), pp. 73–79 suggested two loans; against it Thür (1988), p. 230; recently also De Romanis (2014), pp. 79–80.
115. There is no deadline in the papyrus for the repayment of the loan in Alexandria. De Romanis (2014), pp. 82–89 has suggested that there was no deadline at all; the time of return was evident from the sailing season. In my view, a transmarine loan without a deadline is rather unlikely: Callimachus' contract and all the loans treated above had a strict deadline.
116. Thür (1987), pp. 234 and 240.
117. Nov. 106 pr. (AD 540): on which, see the chapter by P Candy later in this volume; also, Rougé (1966), p. 347. Schuster (2005), pp. 66–67 doubted whether the twenty days can be considered as customary law in trading.
118. Camodeca (1994), pp. 109–110.
119. When setting up legal documents, their outer form was regulated by the *SC Neronianum* (AD 61). See Meyer (2004), pp. 126–134; Jakab (2014b), pp. 333–334.
120. Camodeca (1999), p. 121.
121. Wolf (2010), pp. 29–30.
122. *Chirographa* were mostly written with the own hand, but not exclusively: see Jakab (2011), pp. 287–290.
123. On the *horrearius* see Alzon (1965), pp. 26–32; Wacke (1980), pp. 309–311.
124. Mind the *actiones adiectitiae qualitatis*.
125. Macqueron (1979), pp. 204–208; Pozsonyi (2017), pp. 69–73; Mataix Ferrándiz (2018), pp. 101–103. The liability of the parties appears to have been misunderstood by Jaschke (2010), p. 196.

126. Jakab (2006), pp. 95–99.
127. Rathbone (2009), pp. 299–310; Macqueron (1979), pp. 208–211.
128. We will return to this below, when considering *TPSulp.* 46.
129. To the epigraphic sources about the *horrearius* see, recently, Martini (2015), pp. 161–167.
130. Fiori (1999), pp. 45–50. The symbolic *merces* can be explained with reference to the tight relationship between C. Novius Cypaerus and C. Novius Eunus, who was freed by him. He can also be observed as a witness to the letting (*TPSulp.* 45) and in one of the loans (*TPSulp.* 52): Camodeca (1994), pp. 104–105.
131. *Pignus* and *arrabo* are used as synonyms here: see Jakab (2009), pp. 108–109; Gröschler (2008), pp. 317–319; Krämer (2007), pp. 26–27; Abatino (2012), pp. 316–322 (with linguistic arguments). For forfeiture see Schanbacher (2010), p. 146 and Pozsonyi (2017), pp. 100–101.
132. For storage facilities see Rickman (1971), pp. 194–200.
133. Modern authors mainly argue that C. Novius Eunus was in possession at the time: Gröschler (2008), p. 315; Verhagen (2011), p. 28; Krämer (2007), p. 316; though cf Klinck (2015), pp. 61–65.
134. With the term '*preter [sic] alia HS X nummum que alio chirographo meo eidem debo*' any question of novation seems to be excluded.
135. In this sense also Gröschler (2008). p. 315; Krämer (2007), p. 320; Wolf (1989), p. 20.
136. I would interpret the first pledge as a contractual, non-possessory pledge; Euenus Primianus seems to have been given physical control just through hiring the storeroom. Whether C. Novius Eunus can be considered the owner beforehand (as has commonly been assumed) should remain open here.
137. The economic contact between Hesychus and C. Novius Eunus continued: on 29 August, AD 38, Hesychus lent him 1,130 sesterces and a further 1,250 sesterces on 15 September, AD 39 (*TPSulp.* 67 and 68). Camodeca (1994), p. 105 rightly suspects that these loans have nothing to do with the business conducted in 38. Speculations about the indebtedness of C. Novius Eunus, such as those made by Jaschke (2010), pp. 199–204 are by no means compelling.
138. The legal background of warehouse rentals has also been analysed by Virlouvet (2000), pp. 134–139.
139. For the everyday use of real security see Schanbacher (2006), pp. 69–70; Gröschler (2008), pp. 301–309; Chevreau (2009), p. 188; Verhagen (2011), p. 28; Klinck (2015), pp. 64–66.
140. Recently Finkenauer (2018), pp. 179–181.
141. The grain should have arrived freshly from Egypt. Recent research showed that trade ships were also on the move in winter: see Horden and Purcell (2000), p. 139; Sirks (2002), pp. 135–141; also, the chapter by P Campbell earlier in this volume.
142. Tab. III, pag. 6: '*Chirographum Nardi Publii Anni Seleuci servi conductionis*'.
143. The *horrea* were built on the property of Domitia Lepida: Jakab (2014b), pp. 335–338; Chevreau (2009), pp. 189–191; Klinck (2015), pp. 60 and 62–64; Klinck (2019), pp. 360–361 and 364–366.
144. Rathbone (2003), pp. 199–203.
145. On the other hand, Wolf (2010), p. 128, thinks that the grain in the warehouse was poured together with that of other merchants.
146. Jakab (2006), pp. 92–97; Fiori (2018), pp. 512–519.
147. Jakab (2009), pp. 233–242. Pozsonyi (2017), pp. 88–89 considers that the pledged grain was thus removed from a larger stock of the debtor.

148. Weighing out is not to be confused with the *horrearius'* liability for *custodia*.
149. Camodeca (1999), p. 181 specified the deed as *pignoris datio*. For the practice of real security in the archive see also Pellecchi (2018), pp. 464–469.
150. Maybe a link to the edict concerning the *actio Serviana*: see Chevreau (2009), p. 187.
151. The otherwise highly important terms of the *pactum de vendendo* must be left out here.
152. For the impact of Greek law generally see Schanbacher (2006), pp. 51–55.
153. Sirks (2002), pp. 134–140; *Id.* (1991), pp. 256–257.
154. Chevreau (2009), pp. 195–196; cf Verhagen (2011), pp. 35–46.
155. Chevreau (2009), p. 196. Several authors also argue that the interest on transmarine loans was often capitalised.
156. Rathbone (2003), pp. 213–215.
157. Rathbone and Temin (2008), pp. 375–376:

'Provincials had their own legal traditions which the Romans largely respected. There was mutual influence between Roman legal principles and practice and some Hellenistic types of contract, such as maritime loan, resulting in common hybrid forms of contract. In normal practice Roman courts, at least in the provinces and port towns of Italy, would hear disputes about almost any agreement, however made'.

See also Schuster (2005), pp. 183–188.
158. von Lübtow (1976), p. 338.
159. The short deadlines were treated above; it is not clear if the maritime loan was about HS 10,000.
160. The patron allowed no special terms for his freedman here.
161. Broekaert (2017), p. 406, comes to a similar conclusion about enforcement among businessmen in Puteoli: 'The Sulpicii archive clearly suggests that the procedures of Roman law alone did not provide businessmen with efficient tools to resolve conflicts'.

Chapter 9

Credit for Carriage: *TPSulp.* 78 and P. Oxy. XLV 3250

Peter Candy

TPSulp. 78 takes us into the heart of Puteoli, a thriving port town on the Bay of Naples that flourished until its destruction by the eruption of Vesuvius in AD 79.[1] The tablet was discovered in 1959 at a site near to Pompeii, among a collection of over 100 *tabulae* kept by a moneylending business that was operated by the Sulpicii during the middle part of the first century AD. This particular tablet has generated almost as many different interpretations as there are chapters in this volume. Even so, I believe that the arrangement documented within it may well be an example of a method of contracting that has remained largely unnoticed by scholars of the Graeco-Roman world: an interlinked contract, in which credit and carriage agreements were bundled together into a single transaction.[2] To this end, the contribution will be divided into three parts: first, an overview of the literature; second, my own interpretation of the tablet; and third, its mutual interpretation with a roughly contemporaneous freight contract from Roman Egypt.

'TPSulp. 78 (= Tab. Pomp. 13)
p. 1 Ἐπὶ ὑπάτων Μάρκου Ἀκύλα Ἰουλι–
       ανοῦ καὶ Ποπλίου Νωνίου Ἀσ–
       πρήνα πρὸ τριῶν εἰδῶν
   Ἀπριλίων ἐν Δικαρχήᾳ.
5   Μενέλαος Εἰρηναίου Κερα–
       μιήτης ἔγραψα ἀπέχιν μαι
       παρὰ Πρίμου Ποπλίου Ἀττίου Σεβή–
       ρου δούλου{λου} δηνάρια χίλια
       ἐκ ναυλωτικῆς ἐκσφραγισμένης,
10   ἃ καὶ ἀποδώσω ἀκ{ου}λούθως
   τῇ ναυλωτικῇ, ῆ<ν> πεποίημαι πρὸς
   αὐτόν. Κατέστησα δὲ ἔγγυον
p. 2   εἰς ἔκτισιν τῶν προγεγραμμένων
δηναρίων χιλίων Μάρκον Βαρ–
   βάτιον Κέλερα.
      Q(uintus) Aelius Romanus *scripsi rogatu et*

5   *mandatu* M(*arci*) *Barbati Celeris coram*
        ipso, quod is litteris nesciret, eum
            sua fide iubere eos * ∞, q(*ui*) s(*upra*) s(*cripti*) *sunt,*
        Primo P(*ublii*) *Atti Severi* ser(*vo*) *pro Menela–*
            uo Irenaei f(*ilio*) *Ceramietae, ita*
10   *uti supra scriptum es*[t]. (S) (S) (S)

On the 3rd of the ides of April under the consulate of M. Aquila Iulianus and P. Nonius Asprenas at Dicearcheïa, I, Menelaos, son of Irenaos, from Keramos, hereby acknowledge that I have received from Primus, slave of Publius Attius Severus, the sum of 1000 *denarii* according to the duly signed *naulotike* we have concluded. I will repay willingly the money that I have taken out according to the agreement that I have made with him. And I have set as surety for the payment of the above-mentioned 1000 *denarii*, Marcus Barbatius Celer.

I, Quintus Aelius Romanus, have written on behalf and in the presence of Marcus Barbatius Celer at his request and by his mandate, because he says that he does not know his letters, that he [Celer] guarantees the above-mentioned 1000 *denarii* to Primus, slave of Publius Attius Severus, on behalf of Menelaos, son of Irenaos, from Keramos – as has been written above. (Three seals of Menelaos, Q. Aelius Romanus, and M. Barbatius Celer.)'

CONTEXT AND SCHOLARSHIP

TPSulp. 78 consists of a diptych of wax tablets made up of two *chirographa* dated 11 April 38.[3] The first chirograph, which was written in Greek, contained declarations made by an individual called Menelaos, son of Irenaos, who hailed from Keramos in Caria (Asia Minor). In the document Menelaos declared: first (p.1, ll. 5–9), that he had received 1,000 *denarii* (= HS 4,000) from a certain Primus, slave of P. Attius Severus, 'arising from' a sealed ναυλοτικῆ ('ἐκ ναυλωτικῆς ἐκσφραγισμένης'); second (p.1, ll. 10–12), that he would willingly repay the money 'according to' the ναυλοτικῆ concluded between them; and third (p. 1, l. 12 – p. 2, l. 3), that a certain M. Barbatius Celer would stand as surety in his stead.[4] The second chirograph, which was composed in Latin, contained a declaration made by a certain Q. Aelius Romanus that, because Celer was illiterate, he was acting on his behalf and that the latter agreed to guarantee Menelaos' repayment of the money.

What little is known about the actors may be disposed of quickly. There is no more information about Menelaos than appears in the *chirographa*. In all likelihood he was a peregrine trading between Asia Minor and the Bay of Naples, probably as a merchant, carrier or some combination of the two. As for Primus, his master – Publius Attius Severus – is very likely the same P. Attius Severus whose name is inscribed on *tituli picti* dating to the same period, which show that he was a trader in *garum* between Italy and Baetica.[5] M. Barbatius Celer, the illiterate guarantor, may be the same M. Barbatius who appears elsewhere in the archive as an arbitrator, in which case he was likely a resident of Puteoli.[6] Nothing can be said about Q. Aelius Romanus, other than that he possessed the *tria nomina* of a Roman citizen.

What was the structure of the arrangement? Three issues require to be addressed: first, the intention behind the transfer of the 1,000 *d.* from Primus to Menelaos; second, the identity of the document referred to as a 'ναυλοτικῆ' (*naulotike*); and third, the relationship between the 1,000 *d.* and the ναυλοτικῆ. Before offering my own interpretation, it serves to provide an overview of how each of these questions has been approached by scholars working on the tablet over the past forty years.[7]

The 1,000 *denarii*:

The language in the *chirographa* gives the transfer of the 1,000 *d.* to Menelaos the appearance of a loan. This emerges from two discrete features: first, as JA Ankum noticed, the phrase 'ἔγραψα ἀπέχιν μαι' is a translation into Greek of the formulaic expression '*scripsi me accipisse*', which is standard terminology in Roman loan documentation for the receipt of a *mutuum*; and second, the verb ἀποδώσω (l. 10), used here to indicate Menelaos' commitment to repay, is consistently used in the Graeco-Roman papyri to indicate the commitment by the author to repay money given as a loan.[8] Together, these two features have persuaded most scholars to accept that the 1,000 *d.* was extended as credit. The one exception remains JG Wolf, for whom Menelaos received the coins from Primus in his capacity as carrier on condition that he transport it and pass it on to Primus' agents at some far-flung destination.[9] Though not inconceivable, I think this unlikely. As É Jakab has pointed out, the use of ἀποδώσω rather than παραδώσει (which is the word commonly used in the papyri to indicate the return of property subject to a freight contract) is problematic[10]; and in any case, as the wreck evidence shows, coins were only very rarely transported on seagoing vessels before about the third century AD.[11]

THE ναυλοτικῆ:

The identification of the ναυλοτικῆ as a maritime freight agreement is also relatively uncontroversial. The term is derived from the word ναῦλον, which means 'passage-money, fare or freight'. According to AJM Meyer-Termeer, who conducted a thorough study of the freight agreements preserved in the papyri, the expression ναυλωτικαὶ συγγραφαί refers to 'written documents in which a carrier confirms the receipt and/or loading of goods, whereby he expressly or tacitly undertakes to transport them by ship and to deliver them to a specific destination'.[12] The sense is therefore clear: these were freight contracts in which carriers agreed to transport goods in their ship for a fee.

Until recently, only Ankum, writing in the late 1970s, took a different approach. He understood the ναυλοτικῆ to be a maritime loan contract, on the basis that the expression '*contractus traiecticius*', used in a Justinianic constitution of 528, was already in use by the late Republican or classical period and was translated into Greek by the scribe responsible for writing the tablet as 'ναυλοτικῇ (συγγραφῇ)'.[13] However, as Ankum himself later acknowledged, this argument is difficult to sustain: Jakab's demonstration in the early 2000s that the ναυλοτικῇ was a maritime freight agreement similar to those documented in the papyri was, by this time, irresistible; and in any case, maritime loan contracts are consistently referred to elsewhere as ναυτικαὶ, rather than ναυλωτικαὶ, συγγραφαί. Ankum therefore eventually abandoned his original position and declared for Wolf.[14]

In a recent volume dedicated to E Lo Cascio, however, F De Romanis has argued for a reinterpretation that requires an alternative understanding of the identity of the documents.[15] Arguing by comparison with an arrangement reported in the speeches of Demosthenes,[16] his conclusion is that Menelaos was not a carrier (as is usually supposed) but rather a merchant (*emporos*) trading between Puteoli and Asia Minor on a seasonal basis. On this account, Menelaos borrowed money from Primus to cover the cost of freight once he had arrived in Puteoli. Celer, the surety, then purchased goods from Menelaos, which furnished him with the capital to repay the loan. The *naulotike* therefore consisted of an agreement that Primus would supply Menelaos with 1,000 *d.* when he arrived in Puteoli so that he could pay an otherwise unidentified carrier for the freight, and the chirograph made provision for this arrangement by documenting the loan. However, as De Romanis himself admits, the interpretation encounters some difficulties. The arrival of Menelaos at Puteoli in April, at the beginning of the sailing season, would only be explicable through some unlikely (though not impossible) chain of events; and more fundamentally, the document referred to as a *naulotike* would on this account consist of an agreement between a lender and a merchant, which would run counter to its conventional meaning in the papyri.

The relationship between the 1000 *d.* and the ναυλοτικῇ:

Accepting, then, that the 1000 *d.* was given by Primus to Menelaos as a loan and that the *naulotike* was a maritime freight contract similar to those documented in the papyri, it remains to consider the several interpretations that have been put forward on this basis. Both D Gofas and G Thür have understood the transaction as possessing an insurance function. For Gofas, the money was given as a '*Versicherungsdarlehen*' ('insurance loan').[17] Relying heavily upon comparative evidence, he sought to show how carriers in the Medieval period were accustomed to giving loans equivalent to the value of the cargo, the repayment of which was conditional upon the safe arrival of the ship at its destination. If the ship sank in transit the merchants whose goods had perished would have no obligation to repay, so that the retention of the loan proceeds had the effect of an insurance payout. In *TPSulp.* 78, however, the roles of the parties are not exactly aligned,[18] and in the absence of any positive evidence from the Roman period, Gofas' remedy – that the loan given by Primus was fictitious – is therefore difficult to support.[19] Thür, on the other hand, argued that the 1000 *d.* was intended as an '*Aestimationsabrede*'.[20] On this

account, the sum represented a valuation of the cargo received by Menelaos under
the freight agreement, for which Menelaos as carrier had assumed the risk during
transport. The valuation was dressed as a loan so that, in the event the ship did
not return, the lender could sue using a simple *condictio*. In this way, the loan was
just an 'empty form', such that in return for assuming the risk for the merchandise
the carrier increased the charge on the freight.[21] Again, however, the papyrological evidence tends to show that estimations of this kind could be included in the
main body of agreements without difficulty and need not have been recorded in a
separate document.[22]

Finally, according to Jakab, the transaction between Primus and Menelaos is
best understood with reference to an extract drawn from the thirty-second book of
Ulpian's commentary *ad edictum*, in which the jurist reported a rescript of Caracalla
to the effect that a person who had paid for the transport of their goods in advance
could seek a remission of the *merces* if the ship was lost in transit.[23]

'D. 19.2.15.6 (Ulp. 32 *ad ed.*):
Likewise, when someone was asked, having lost his ship, to return freight he accepted
as loan, it was replied in a rescript by Antoninus Augustus that it is not without cause
for the emperor's procurator to ask him the restitution of the freight, because he did
not fulfil the duty to convey: a rule that should hold for all persons alike.'[24]

Now, the Byzantine commentators on the text understood the expression '*pro
mutua*' as synonymous with the Greek concept of 'προχρεία', which in the papyri
refers to the paying of money in advance without interest, especially in connection with the performance of services. In practice, this amounted to an advance
payment by the person receiving the services that was documented as though it
had been given as a loan. Until the services were performed, the 'creditor' kept
the document as protection against non-performance (in which case they could
reclaim the money); but as soon as performance was made, it was handed back to
the 'debtor', who retained the sum given as payment. The particular context of
this rescript was that if the freight was paid 'as a loan', the contract would be interpreted as a charter party in which the carrier was engaged to transport goods from
one port to another, the freight only being due on delivery (i.e. a voyage charter
'*de résultat*'). This being the case, the failure of the carrier to deliver, whatever the
cause, would entitle the 'creditor' to claim back the money 'because he did not
fulfil the duty to convey'. On this reading, then, Primus had engaged Menelaos
to carry his goods to a certain port, paying the freight in advance *pro mutua* and
keeping a copy of the loan receipt with the Sulpicii until such time as delivery was
achieved. If Menelaos succeeded, he retained the advance payment as freight; if
not, Primus was entitled to its return. Of course, if Menelaos was unable to repay,
Primus could proceed against the surety, Celer, in his stead.

Though this explanation has much to commend it, perhaps the greatest concern is the size of the sum advanced, which is far in excess of even the highest
charges paid for freight in the papyri. There, the highest freight paid was 640

drachmas for the carriage of 800 *keramia* of wine to the II *Traiana Fortis* legion in the mid-third century AD (also a time of high inflation).[25] This led both D Rath-bone and DF Jones to suggest an alternative explanation: that the money was intended to cover the payment of customs duties (*portoria*) and other expenses.[26] Possibly this is right – as we shall see, carriers sometimes undertook to pay taxes on the merchant's behalf – but again we are left wondering why the parties went to the trouble of disguising the advance as a loan.

TPSULP. 78: CREDIT FOR CARRIAGE

One would be forgiven, on the basis of this survey, for thinking that the scope for interpretation had been exhausted. In my view, however, the transaction docu-mented in *TPSulp.* 78 can be perfectly well understood by triangulating it within three related contexts: first, the loan documentation in the archive of the Sulpicii; second, loan documentation in the papyri; and third, ancient Mediterranean cus-tomary maritime commercial practice.

As for the archive, there are sixty-one records of payments or acknowledg-ments of debt amounting to a total value of HS 1,022,000.[27] One remarkable fea-ture, however, is that very few contain a due date for repayment, and none appear to make provision for the payment of interest. Since the Sulpicii and their clients can hardly have been in the business of lending gratuitously, this peculiarity – like the tablet under discussion – has given rise to several explanations: (i) that inter-est was paid monthly on the basis of pacts[28]; (ii) that stipulations for interest were recorded in the loan dossiers for each transaction, but in the separate *cautiones* that have not survived[29]; (iii) that the lender deducted interest in advance from the sum paid out to the debtor, so that the amount of the principal was effectively overstated[30]; and (iv) that after the lender had counted out the principal to the borrower, a portion was immediately and voluntarily paid back in the name of 'future interest'.[31]

If we hold these possibilities in mind, a similar phenomenon – of loans apparently given without interest – can be observed in the papyrological loan documentation. According to PW Pestman, whose survey of the documenta-tion was published in 1971, it is common in the papyri to find loans in which the stated sum was intended to represent the total amount that the debtor was obliged to repay.[32] From here, Pestman identified three possibilities: (i) that the borrower simply received a gratuitous loan; (ii) that they received the sum stated, but owed the yield in some other form (e.g. as a *quid pro quo*); or (iii) that they received less than the sum stated since the yield was already included in the amount represented as the principal.[33] Now, it will be apparent that the third and final of Pestman's hypotheses covers the same ground as the third and fourth hypotheses advanced in connection with the Sulpician tablets: namely, that the sum represented in the document was intended as an acknowledgment of the whole debt, including both principal and yield. In contrast, however, Pestman's second hypothesis, that the yield might have consisted wholly or partly of a *quid pro quo*, has not been considered from the perspective of the tablets in the Sulpician archive. Could this have been the structure adopted here?

The third and final step is to compare this range of possibilities with the customary practices reported by a group of carriers whose testimony is reported in a Novel issued by the emperor Justinian in the year 540. The background to the constitution is that two moneylenders – Petros and Eulogetos – had approached Justinian's praetorian praefect, John the Cappadocian, with a petition concerning disputes that had arisen with merchants (*emporoi*) and carriers (*naukleroi*) over the customs surrounding maritime loans. Their request, which was communicated by John to Justinian, was for the prevailing usages to be clarified by imperial decree. Justinian, acquiescing to the proposal, instructed John to make further inquiries, so that once the nature of the dispute had been made clear he could 'include our decision in a permanent law'. John therefore convened a conference of *naukleroi* so that they could testify to the 'ancient custom' (*antiqua consuetudo*) under oath. His report was as follows:

'The evidence they gave, with the extra backing of an oath, was that such loans were of various kinds. Should the lenders have so chosen, they would load one modius of wheat or barley aboard the ship for each coin of whatever sum they lent, without making any payment on it to the public tax-collectors; as far as they were concerned, the vessels would sail tax-free, and they would have that as profit on what they had lent. Additionally, they would receive interest at just one gold piece in ten, with the risk of the venture being the regard of the lenders themselves. However, should the lenders not choose that method, they would receive interest at one-eighth on each coin. This would not be counted as due on any definite date, but only on the ship's safe return; and under that arrangement, it might happen that the time extended up to even a year, should the ship have spent so long away that the year had actually come to an end, or even been exceeded – whereas, if she had returned sooner, and the time only lasted a month or two, they still had the benefit of the three carats [i.e., one-eighth of a 24-carat solidus] whether the elapsed time was as short as that, or whether the loan had remained with the borrower for longer. Just the same thing applied if the traders chose to make another consecutive voyage, so that the form of the loan was fixed for one shipment at a time: it depended on the agreement reached between the parties whether it should stay the same, or be altered. However, if they should have come back, on the ship's safe return, when she could not sail again because of the season, a time-limit was given to the borrowers by the lenders of just twenty days, during which no demand for interest on what was owing could be made until sale of the shipment had taken place. Should the debt remain outstanding for longer than that, the nature of the loan changed at once and became a terrestrial one, as the lenders no longer had the worry over the perils of sea-going, and interest of two-thirds of one per cent was payable to the owners of the capital. That is what they all said, giving their evidence on oath; and that is the information you gave us, for us to put our decision into legislation . . .'[34]

The *naukleroi* testified that maritime loans could be structured in a number of different ways. In one method, the creditor assumed the risk and required the borrower to carry and pay duties on one *modius* of grain or barley per *solidus* lent, in addition to paying one *aureus* for each ten *modii* received. In another method, the creditor simply demanded a yield equivalent to an eighth part of the capital, not calculated with reference to a definite due date, but owing instead on the ship's safe return. In both structures, the uncertain due date meant that there was no relation between the calculation of the yield and the time taken to complete the enterprise; rather, the creditor was entitled to a fixed sum whatever the voyage's duration. The parties could also agree to repeat the transaction multiple times during a sailing season, building up a debt until when no more shipments could be made. Once the final journey of the season had been completed, it was customary – so the carriers claimed – for the borrower to be allowed a twenty-day grace period to sell the last freight and repay what was owed, after which time the loan would be placed on a landed (ἔγγεια) footing and accrue interest at the maximum rate for business loans of two-thirds of a one hundredth part per month (i.e. 8.33 per cent per annum). According to the *naukleroi*, then, there were (at least) two ways of demanding the yield in a maritime loan: the first involving the combination of a financial yield with a *quid pro quo* (i.e. the service of carrying and paying tax on the goods); the second expressed solely in financial terms.

Taken together, these three overlapping sets of evidence provide the context within which *TPSulp.* 78 can be properly understood. The starting point here is the identification of the *naulotike* with a maritime freight agreement and the understanding that Menelaos received the 1000 *d.* as a loan. Assuming that the identification of the *naulotike* with those freight documents preserved in the papyri is correct, this would have contained the details of a freight contract that, among other things, made provision for Menelaos' carriage of Primus' goods. The second point, that Menelaos received the money as a loan, has already been made out: the verb ἀποδώσω and the expression ἔγραψα ἀπέχιν μαι are both indicative of this intention. A plain reading of the chirograph therefore indicates two main features: on the one hand, a loan given by Primus to Menelaos, and on the other, a *naulotike*, or maritime freight agreement. Recalling now the first loan structure spoken to by Justinian's *naukleroi*, there the creditor lent a sum of money for which he assumed the risk and demanded in return both a financial yield and the borrower's services in carrying and paying taxes on his goods. In other words, the parties agreed that part of the yield due on the loan was to consist of services performed by the carrier. Turning to the present transaction, *TPSulp.* 78 is amenable to interpretation in these terms: Menelaos (a *naukleros*) received 1000 *d.* as a loan and agreed in the *naulotike* to offer his services partly or wholly in place of paying a financial yield.

On this interpretation, Primus and Menelaos were not only lender and carrier but also traders in their own right. Nor is this unlikely. As we saw earlier, one of the few salient facts about the parties to the transaction was that Primus was owned by P. Attius Severus, who is very likely the same person whose trading interests are attested to by the *tituli picti*. It would not therefore be surprising if Primus, like his master, was not only a moneylender but also directly engaged in long-distance trade. We also know from the wreck evidence that merchant vessels frequently held consignments owned by multiple traders at the same time as transporting goods belonging to the carrier themselves.[35] Most likely, then, Menelaos was a merchant shipowner and Primus a lender with trading interests. The result was an 'interlinked contract' – credit for carriage – in which a credit agreement and freight contract were rolled into one: Menelaos received the 1000 *denarii* as a loan and offered his services as a carrier either wholly or partly in the place of the yield.

This interpretation has three principal advantages. First, it explains the lack of an explicit 'yield' in Menelaos' acknowledgment of the debt with reference both to the other loans within the Sulpician archive and to the lending methods documented in the papyri. These, too, align neatly with the customary lending practices attested to in Nov. 106. Second, the interpretation relies on a plain reading of the evidence and a reconstruction of the most likely scenario, which is that Menelaos was a (merchant) carrier departing Puteoli with Primus' goods at the opening of the sailing season (*pace* De Romanis). Third, it accounts for the awkward sum of 1,000 *denarii*, which is both substantially higher than all the freight charges documented in the papyri (*pace* Jakab) and too low to reasonably constitute a maritime loan (the position Ankum abandoned). If, then, the 'yield' on the loan would have been somewhere between one-eighth and one-quarter of the sum lent (depending partly upon whether Primus, as the lender, shouldered the risk, for which we have no evidence either way), then the freight charge against which it was set off would have been somewhere in the region of 125–250 *denarii*: well within the range of the majority of freight charges in the papyri, many of which were paid during the same period.

TPSULP. 78 + P. OXY. XLV 3250: TWO SIDES OF THE SAME TRANSACTION?

'P. Oxy. XLV 3250:[36]

Anoubas, son of Hermias, (. . .) captain (κυβερνήτης) of the riverboat (σκάφη ποταμία), property of the centurion Marcus Cornelius Turullus, the legal capacity of burden of which is 500 *artabae*, has entered into a freight contract (ἐναύλωσεν) with Polytimos, slave of Caius Norbanus Ptolemy, concerning the aforesaid vessel with its crew. In this he will load in whatever port he will find in the Hermopolite, 500 *artabae* of chickpeas, measured using Athenaios' measure, 12 ½ *artabae* per 100 *artabae* being exempt from payment. These he will restore at Akanthôna and Lilê, in the Oxyrhynchite, at the agreed price of 28 silver drachmas per 100 *artabae*, for a total of 140 drachmas, of which Anoubas acknowledges that he has received from Polytimos 72 drachmas at the signing of the agreement. The remaining 68 will be paid to him at the unloading of the chickpeas. He will have the boat ready for sailing upstream on the 21st of the next month of Augustus; will sail to the ports of the Hermopolite, receive the chickpeas and be liable for this; leave without delay and comply with all the safety rules. Let any present expenditure be his. Let him furnish the boat with a skilled crew. And let it not be permissible for him to sail at night, nor when there is stormy weather. Let him anchor each day in the safest harbours. Anoubas will provide the hampers in the Hermopolite; in the Oxyrhynchite [they will be provided] by Polytimos. The chickpeas will be handed over to Polytimos or to his representatives at the ports of Akanthôna and Lilê and will be measured with the measure that will be found there. Any overflowing surplus will be the property of Polytimos or will be bought from him at the price of [---] per [---] . . . (trans. Arnaud, adapted.).'

P. Oxy. XLV 3250 consists of a freight agreement for the fluvial transport of 500 *artabae* of chickpeas between the Hermopolite and Oxyrhynchite nomes on the Nile delta that was concluded in or around the year AD 63.[37] The actors' biographical information can be dealt with swiftly. The ship's captain was an individual named Anoubas, who had been appointed to the role by a Roman centurion called M. Cornelius Turullus, about whom nothing else is known other than that he was the owner of the vessel.[38] Polytimos, the shipper, appears to have been the slave of C. Norbanus Ptolemaios, who is identified elsewhere as head of the department of the Idios Logos and *iuridicus*, second only in command to the praetorian praefect in 63.[39] The discovery of several amphora stamps bearing the inscription Ptolem. C. Norbanus at Koptos also combine with a number of other references to a landowner and businessman of the same name who was already active in central Egypt under Caligula.[40] On the other hand, as A Jördens has shown, there is little chance that the Norbanus named in the contract is the same individual as the one who was previously identified as praetorian praefect under Domitian in 96.[41]

The transaction would appear to have been straightforward enough. Anoubas agreed to load the cargo in the Hermopolite and carry it to the Oxyrhynchite where it would be discharged. It was his responsibility to furnish the ship with a crew and to bear the expenses of the voyage. Clauses were inserted concerning the responsibility for providing containers and for the measurement of the merchandise during loading and unloading. A 'navigationsklausel' was also included, governing the conditions in which Anoubas was allowed to sail and the character of the places where he should drop anchor each day.[42] As for the shipper, Polytimos agreed to pay 28 drachmas per 100 *artabae*: a total of 140 drachmas, of which Anoubas acknowledged that he had already received 72 as an advanced payment, the remaining 68 to be paid on unloading at Akanthôna and Lilê.[43]

The outstanding feature from our perspective is the otherwise unexplained discount in the cost of the freight, which entitled Polytimos to an exemption from payment on 12.5 *artabae* out of every 100. Why the figure of 12.5? Returning momentarily to Nov. 106, it just so happens that this was also the figure given by the *naukleroi* in connection with the second loan structure, according to which it was customary for creditors to lend *pecunia traiecticia* at their own risk for a fixed yield of one-eighth of the principal, or 12.5 per cent. Nor does this appear to be entirely coincidental: one-eighth was also the yield reported by Demosthenes in relation to a maritime loan given for a short one-way journey between Sestos and Athens in the fourth century BC.[44] The same figure appears again in the context of maritime loans connected to voyages along the Egyptian and Levantine coasts during the third century BC and the second century AD, and in a joke about a loan given to a *naukleros* recorded in the fourth- or fifth-century *philogelos*.[45] Altogether, the evidence suggests that it was customary to demand a yield of one-eighth on a maritime loan, at least for voyages of short duration (that is, of no more than several days).

Now, though there is nothing in this particular *naulotike* to indicate the reason for the discount, an explanation can be supplied by interpreting *TPSulp.* 78 and P. Oxy. XLV 3250 together. The exercise begins from a strong foundation: both documents are dateable to within a thirty year period around the middle of the first century AD, each representing one component of what was often a larger dossier of contractual documentation. On the one hand, where part of the agreement was that a carrier would borrow a sum of money from a merchant-cum-lender, it was fairly standard for them to acknowledge the debt in a chirograph such as the one preserved in the Sulpician archive. On the other hand, if the arrangement involved the transport of the merchant's goods by the carrier, then one would expect the parties to conclude a *naulotike* between them. Where the agreement involved the combination of these two elements one would expect to find both documents, each possibly bearing some trace of interlinkage with the other.

On this basis, one might suppose that Polytimos had lent money to Anoubas, but instead of demanding a yield on the loan, he negotiated a reduction in the freight charge of the equivalent 12.5 per cent (that is, one eighth) in its place. In the *naulotike* concluded by Menelaos and Primus, one could equally conjecture a similar construction: Menelaos reduced or otherwise set the freight off against the yield that would otherwise have been demanded on the 1,000 *denarii*. This would explain not only the loan's apparent gratuity, but also why it was described as having been given in connection with the *naulotike*. Perhaps – and we can only say perhaps – the Sulpician *chirographum* and the Egyptian *naulotike* were two sides of the same transaction: credit for carriage or some combination thereof.

BIBLIOGRAPHY

Andreau, J. (1999), *Banking and Business in the Roman World* (Cambridge: Cambridge University Press).

Ankum, J.A. (1978), 'Tabula Pompeiana 13: ein Seefrachtvertrag oder ein Seedarlehen?' *IVRA* 29, pp. 156–173.

Ankum, J.A. (1988), 'Minima de Tabula Pompeiana 13', *Cahiers d'histoire. Navires et commerces de la Méditerranée antique. Homage à Jean Rougé* 33, pp. 271–290.

Ankum, J.A. (1996), 'Observations sur le prêt maritime romain, sujet cher à Henryk Kupiszewski', in W. Wołodkiewicz and M. Zabłocka (eds), *Le droit romain et le monde contemporain: Melanges à la mémoire de Henryk Kupiszewski* (Warsaw: University of Warsaw), pp. 59–68.

Ankum, J.A. (2003), 'Noch einmal: die Naulootike des Menelaos in TP 13 (=TPSulp. 78) - Ein Seedarlehen oder ein Seefrachtvertrag?', in J. Sondel, P. Ścislicki, and J. Reszczynski (eds), *Roman Law as Formative of Modern Legal*

Systems: Studies in Honour of Wieslaw Litewski (Krakow: Jagiellonian University Press), pp. 15–23.

Arnaud, P. (2011), 'Ancient Sailing-Routes and Trade Patterns: The Impact of Human Factors', in D. Robinson and A.I. Wilson (eds), *Maritime Archaeology and Ancient Trade in the Mediterranean* (Oxford: Oxford Centre for Maritime Archaeology), pp. 61–80.

Balogh, E. and Pflaum, H.G. (1952), 'Le consilium du préfet d'Egypte. Sa composition', *RHD* 29, pp. 117–124.

Bell, C. (1988), 'Credit Markets and Interlinked Transactions', in H. Chenery and T.N. Srinivasan (eds), *Handbook of Development Economics*, Vol. 1 (Amsterdam: Elsevier), pp. 763–830.

Bove, L. (1984), *Documenti di operazioni finanziarie dall'archivio dei Sulpici: Tabulae Pompeianae di Murécine* (Naples: Liguori).

Brunt, P.A. (1975), 'The Administrators of Roman Egypt', *JRS* 65, pp. 124–147.

Camodeca, G. (1992), *L'archivio puteolano dei Sulpicii* (Naples: Università Napoli Federico II).

Camodeca, G. (1999), *Tabulae Pompeianae Sulpiciorum (TPSulp.). Edizione critica dell'archivio puteolano dei Sulpicii*, Vol. 2 (Rome: Quasar).

Camodeca, G. (2003), 'Il credito negli archivi campani: il caso di Puteoli e di Herculaneum', in E. Lo Cascio (ed), *Credito e moneta nel mondo romano: atti degli Incontri capresi di storia dell'economia antica (Capri 12–14 ottobre 2000)* (Bari: Edipuglia), pp. 69–98.

Casson, L. (1995), *Ships and Seamanship in the Ancient World* (Baltimore, MD: John Hopkins University Press).

Cohen, E.E. (1989), 'Athenian Finance: Maritime and Landed Yields', *Classical Antiquity* 8, pp. 207–223.

Connolly, A. (1991), 'The Meaning of ἀνορμίζω and the Possible 'Addendum Lexicis' ἀνορμέω', *ZPE* 86, pp. 35–40.

Cuvigny, H. (1998), 'Bouchons cachetés des fouilles d'Adolphe Reinach à Coptos', *Bulletin des Musées et Monuments Lyonnais* 4, pp. 2–7.

De Romanis, F. (2019), 'Timoteo, Apollodoro e i chirographa di TPSulp. 78', in M. Maiuro, G.D. Merola, M. De Nardis, and G. Soricelli (eds), *Uomini, istituzioni, mercati. Studi di storia per Elio Lo Cascio* (Bari: Edipuglia), pp. 443–448.

Gofas, D. (1994), 'Encore une fois sur la Tabula Pompeiana 13 (essai d'une interprétation nouvelle)', in G. Thür (ed), *Symposion 1993. Vorträge zur griechischen und hellenistischen Rechtsgeschichte (Graz-Andritz, 12–16 September 1993)* (Cologne: Böhlau), pp. 251–266.

de Graaf, R.P.J. (2019), *Het Contract van Schipper Menelaos: TPSulp. 78 en de Internationaliteit van Handel en Recht in een Romeins-hellenistische Wereld* (Nijmegen: Radboud University).

Gröschler, P. (1997), *Die Tabellae-Urkunden aus den pompejanischen und herkulanensischen Urkundenfunden* (Berlin: Duncker und Humblot).

Gröschler, P. (2006), 'Die Konzeption des Mutuum cum Stipulatione', *RHD* 7, pp. 261–287.

Gröschler, P. (2009), 'Darlehensvalutierung und Darlehenszins in den Urkunden aus dem Archiv der Sulpizier', in H. Altmeppen, I. Reichard, and M.J. Schermaier (eds), *Festschrift für Rolf Knütel zum 70. Geburtstag* (Heidelberg: C.F. Müller), pp. 387–399.

Guarino, A. (1989), *Giusromanistica elementare*, 2nd edn (Naples: Jovene).

Harris, W.V. (2019), 'A Strange Fact about Shipboard Coin Hoards Throws Light on the Roman Empire's Financial System', *Athenaeum* 107, pp. 150–155.

Jakab, É. (2000), 'Vectura pro mutua: Überlegungen zu TP 13 und Ulp. D. 19, 2, 15, 61', *ZRG RA* 117, pp. 244–273.

Jakab, É. and Manthe, U. (2003), 'Recht in der römischen Antike', in U. Manthe (ed), *Rechtskulturen der Antike* (Munich: C.H. Beck), pp. 239–309.

Jones, D.F. (2006), *The Bankers of Puteoli: Finance, Trade and Industry in the Roman World* (Stroud: Tempus).

Jördens, A. (2007), 'Noch einmal: Norbanus "praefectus Aegypti"?', *ZPE* 163, pp. 195–199.

Meyer-Termeer, A.J.M. (1978), *Die Haftung der Schiffer im griechischen und römischen Recht* (Zutphen: Terra).

Miller, D.J.D. and Sarris, P. (2018), *The Novels of Justinian: A Complete Annotated English Translation*, Vol. 2 (Cambridge: Cambridge University Press).

Pestman, P.W. (1971), 'Loans Bearing No Interest?', *JJP* 16–17, pp. 7–29.

Purpura, G. (1984), 'Tabulae pompeianae 13 e 34; duo documenti relativi al prestito marittimo', in *Atti del xvii Congresso internazionale di papirologia (Napoli, 19–26 maggio 1983)* (Naples: Centro internazionale per lo studio dei papiri ercolanesi), pp. 1245–1266.

Rathbone, D. (2003), 'The Financing of Maritime Commerce in the Roman Empire I-II AD', in E. Lo Cascio (ed), *Credito e moneta nel mondo romano: atti degli Incontri capresi di storia dell'economia antica (Capri 12–14 ottobre 2000)* (Bari: Edipuglia), pp. 197–229.

Rathbone, D. (2007), 'Merchant Networks in the Greek World: The Impact of Rome', *Mediterranean Historical Review* 22, pp. 309–320.

Schuster, S. (2005), *Das Seedarlehen in den Gerichtsreden des Demosthenes: mit einem Ausblick auf die weitere historische Entwicklung des Rechtsinstitutes: dáneion nautikón, fenus nauticum und Bodmerei* (Berlin: Duncker & Humblot).

Thür, G. (1994), 'Die Aestimationsabrede im Seefrachtvertrag: Diskussionsbeitrag zum Referat Dimitri C. Gofas', in G. Thür (ed), *Symposion 1993. Vorträge zur griechischen und hellenistischen Rechtsgeschichte (Graz-Andritz, 12–16 September 1993)* (Vienna: Böhlau), pp. 267–271.

Van der Mieroop, M. (2005), 'Sumerian Loans', in W.N. Goetzmann and K.G. Rouwenhorst (eds), *The Origins of Value. The Financial Innovations that Created Modern Capital Markets* (Oxford: Oxford University Press), pp. 17–30.

Verboven, K. (2003), 'The Sulpicii from Puteoli and Usury in the Early Roman Empire', *RHD* 71, pp. 7–28.

Verboven, K. (2016), 'Currency and Credit in the Bay of Naples in the First Century AD', in M. Flohr and A.I. Wilson (eds), *The Economy of Pompeii* (Oxford: Oxford University Press), pp. 363–386.

Wolf, J.G. (1979), 'Aus dem neuen pompejanischen Urkundenfund. Der See-frachtvertrag des Menelaos', *Freiburger Universitätsblätter* 65, pp. 23–36.

Wolf, J.G. (2001), 'Aus dem neuen pompejanischen Urkundenfund: Die 'naulo-tike' des Menelaos – Seedarlehen oder Seefrachtvertrag?', in *Iuris vincula: studi in onore di Mario Talamanca* (Naples: Jovene), pp. 423–463.

Wolf, J.G. (2015), 'Documents in Roman Practice', in D. Johnston (ed), *The Cambridge Companion to Roman Law* (Cambridge: Cambridge University Press), pp. 61–84.

NOTES

1. I would like to take the opportunity to thank É Jakab for her constructive comments in the preparation of this chapter. Any errors are my own. For some remarks concerning the role and history of Puteoli as a trading port, see the chapter by É Jakab earlier in this volume.

2. Cf the antichretic loans that were common in Babylonia: van der Mieroop (2005), p. 27. For the structure of interlinked contracts from an economic perspective, see Bell (1988), pp. 797–798.

3. Chirographs were declarations, written in the first person and by the author's own hand, that were intended to be kept as proof that the speaker had made the declaration in question. To strengthen the probative value of the document, the author often added their seal below the writing, and though not required, witnesses were sometimes supplied as well: Wolf (2015), pp. 63–65. The presence of two *chirographa* in the same document is unusual, but not unique: Camodeca (1999), Vol. 2, p. 178; also, Wolf (2001), p. 426.

4. See Rathbone (2003), pp. 208–209.

5. *CIL* XV 3642–5 and 4748–9 (Dressels 7–11 and 20): on which, Camodeca (1999), p. 179.

6. *TPSulp.* 34, 35 and 36.

7. For a thorough and (almost) up-to-date account of the different interpretations given to the text, see de Graaf (2019), pp. 32–37.

8. Camodeca (1999), p. 179.

9. Wolf (1979), p. 34.

10. See, e.g. Jakab (2000), p. 250.

11. Harris (2019).

12. Meyer-Termeer (1978), p. 75: 'ναυλωτικαὶ συγγραφαί sind in griechischer Sprache abgefasste Urkunden, in denen jemand, der Güter per Schiff befördert, den Empfang und/oder das Einladen von Gütern bestätigt, wobei er sich ausdrücklich oder stillsch-weigend verpflichtet, diese Güter mit seinem Schiff zu befördern und an einem bestimm-ten Ort abzuliefern'.

13. C. 4.32.26.2 (*Iust.*, 528): Ankum (1978), pp. 168–169; also, *Id.* (1988), p. 282; and *Id.* (1996), pp. 67–68.

14. Ankum (2003), p. 454.

15. Generally, De Romanis (2019).

16. Dem. 49.26–42.

17. Gofas (1994); followed by Arnaud (2011), p. 68.

18. Jakab (2000), p. 253.

19. Gofas (1994), p. 265.
20. Thür (1994), pp. 267–271. In agreement, Camodeca (1999), pp. 178–179; also, *Id.* (2003), pp. 88–89.
21. Thür (1994), p. 271.
22. Jakab (2000), pp. 253–254.
23. D. 19.2.15.6 (Ulp. 32 *ad ed.*): '*Item cum quidam nave amissa vecturam, quam pro mutua acceperat, repeteretur, rescriptum est ab Antonino Augusto non immerito procuratorem Caesaris ab eo vecturam repetere, cum munere vehendi functus non sit: quod in omnibus personis similiter observandum est*'.
24. Trans. Fiori, in Ch.10 of this volume.
25. P. Oxy. XLIII 3111.
26. Cf Rathbone (2003), pp. 208–209, who initially sought to develop the thesis advanced by Jakab (2000) by suggesting that the loan was fictive; but who has subsequently argued in favour of a (possibly fictive) loan for the purpose of paying customs duties: Rathbone (2007), p. 315. See, also, Jones (2006), pp. 103–117.
27. Verboven (2016), p. 372.
28. Guarino (1989), p. 205; also, Gröschler (2009), pp. 398–399; and *Id.* (1997), pp. 165–177.
29. Purpura (1984); also, Andreau (1999), pp. 98–99; and Wolf (2015), p. 78.
30. See Plut. *De vitando.* 5; also, Ps.-Asc. *in Cic. Verr.* II 1.36.91: on which, Bove (1984), pp. 41–42 and 47–48; Camodeca, (1992), pp. 174–177; *Id.* (1999), p. 134; and now, Gröschler (2006), pp. 267–269.
31. Verboven (2003), 17–19.
32. Pestman (1971), p. 24.
33. Pestman (1971), pp. 24–26.
34. Trans. Miller and Sarris (2018), pp. 697–700.
35. See, e.g. the wreck at Dramont A, where the name of a certain Sex. Arrius appears inscribed on both the anchor and several amphora stamps.
36. P. Oxy. XLV 3250:

ἐναύλωσεν Ἀν[ο]υβᾶς Ἑρμίου τῶν ἀπὸ Ὑφαντῶνος τοῦ Ἑρμοπολείτου
Πέρσης τῆς ἐπ[ι]γονῆς κυβερνήτης τῆς Μάρκου Κορνηλίου Το-
ρούλλου ἑκατοντάρχου σκάφης ποταμίας ἀγωγῆς ἀρταβῶν
πεντακοσίων Πολυτίμῳ Γαΐου Νορβανοῦ Πτολεμαίου
τὴν δηλουμένην σκάφην σὺν τῇ ναυτείᾳ, εἰς ἣν καὶ ἐμβαλεῖ-
ται ἀφ' ὧν ἐὰν αἱρῆται τοῦ Ἑρμοπολείτου νομοῦ ὅρμον ἄρακος
μέτρῳ Ἀθηναίου ἀρτάβας πεντακοσίας καὶ τῶν ἑκατὸν
ἀρταβῶν ἀναυλὶ ἀρτάβας δέκα δύο ἥμισυ, ὥστε ἀποκατασ-
τῆσε εἰς Ἀκανθῶνα καὶ Λιλῆ τοῦ Ὀξυρυγχείτου, ναύλου τοῦ
διεσταμένου πρὸς ἀλλήλους τῶν ἑκατὸν ἀρταβῶν
ἀργυρίου δραχμῶν εἴκοσι ὀκτὸ, ὥστ' εἶναι δραχμὰς ἑκατὸν
τεσσεράκοντα, ἀφ' ὧν ὁμολογεῖ ὁ Ἀνουβᾶς ἐσχηκέναι παρὰ
τοῦ Πολυτείμου ἐπὶ τῶν τόπων δραχμὰς ἑβδομήκοντα
δύο . τὰς δὲ λοιπὰς τοῦ ναύλου δραχμὰς ἑξήκοντα ὀκτὼ
ἀποδότω αὐτῷ ἐπὶ τῆς ἐγβολῆς τοῦ ἄρακος. παραστησάτω
οὖν τὴν σκάφην ἑτοίμην πρὸς τὸν ἀνάπλουν τῇ μιᾷ καὶ εἰκά-
δι τοῦ ἐνεστῶτος μηνὸς Σεβαστοῦ, καὶ γενόμενος
ἐπὶ τῶν τοῦ Ἑρμοπολείτου ὅρμων καὶ ἀναλαβὼν καὶ πα-
ραλαβὼν τὸν ἄρακα ἀποπλευσάτω ἀνυπερθέτως
μετὰ πάσης ἀσφαλείας, ἑαυτῷ παρεχόμενος ἐν τῷ ἀνά-

πλῳ καὶ κατάπλῳ τὴν τῆς σκάφης χορηγίαν πᾶσαν ἐντελῆ
καὶ ναύτας ἱκανούς, καὶ μὴ ἐξέστω αὐτῷ νυγτοπλοεῖν μηδὲ
χειμῶνος ὄντος. ἀνορμίτω καθ᾽ ἑκάστην ἡμέραν
ἐπὶ τῶν ἀσφαλεστάτων ὅρμων, τῶν διεραμάτων τοῦ
Ἑρμοπολείτου ὄντων πρὸς τὸν Ἀνουβᾶν, τῶν δὲ τοῦ Ὀξυρυγχείτου ὄντων πρὸς τὸν Πολύτιμον. τὸν δὲ ἄρακα παρα-
δότω τῷ Πολυτίμῳ ἢ τοῖς παρ᾽ αὐτοῦ ἐπὶ τοῦ τῆς Λιλῆ καὶ
Ἀγανθῶνος ὅρμο μέτρῳ ᾧ ἐὰν παραλάβῃ, τοῦ ἐγβησομέ-
νου ἐκ τῆς κοίλης ὄντος τοῦ Πολυτίμου ἢ ἀποτισάτω
αὐτῷ τιμὴ[ν] ἑκαστη[ς - ca.25 -].

37. ἐναύλωσεν is a form of ναυλόν: Meyer-Termeer (1978), p. 246 nt. 1.
38. The designation *kybernetes* is equivalent to the Latin *gubernator*, or 'pilot': Casson (1995), p. 316.
39. P. Faoad I 21 (= FIRA III 171a, 5–6): on which, Jördens (2007), p. 196.
40. Cuvigny (1998).
41. Jördens (2007). Cf, e.g. Balogh and Pflaum (1952), pp. 419–420; Brunt (1975), p. 144.
42. Meyer-Termeer (1978), p. 63 nt. 21; also, Connolly (1991).
43. For other examples of advanced payments, Meyer-Termeer (1978), p. 43 nt. 166.
44. Dem. 50.17: on which, Cohen (1989), p. 215 and 219–220.
45. P. Cair. Zen. I 59010, SB VI 9571, and *Philogelos* 50.

Chapter 10

The Allocation of Risk in Carriage-by-Sea Contracts

Roberto Fiori

INTRODUCTION

According to the traditional view, in Roman law the contract of letting and hiring (*locatio conductio*) had a threefold structure: (a) when one contractual party granted the other the enjoyment of a thing in exchange for a price, the contract was called *locatio conductio rei*; (b) when the exchange regarded the daily activities of one of the parties, it was named *locatio conductio operarum*; and (c) when the price was paid for an amount of work, taken as a whole, the contract was a *locatio conductio operis*. An important addition to this view is that the distinction between *locatio conductio operarum* and *operis* has produced in civil law the important theoretical dichotomy between *obligation de moyens* and *obligation de résultat*[1] – that is, broadly speaking, between a duty to perform with reasonable care and a duty to attain a specific result.

The problem with this theory is that it does not explain why the Romans would have given the same name of *locatio conductio* and the same procedural remedies to very different contractual patterns: from the rental of agricultural land to the lease of houses, from labour to building contracts and so forth. In a work of a few years ago I suggested that the peculiarity of Roman law, and our difficulty in understanding it, derives from the different ways in which 'contract' is conceived in ancient and modern law.[2] In the latter – at least in civil law – the contract is understood as an agreement between two or more parties with respect to the content or 'object' of the transaction. In this perspective, since agreement is common to every transaction, the differences among contracts depend upon the differences between their objects, while the duties of the parties (the obligations) are considered 'effects' of the contract. Because of this idea, the civilian tradition has created different kinds of *locatio conductio*, one for each 'object' (*res*, *opera*, *opus*), so that by the publication of the German *Bürgerliches Gesetzbuch* of 1900, the traditional unity was abandoned and letting and hiring fragmented into a number of distinct contracts. In Roman law, on the contrary, the contract was identified with the obligation, of which the agreement was only the premise: therefore, as long as the obligation was the same, the contract was one, regardless of the diversity of the objects.[3] Since in *locatio conductio* every contractual pattern consisted of the same mutual obligations – that is: the exchange of enjoyment (*uti frui*, for the enjoyment of things; *opera*, *opus*, for the enjoyment resulting from the activity of persons) against a price (*merces*) – each pattern fell into the contract of letting and hiring. The structure was such that the contract was one but the nego-tiation patterns could be modified and adapted infinitely by the parties, far beyond the traditional tripartite division of the so-called *locatio rei*, *operarum* and *operis*.

In my previous study, although I had all this in mind, I could not free myself from the traditional view when dealing with carriage-by-sea contracts. I therefore used the trichotomy and distinguished the hiring of a ship (*locatio rei*, in the form of the *conductio navis*), the transport contract (*locatio operis*, in the form of *locatio mercium vehendarum*), and the labour contract between the entrepreneur and the sailors (*locatio operarum*).

In this paper, I would like to reconsider the matter and correct my earlier ideas by taking into account a privileged point of view, the problem of the allocation of risk.[4]

THE DEAD SLAVE

The first relevant text is a fragment taken from Labeo's *pithaná* (first century AD), summarised and commented upon by Paul (third century AD):

> 'D. 14.2.10 pr. (Lab. 1 *pith. a Paulo epit.*): *si vehenda mancipia conduxisti, pro eo mancipio, quod in nave mortuum est, vectura tibi non debetur.* Paulus: *immo quaeritur, quid actum est, utrum ut pro his qui impositi an pro his qui deportati essent, merces daretur: quod si hoc apparere non poterit, satis erit pro nauta, si probaverit impositum esse mancipium.*
>
> If you were entrusted with the carriage of slaves, you will not be entitled to freight for the slave who dies en route. *Paul*: But this depends on the agreement, whether freight was payable for the slaves who were loaded or for those who were carried to destina-tion. If it is not clear what the agreement was, it will be enough for the captain to prove that a slave was put on board.'

Labeo's solution looks like the perfect example of *locatio operis* as *obligation de résultat*: the obligation is fulfilled only when the foreseen result has been reached. What is not clear is Paul's notation: why, in a *locatio operis*, should the freight be calculated on the loaded (*impositi*) slaves rather than on those actually carried to destination (*deportati*)? And why should it be better to presume, in case of doubt, that the parties had preferred this arrangement over the other? The usual expla-nation is that Paul distinguishes between the *locatio operis* of carrying the slaves (the case discussed by Labeo) and the *locatio rei* of the whole ship or of its parts: in the first case, the freight is not due because the slave has not reached the harbour; in the other it is due because the freight is intended for the lease of the ship.[5]

What has not been considered by the interpreters is that this text clearly makes reference to documentary practices that we know were widespread in the Mediterranean, at least from the first century AD, which have come down to us thanks to the Graeco-Egyptian papyri. An examination of these texts shows that carriage-by-sea contracts were arranged according to several patterns.

The simplest is the lease of the ship. This is a contract between a shipowner (*locator*) and an entrepreneur (*conductor*) in the area of water transportation. The *locator* provides the ship while the *conductor* has to pay the rent and give back the ship and its equipment without damage, apart from those resulting from age, use and acts of God (storm, fire and looting of enemies or pirates) that they could prove.[6] The *conductor* receives the ship assuming full management and will pay the rent in any case, even if the ship is not used at all.[7]

In other cases, the contract is between a cargo owner and a carrier, entrusted with the transportation of goods at the carrier's risk (τῷ ἐμαυτοῦ κινδύνῳ). This clause – the so-called κίνδυνος-*Klausel* – makes the carrier not only liable for any harm suffered by the cargo (this was provided by the so-called σῶος-*Klausel*) but also bound them to hand over the cargo at any cost[8]: it is probably not a coincidence that all known contracts with this clause concern the delivery of fungible goods.[9] Under these conditions, if the carrier is not able to deliver the goods at the destination, they do not receive any freight: this arrangement is therefore a clear case of *obligation de résultat*.

Alongside these two patterns – which easily fit into the traditional patterns of *locatio rei* and *operis* – there is, however, a third, in which the carrier is entrusted with the transportation of goods, but under the instructions of the cargo owner who could demand that the ship sails only by day when the water is calm and dropping anchor each day in the safest ports. All these prescriptions are set in a contractual clause that the scholars call a 'navigationsklausel'. The obligation of the carrier is therefore to put at the disposal of the cargo owner a seaworthy ship, a crew and their seamanship, and to keep the cargo safe – but not at any cost: they are explicitly exempted from acts of God, so that if the cargo or part of it cannot be delivered at destination and the carrier cannot be blamed for it, they are entitled to receive the freight. This arrangement is a case of *obligation de moyens*.

Although there are such differences of geographical, social and legal context between the trades described by Roman jurists and those attested to by the contemporary Graeco-Egyptian papyri, that the comparison should be very cautious,[10] this survey has shown a clear similarity to the arrangements described in D. 14.2.10 pr. Indeed, the arrangement discussed by Labeo is similar to the second pattern (freight due in proportion to the discharged cargo), while Paul also takes into consideration the third pattern, where the freight is due for the undelivered cargo as well. It is clear that if the freight can be calculated on the loaded (*impositi*) slaves rather than on those carried to destination (*deportati*), it implies that the carrier cannot be held responsible for acts of God, as in the case of a slave who dies on board.

This shows all the limits of the traditional trichotomy of *locatio conductio*: the third pattern is certainly not a *locatio rei*, because the carrier is obliged to convey the goods, nor a *locatio operarum*, because the carrier does not work for the cargo owner on a temporal basis, but rather is entrusted with the overall task of transporting the goods from one place to another. However, it is not even a *locatio operis* conceived as an *obligation de résultat*, because if the carrier has performed all their duties, they must be paid even in the case that the goods are not delivered.

INTERLUDE: FROM ROMAN LAW TO ENGLISH LAW

The inadequacy of the threefold division is confirmed by the historical develop-ment of these rules in the history of maritime law.

It has to be considered that for centuries,[11] in the civil law, all maritime con-tracts have received the name of 'affreightment', generally understood as the con-tract in which a freight is paid and which can, therefore, be configured either as a simple lease of the ship or as a lease of the ship and of the carrier's activity. In the latter case, however, the freight could be calculated either: (a) on the goods loaded, so that the carrier received the freight even if the cargo was lost and their activity (*opus*) was compensated even if the expected result was not obtained; or (b) on the goods delivered, so that the carrier received the freight only if the cargo was carried to its destination, and their activity (*opus*) was compensated only if the expected result was obtained. This is clearly the system attested in Paul: the only difference is that when an express convention was lacking, it was presumed that the parties had agreed on (b) instead of (a), with the sole exception of oceanic journeys – probably because, with respect to antiquity, greater security was achieved in short journeys.

Through the *Ordonnance de la marine* issued by Louis XIV in 1681, this system was adopted in the nineteenth century by the codes of commerce of the civil law countries – even in Germany, where the *Bürgerliches Gesetzbuch* had fragmented letting and hiring into a number of contracts. However, in the most recent codes – the Italian *Codice della navigazione* (1942), the French *Code des transports* (2010) and the German *Handelsgesetzbuch* (2013) – the general 'affreightment' has been divided into four species:

(1) The hiring of the bare ship (*locazione della nave/affrètement coque nue/ Schiffsmietvertrag*),[12] in which case the price is due even if the ship does not travel.

(2) the hiring of the ship and the crew for a certain time (*noleggio a tempo/affrète-ment à temps/Zeitchartervertrag*)[13]: also, in this case the price is due even if the ship does not travel.

(3) The hiring of the ship and the crew for a specific journey (*noleggio a viaggio/ affrètement au voyage/Reisefrachtvertrag*),[14] in which case the freight is due if there is a journey, but the carrier is not held responsible for non-delivery: it is an *obligation de moyens*.

(4) The entrusting of the carrier with the transport of goods or people from one port to another (*contratto di trasporto/contrat de transport/Stückgutfrachtvertrag* or *Personenbeförderungsvertrag*),[15] in which case the freight is due only if the cargo or the people are delivered: it is an *obligation de résultat*.

For our purposes, however, the English system is the most interesting, because it is the one that has preserved and developed regulations that are the most similar to Roman law (in fact, English maritime law has long been modelled on civil law[16] and did not lose its characteristics even when, in the seventeenth century, the matter passed into the jurisdiction of the common law courts).[17] Apart from the so-called 'bills of lading', when carriers accept cargo from all-comers for a particular voyage, English maritime law knows basically two contractual patterns.[18]

The first pattern coincides with either: (1) a lease of the vessel ('bareboat charter'); or (2) a hiring of the vessel and the crew for an agreed time ('time charter'). In both cases the freight must be paid even if the charterer does not use the boat, and all risks not related to the condition of the ship and (in the time charter) of the crew are borne by the charterer. Furthermore, in both cases, if the contract is ended due to frustration a payment is due in proportion to the utility obtained from the provision of the ship (and possibly the crew) to that time.

In the second pattern, the carrier provides the charterer with the ship and the crew for one or more specific journeys ('voyage charter'), which includes both the case in which the performance of the carrier is only to transport, and that in which their performance is to deliver. Historically, the distinction is based on the exegesis of Paul's passage: during the seventeenth century the fragment was cited even by those most in favour of a transfer of maritime law to the common law courts, and in the nineteenth century it was further elaborated. What is important to us is that according to the English law there are two clues to discern whether in a voyage charter the duty of the shipowner is to transport or to deliver:

(1) if nothing has been explicitly agreed by the parties, it is presumed that the obligation is to deliver, so that in case of non-delivery freight is not due[19]; and

(2) on the contrary, if there is an express clause that calculates the freight on the loaded cargo, freight is due even in case of non-delivery.[20]

In other words, while civil law has created different contracts for the voyage charter, depending on whether it is structured as *obligation de moyens* or *obligation de résultat* (in the preceding paragraphs), in English law it is a unitary contract, and the obligations of the carrier are distinguished in (1) and (2) directly above by taking into account the way the freight is calculated. The regulations of English law are historically based on the Roman rules and have not been influenced by the civil law parallelism between *obligations de moyens* = *locatio operarum* and *obligation de résultat* = *locatio operis*. They therefore confirm the interpretation of D. 14.2.10 pr. given previously: in Roman law, a *locatio operis* did not necessarily imply an *obligation de résultat*.

THE NAVIS ONERARIA

As we have seen, English maritime law can be of help in understanding the Roman carriage-by-sea contracts. We have a further example in another opinion by Labeo, preserved in the same fragment:

'D. 14.2.10.2 (Lab. 1 *pith. a Paulo epit.*): *si conduxisti navem amphorarum duo milium et ibi amphoras portasti, pro duobus milibus amphorarum pretium debes.* Paulus: *immo si aversione navis conducta est, pro duobus milibus debetur merces: si pro numero impositarum amphorarum merces constituta est, contra se habet: nam pro tot amphoris pretium debes, quot portasti.*

If you hire a ship capable of carrying two thousand jars and you load jars on it, you must pay freight for two thousand jars. *Paul:* But the freight for two thousand jars will only be payable if the ship was hired at a flat rate. If the freight was fixed in relation to the number of jars loaded, the result is different, for you will only owe freight for the number of jars you carried.'

The usual interpretation of this fragment is that Labeo is speaking of the hiring of a ship (that is, of a bareboat charter).[21] However, this interpretation makes Labeo say something obvious: it is clear that, if one hires a thing and decides not to use it, the price is due in full. Actually, Labeo says something different: he states that if the freight is calculated on the tonnage of the ship, it is due regardless of the quantity of goods actually transported. Now, in English law the calculation of the freight on the tonnage of the ship is typical of the time charter.[22] The possibility that Labeo is also referring to this contract becomes convincing when we consider that the bareboat charter was usually between a shipowner and an entrepreneur, while this contract was aimed at a specific transport and was therefore between a carrier and a cargo owner. What Labeo wants to make clear, therefore, is that, while in a voyage charter freight is normally computed on the cargo, in a time charter it is due regardless of the actual load.

The distinction becomes explicit in Paul's comment. This is usually explained as if he were opposing a bareboat charter to a voyage charter '*de résultat*'[23] or to a 'slot charter'[24] (that is, to the hiring of a section of the ship). However, Paul speaks of a freight calculated on the loaded (*impositae*) amphorae, which is a clause that we have seen connected with the voyage charter '*de moyens*'. It therefore becomes more probable that he is distinguishing between a time charter and a voyage charter '*de moyens*'. There is actually need for such a distinction: in both charters the cargo owner entrusts the carrier with their goods in order to have them carried on a specific ship, and therefore both charters are described as *conducere navem*.[25] Moreover, in both charters freight is due even if the destination port is not reached. Confusion may therefore arise about the charter that the parties agreed upon. The jurist makes clear that in a time charter the freight is calculated on the tonnage of the ship and in a voyage charter '*de moyens*' on the tons of the actual cargo.

THE CHANGE OF SHIP

Another interesting text is:

'D. 14.2.10.1 (Lab. 1 *pith. a Paulo epit.*): *si ea condicione navem conduxisti, ut ea merces tuae portarentur easque merces nulla nauta necessitate coactus in navem deteriorem, cum id sciret te fieri nolle, transtulit et merces tuae cum ea nave perierunt, in qua novissime vectae sunt, habes ex conducto locato cum priore nauta actionem.*

If you chartered a ship for the carriage of your cargo and the *nauta* needlessly transhipped the cargo to a less good vessel, knowing that you would disapprove, and your cargo went down with the ship lastly carrying it, you have an action on hire and lease against the original *nauta*.'

Labeo describes the case as a *conductio navis* aimed at carrying the cargo of a *dominus mercium*. The carrier transfers the goods in a worse ship against the will of the cargo owner and the goods are lost: Labeo says the cargo owner has an action *ex locato conducto*. The interpretation of the arrangement is not difficult: it is not a bareboat charter, because the carrier has been entrusted with the transport; it is also unlikely to be a time charter, because the case refers to a specific journey; rather, it is a voyage charter in which the cargo owner has chosen the ship – in other words, a voyage charter '*de moyens*'.

What is interesting is that the case is described as a *locatio mercium vehendarum* in Paul's comment (' . . . *devehendas eas merces locasset* . . . ') and in another fragment of Labeo's dealing with the same case:[26]

'D. 19.2.13.1 (Ulp. 32 ad ed.): *si navicularius onus Minturnas vehendum conduxerit et, cum flumen Minturnense navis ea subire non posset, in aliam navem merces transtulerit eaque navis in ostio fluminis perierit, tenetur primus navicularius? Labeo, si culpa caret, non teneri ait: ceterum si vel invito domino fecit vel quo non debuit tempore aut si minus idoneae navi, tunc ex locato agendum.*

If a *navicularius* was entrusted with the transport of cargo to Minturnae and then, since the ship could not go upstream Minturnae's river, transferred the goods onto another ship and the second ship foundered at the river's mouth, is the first *navicularius* liable? Labeo says he is not liable if he is free from fault; different is the case if he acted against the cargo owner's will or in a circumstance when he should not or by using a less suitable ship: then there should be an action on lease.'

The voyage charter '*de moyens*' can be represented either as a *conductio navis* or as a *locatio mercium vehendarum*, because on the one hand the carrier gives the cargo owner the use of the ship, and on the other hand they are obliged to transport. Therefore, if the cargo owner must sue the carrier for not having made the ship available, they will have the action *ex conducto*; if, on the contrary, they sue them for not having carried the goods, they will have the action *ex locato*; and if they sue for both obligations, as in D. 14.2.10.1, they will have both actions (*ex locato conducto*).

THE DETAINED SHIP

Another example of freight calculated on the loaded cargo is in an opinion by Cervidius Scaevola (second century AD):

'D. 19.2.61.1 (Scaev. 7 dig.): *navem conduxit, ut de provincia Cyrenensi Aquileiam navigaret olei metretis tribus milibus impositis et frumenti modiis octo milibus certa mercede: sed evenit, ut onerata navis in ipsa provincia novem mensibus retineretur et onus impositum*

commisso tolleretur. quaesitum est, an vecturas quas convenit a conductore secundum loca-
tionem exigere navis possit. respondit secundum ea quae proponerentur posse.

A man hired a ship to sail from the province of Cyrene to Aquileia with the condition
that 3000 measures of oil and 8000 *modii* of corn would be loaded for a specified freight:
but, as it turned out, the loaded ship was detained in that province for nine months and
the loaded cargo was unloaded and confiscated. It was asked whether the ship could
demand from the lessee the freight agreed on in the lease. He [Scaevola] responded
that, according to what had been illustrated, it could.'

This contract has been often interpreted as a bareboat charter,[27] without considering that in the agreement the route was specified – which, in a bareboat charter,
would have been unnecessary – and that the freight was called *vectura* (the usual
term for the *locatio mercium vehendarum*) and not *merces* (the usual term for the
locatio rei). However, even if this were the case, Scaevola's solution would appear
very dubious. In a *locatio rei* the lessor should not simply provide the *res*, but also
the actual chance of its enjoyment: when this was not possible because of some
unforeseen circumstances, the price was proportionally reduced or completely
cancelled (*remissio mercedis*).[28] In the present case, the carrier had placed the ship
at the disposal of the cargo owner, but since the vessel had been detained in the
port the carrier could not guarantee its use and the freight should not be due.[29]

Scaevola's solution cannot be explained even by thinking of a voyage charter
'*de résultat*'. The scholars who have proposed such an interpretation have tried to
justify the jurist's answer by presuming that the cargo owner was responsible for
committing an administrative offense that had caused the blockage of the ship
and the confiscation of the cargo.[30] However, nothing like this is in the fragment.[31]

In fact, since the *merces* is calculated on the loaded cargo, the case discussed
by Scaevola probably regards a contract in which the carrier takes on the obligation of transporting cargo on a specific ship but is not responsible for its delivery.
In other words, it is a voyage charter '*de moyens*', where all risks arising after loading are borne by the cargo owner.

This solution may seem unjust at first sight, but on closer inspection it is what
happens today in English law: while in a bareboat charter or in a time charter, in
case of frustration of the contract, the charterer has a right to a reduction of the
freight proportional to the utility actually received, in a voyage charter the freight
is due when calculated on the loaded cargo and not due when calculated on the
cargo delivered at the destination port. These contractual clauses are aimed at
regulating the risk allocation regime agreed upon by the parties.[32]

THE ADVANCE FREIGHT

It is now time to examine a well-known fragment by Ulpian:

'D. 19.2.15.6 (Ulp. 32 *ad ed.*): *item cum quidam nave amissa vecturam, quam pro mutua*
acceperat, repeteretur, rescriptum est ab Antonino Augusto non immerito procuratorem

Caesaris ab eo vecturam repetere, cum munere vehendi functus non sit: quod in omnibus personis similiter observandum est.

Likewise, when someone was asked, having lost the ship, to return the freight he accepted as loan, it was replied in a rescript by Antoninus Augustus that it is not without cause for the emperor's procurator to ask him the restitution of the freight, because he did not fulfill the duty to convey: a rule that should hold for all persons alike.'

The passage is generally interpreted in the sense that the freight should be returned because the carrier did not fulfil the *obligation de résultat* of the contract, as in the case discussed by Labeo in D. 14.2.10 pr.[33] However, if this were the case, and if it had been undisputed for centuries, why would the parties need an imperial intervention and why would Ulpian report it?[34] I think we should be more cautious in identifying the nature of the contract.

The parties certainly agreed upon a duty of the carrier to convey the cargo with his own ship, and the contract was therefore certainly a voyage charter: however, it is not clear whether the obligation of the carrier was *de moyens* or *de résultat*.

To solve the problem, it may be useful to concentrate on terminology. Ulpian says that the freight has been accepted by the carrier *pro mutua*. This expression is usually interpreted as a reference to the contract of loan (*mutuum*) alongside a voyage charter '*de résultat*',[35] but in this case the clarification would be completely unnecessary: if the freight should be returned because there was no delivery, why add that the sum had been initially taken as a loan? In this reconstruction, the words *pro mutua* are so redundant that the majority of scholars commenting the text does not mention them.[36] However, the Byzantine commentators of the text translate *pro mutua* – here and in other cases[37] – with προχρεία[38]: a word that in the Graeco-Egyptian papyri means the giving of money in advance without interest, especially in relation to work performances.[39] The practice is shown once again by the papyri: when the parties agreed on an advance payment or delivery in a contract, the creditor was given a document referring to a (fictitious) loan[40]; when the future service for which the advance money had been paid or the thing had been delivered was performed, the document was returned to the debtor. Therefore, before the debtor's performance, the creditor was guaranteed by the document attesting his credit as a loan; after the performance, the payment or delivery anticipated by the creditor took on the role of counter-performance.[41]

A useful comparison is offered once again by English law, where the judges face the same problems. At the beginning of the nineteenth century – though from the tone of the discussion it is clear that the matter was not new – the question was posed whether an advance payment in favour of the carrier should be interpreted as freight or as a loan.[42] The answer was that, in case of loss of the ship the money paid in advance: (a) should be returned if it is a loan or if it is freight and the obligation of the carrier is '*de résultat*', because in this case the freight is not earned until the cargo is delivered at the destination; (b) should not be returned if it is freight and the obligation of the carrier is '*de moyens*', because in this case the freight is earned on departure. In the first case the risk is borne by the carrier, in the second by the cargo owner.[43]

The *rescriptum* in D. 19.2.15.6 was aimed, in my opinion, at clarifying the distinction between the two forms of voyage charter. In Roman law the voyage charter '*de moyens*' was the basic form, and an advance payment would usually be acquired at any event by the carrier, even if it was not specified that the freight was computed on the loaded goods (see above). In this case, on the contrary, the freight was accepted 'as loan' and that implied it could not be considered as earned until delivery: the contract was a voyage charter '*de résultat*'.[44]

CONCLUSION

The Roman jurists adapted the commercial customs of Mediterranean trade to the structure of the contract of *locatio conductio*. Since in Roman law every exchange between enjoyment and price fell within this contract, the differences among the arrangements chosen by the parties did not create different contracts but, rather, were distinguished from one another by contractual clauses.

Differences in terminology have misled modern interpreters, who have rigidly distinguished between a *conductio navis* conceived as a (modern) *locatio rei* and a *locatio mercium vehendarum* conceived as a (modern) *locatio operis*, that is, as an *obligation de résultat*. The picture is, however, much more complex. *Conductio navis* means that the *conductor* has chosen the ship: still, the contract may consist in the simple granting of a seaworthy vessel (bareboat charter), in the obligation to supply the ship and the crew for a certain time (time charter), or in the obligation to make a specific journey at the cargo owner's instructions (voyage charter '*de moyens*'). *Locatio mercium vehendarum* means that the carrier was entrusted with a specific transportation: but the contract may consist either in a voyage charter '*de moyens*' or '*de résultat*', depending on the specific contractual clauses.

Terminology was, however, important when the parties went to trial, for it distinguished the actions from one another, helping the judge to understand the claim of the plaintiff – although a mistake could lead to the absolution of the defendant. The cargo owner was actually *conductor* in a time charter and in a voyage charter '*de moyens*', having an *actio ex conducto* for the unseaworthiness of the ship, the insufficiency of the crew, and so forth. He was instead *locator* in a voyage charter, both '*de moyens*' and '*de résultat*', having an action *ex locato* for claims regarding the obligation of the carrier to convey the goods. In fact, it is likely that in a voyage charter '*de moyens*' the Romans split the carrier's obligations, granting the cargo owner two actions, one *ex conducto* and the other *ex locato*.

According to the sources, however, there were cases so complex that it was impossible to discern whether the plaintiff was *conductor* or *locator*, so that an atypical civil action was resorted to. This situation is described once again by Labeo, who also proposes the remedy:

'D. 19.5.1.1 (Pap. 8 *quaest.* = Lab. *ad ed.*, in Lenel, *Pal*, fr. 98): *domino mercium in mag-istrum navis, si sit incertum, utrum navem conduxerit an merces vehendas locaverit, civilem actionem in factum esse dandam Labeo scribit.*

Labeo writes that a civil action describing the case should be given to the owner of cargo against a ship captain when it is unclear whether he hired the ship or entrusted [the captain] with the transportation of cargo.'

The contractual clauses might vary infinitely, giving rise to ever new arrangements, even beyond the four patterns described above for carriage-by-sea contracts, and still the contract remained a *locatio conductio*, because there was an exchange between enjoyment and price and the remedy was a civil law action. This action is to be interpreted as an *agere praescriptis verbis*, that is as an action the formula of which described the case not – as in the *actiones locati conducti* – within the proper formula, but rather in a text that prefaced the formula where no reference was made to the positions of the parties as *locator* or *conductor*.

The problem of the allocation of risk is, I think, one of the best examples of how the traditional trichotomy of *locatio conductio* is an insufficient hermeneutic tool. But it is also a good example of how sometimes it is not enough to limit the study of Roman law to the analysis of the juridical sources contained in the Digest, and that the investigation should be extended to other contemporary ancient sources and to the subsequent developments of law in history, both in the civil and the common law.

BIBLIOGRAPHY

Alzon, C. (1965), *Problèmes relatifs à la location des entrepôts en droit romain* (Paris: Éditions Cujas).
Brecht, Chr. H. (1962), *Zur Haftung der Schiffer im antiken Recht* (Munich: C.H. Beck).
Cerami, P. and Petrucci, A. (2010), *Diritto commerciale romano. Profilo storico* (Turin: Giappichelli).
Coquillette, D.R. (1988), *The Civilian Writers of Doctors' Commons, London. Three Centuries of Juristic Innovation in Comparative, Commercial, and International Law* (Berlin: Duncker & Humblot).
Demogue, R. (1925), *Traité des obligations en général*, Vol. 5 (Paris: Librairie A. Rousseau).
Dernburg, H. (1912), *System des römischen Rechts (Pandekten)*, Vol. II[8] (Berlin: H.W. Müller).
du Plessis, P.J. (2003), *A History of 'Remissio Mercedis' and related Legal Institutions* (Rotterdam: Sanders Instituut).
du Plessis, P.J. (2012), *Letting and Hiring in Roman Legal Thought: 27 bce–284 ce* (Leiden: Brill).
Fercia, R. (2002), *Criteri di responsabilità dell'exercitor* (Turin: Giappichelli).
Fercia, R. (2008), *La responsabilità per fatto di ausiliari nel diritto romano* (Padua: Cedam).

Fiori, R. (1999), *La definizione della 'locatio conductio'. Giurisprudenza romana e tradizione romanistica* (Naples: Jovene).

Fiori, R. (2003), 'Il problema dell'oggetto del contratto nella tradizione civilistica', in R. Cardilli (ed), *Modelli teorici e metodologici nella storia del diritto privato*, Vol. 1 (Naples: Jovene), pp. 169–238.

Fiori, R. (2018), 'L'allocazione del rischio nei contratti relativi al trasporto', in E. Lo Cascio and D. Mantovani (eds), *Diritto romano e economia: Due modi di pensare e organizzare il mondo (nei primi tre secoli dell'Impero)* (Pavia: Pavia University Press), pp. 507–567.

Holdsworth, W.S. (1922), *A History of English Law* I, 3rd edn (Boston: Little, Brown & Co).

Holdsworth, W.S. (1937), *A History of English Law* V, 2nd edn (London: Methuen & Co).

Honoré, T. (2002), *Ulpian. Pioneer of Human Rights*, 2nd edn (Oxford: Oxford University Press).

Jakab, É. (2006), 'Vertragsformulare im Imperium Romanum', *ZRG RA* 123, pp. 71–101.

Jördens, A. (1990), *Vertragliche Regelungen von Arbeiten im Späten Griechischsprachigen Ägypten* (Heidelberg: C.H. Winter).

Mayer-Maly, Th. (1956), *Locatio conductio. Eine Untersuchung zum klassischen römischen Recht* (Vienna and Munich: Herold).

Meyer-Termeer, A.J.M. (1978), *Die Haftung der Schiffer im griechischen und römischen Recht* (Zutphen: Terra).

Quadrato, E. (2007), 'Promutuum', *SDHI* 73, pp. 71–83.

Robaye, R. (1987), *L'obligation de garde. Essai sur la responsabilité contractuelle en droit romain* (Brussels: Bruylant).

Röhle, R. (1968), 'Das Problem der Gefahrtragung im Bereich des römischen Dienst- und Werkvertrages', *SDHI* 34, pp. 183–222.

Thür, G. (2010), 'Fictitious loans and novatio: IG VII 3172, UPZ II 190, and C.Pap.Jud. I 24 reconsidered', in T. Gagos (ed), *Proceedings of the Twenty-Fifth International Congress of Papyrology (Ann Arbor 2007)* (Ann Arbor, MI: Scholarly Publishing Office, The University of Michigan Library), pp. 757–762.

Vacca, L. (2001), *Considerazioni in tema di risoluzione del contratto per impossibilità della prestazione e di ripartizione del rischio nella locatio conductio*, in *Iuris vincula. Studi M. Talamanca VIII* (Naples: Jovene), pp. 247–296.

Wilson, J.F. (2010), *Carriage of Goods by Sea*, 7th edn (Harlow: Longman).

NOTES

1. This distinction was fixed in these terms by Demogue (1925), pp. 538–549, but it was already used in Germany at the end of the nineteenth century, on the basis of the difference between *locatio operarum* and *operis*: Dernburg (1912), pp. 788–789 nt. 3.
2. Fiori (1999). The view has been accepted by, among others, du Plessis (2012).
3. For a more detailed analysis of these problems, see also Fiori (2003).

4. By 'allocation of risk' I mean the rules governing the distribution of losses between the parties when unforeseen circumstances interfere with their performances, making the contract more expensive for one party or less advantageous for the other. I will not deal instead with other issues related to the general subject of 'risk' in maritime law, such as the so-called *lex Rhodia de iactu* or the *receptum nautarum*.

5. This was also my idea in Fiori (1999), pp. 136–152 (with other references at p. 136 nt. 33–34).

6. See, e.g. P. Köln III 147.

7. Other reports involving the hiring of a ship are more complex. In a contract from AD 570 (P. Lond. V 1714) the *conductor* also undertakes to carry out transport activities for the owner and to restore and return the ship, except in the case of *force majeure*. In other cases the hire has a duration of fifty to sixty years and tends to be confused with a sale: these are the much discussed cases of the μισθοπρασία (BGU IV 1157, 10 BC; P. Lond. III 1164, AD 212; P. Oxy. XVII 2136, AD 291).

8. See for all, Jakab (2006), pp. 94–95.

9. Brecht (1962), pp. 61–67.

10. Caution is recommended, especially by Meyer-Termeer (1978), p. 171; see, also, Brecht (1962), pp. 3–27 (on the *receptum nautarum*).

11. For references see Fiori (2018), p. 524 nt. 64.

12. Artt. 376–383 Italian cod. nav.; art. L5423–8 French cod. trasp.; § 553 German HGB.

13. Artt. 384–395 Italian cod. nav.; art. L5423–10 French cod. transp.; § 557 German HGB.

14. Artt. 384–395 Italian cod. nav.; art. L5423–13 French cod. transp.; § 527 German HGB.

15. Artt. 396–456 Italian cod. nav.; art. L5422–1. French cod. trasp.; §§ 481–493 and 536–551 German HGB.

16. See for all Holdsworth (1937), pp. 63–73.

17. On the 'battle for the Law Merchant' of the seventeenth century see for all, Holdsworth (1922), pp. 552–567; Id. (1937), pp. 140–153; and, more recently, Coquillette (1988), pp. 106–114.

18. Those indicated in the text are the most important models but there is also the hiring of the ship's spaces ('slot charter'), the time charter of a ship for a specific cargo voyage ('trip charter'), the time charter of a ship for a series of voyages between designated ports ('consecutive voyage charter'), and the transport of a certain quantity of goods within a certain period of time through an indefinite number of trips (long-term freighting contract). On the types of charters, see Wilson (2010), pp. 3–18.

19. *De Silvale v Kendall* (1815) 4 M&S 37 (at 40) = 105 ER 749 (at 750): 'by the policy of the law of England freight and wages, strictly so called, do not become due until the voyage has been performed'. Other examples include: *Cook v Jennings* (1797) 7 TR 381 = 101 ER 1032; *Osgood v Groning* (1810) 2 Camp. 466 = 170 ER 1220.

20. See again *De Silvale v Kendall* (1815) 4 M&S 37 (at 42) = 105 ER 749 (at 751):

    'if the charter-party be silent the law will demand a performance of the voyage, for no freight can be due until the voyage is completed. But if the parties have chosen to stipulate by express words, or by words not express but sufficiently intelligible to that end, that a part of the freight (using the word freight) should be paid by anticipation, which should not depend upon the performance of the voyage, may they not so stipulate?'.

    Other references in Fiori (2018), pp. 528 nt. 88.

21. I did it myself in Fiori (1999), pp. 139–144.

22. See Wilson (2010), p. 86.
23. Alzon (1965), p. 242 and nt. 1121, followed by Robaye (1987), p. 64 and nt. 14.
24. Fiori (1999), p. 141, followed by Fercia (2002), p. 178; *Id.* (2008), p. 313 nt. 47. Both possibilities are considered by Cerami and Petrucci (2010), p. 253.
25. Cf the sources where the aim of the *locare conducere navem* is made explicit: to carry a cargo (D. 14.2.10.1), to sail from one port to another (D. 19.2.61.1), to carry passengers or cargo (D. 14.1.1.3).
26. See Fiori (1999), p. 149 nt. 70.
27. See literature in Fiori (2018), p. 543 nt. 128.
28. On *remissio mercedis* see for all du Plessis (2003).
29. Obviously, in a bareboat charter, the obligation of the shipowner is not to provide a ship that can only be loaded, but a ship that can actually sail, just as the obligation of the owner of land is not to put at the tenant's disposal any land, even if sterile, but land that can actually be cultivated. This is apparently not perceived by Vacca (2001), p. 285 nt. 73.
30. See for all Mayer-Maly (1956), p. 198; Röhle (1968), p. 219; du Plessis (2012), p. 131. The idea dates back to the seventeenth century: see Fiori (2018), p. 546 nt. 135.
31. Moreover, if there were some responsibility of the cargo owner, the carrier would have probably asked him not only for the payment of the freight but also – according to the general rules (see Fiori (1999), pp. 103–115) – the *id quod interest* for having blocked his activity for nine months.
32. See above, nt. 18. In some decisions it is said that the freight must be returned, but the cases are different: in *Le Buck v van Voisdonck* (1554), in *Select Pleas of the Admiralty (Selden Society)* II 93, no cargo or passengers were loaded; in *Roelandts v Harrison* (1854) 9 Ex 447 = 156 ER 189 the freight was payable on 'final sailing' of the vessel, but the ship foundered in a canal between the docks and the open sea. Another exception is *Thompson v Gillespy* (1855) 5 E&B 209 = 119 ER 459, where the ship had sailed in an unseaworthy condition.
33. Literature in Fiori (2018), p. 547 nt. 139.
34. Ulpian recalls imperial constitutions not only when they are innovative, but also when they confirm a point of view already advanced by jurists: see Honoré (2002), pp. 156–157. However, if the case was undisputed, this time the quotation would have really been useless.
35. See for all Röhle (1968), p. 218.
36. See e.g. Mayer-Maly (1956), p. 146; Vacca (2001), pp. 284–289.
37. Another fragment by the same jurist: D. 32.24.3 (Scaev. 16 *dig.*).
38. See Bas 53.1.59 (Scheltema, A VII, 2439–40) and sch. 5 ad Bas. 20.1.15 (Scheltema, B III, 1182): ὁ προχρήσας, with reference to D. 19.2.15.6; sch. 4 ad Bas. 48.5.41.4 (Scheltema, B VII, 2914), with reference to D. 40.7.40.5 (Scaev. 24 *dig.*).
39. Jördens (1990), pp. 271–285. It is doubtful whether in Scaevola's fragment one should read *pro mutua* or *promutua*: for *promutuus* and *promutuum*: see Caes. *BCiv.* 3.32; D. 40.7.40.5 (Scaev. 24 *dig.*).
40. When the sources deal with a real *mutuum*, they speak of *mutuum accipere*, not of *accipere pro mutuo* (Quadrato (2007), p. 81); moreover, in the whole of Latin literature, the words *pro mutuo* make reference to a contract of *mutuum* only once: D. 46.1.54 (Paul. 3 *quaest.*).
41. Thür (2010), pp. 757–768.

42. Cf *De Silvale v Kendall* (1815) 4 M&S 37 = 105 ER 749; *Manfield v Maitland* (1821) 4 B&A 582 = 106 ER 1049; *Wilson v Martin* (1856) 11 Exch 684 = 156 ER 1005; *Hicks v Shield* (1857) 7 El&Bl 633 = 119 ER 1380; *Droege & Co v Suart (The Karnak)* (1869) 6 Moo PC NS 136 = 16 ER 677; *Allison v Bristol Marine Insurance* (1876) 1 AC 209. The solution was sometimes found thanks to express clauses qualifying the sum in one sense or the other, by identifying who insured the sum (the cargo owner would only insure the freight, because they do not bear the risk of the loan), or based on the presence or not of interest.

43. This is clearly stated in *Compania Naviera General S.A. v Kerametal Ltd. (The Lorna I)* (1983) 1 *Lloyd's Rep* 373 (at 374).

44. The memory of Caracalla's *rescriptum* may be preserved in the *Nómos Rhodíōn nautikós* – the Byzantine collection of navigation rules most likely composed in the seventh or eighth century AD (but based on older materials) – where it is said that if a disaster occurs during navigation, the cargo owner cannot request the part of the freight they have anticipated (ἡμίναυλον), unless they gave it as a προχρεία (*Nóm. naut.* 3.32).

Index